Rebecca Latimer Felton

Nine Stormy Decades

REBECCA LATIMER FELTON
Photograph taken at the time of her appointment as U.S. Senator

Rebecca Latimer Felton
Nine Stormy Decades

By JOHN E. TALMADGE

Published by

UNIVERSITY OF GEORGIA PRESS

Athens

To My Wife

MIRIAM COFFIN TALMADGE

Contents

Illustrations

Frontispiece

REBECCA LATIMER FELTON

Photograph taken at the time of her appointment as U. S. Senator

Following Page 12

CHARLES LATIMER, SR.

ELEANOR SWIFT LATIMER

REBECCA LATIMER FELTON AND HER SISTER
MARY LATIMER McLENDON

FELTON HOME NEAR CARTERSVILLE

MR. AND MRS. WILLIAM H. FELTON

Cartoon: MRS. FELTON CHASTISES BISHOP CANDLER

Preface

ON A TRIP to Cartersville for material on Mrs. Felton, I spent the night with my colleague Dean William Tate at the home of his mother in nearby Fairmount. Mrs. Tate had known Mrs. Felton, and during the evening she gave me information far more entertaining than that I had found at the Bartow County Courthouse. When I was leaving the following morning, she gave me some advice also.

"Young man," she said, "I'd be careful what I wrote about Mrs. Felton."

Feeling obliged to answer in a youthful vein, I assured Mrs. Tate that if Mrs. Felton were living, I wouldn't dare write anything about her.

"Never mind," said Mrs. Tate; "you may run up on her in the next world."

It was not a cheerful thought.

I knew even then that I was not going to write the sort of book Mrs. Felton wanted. When she left her papers to the University of Georgia, she had hoped they would be used some day to vindicate the long fight her husband made, with her help, against the Democratic overlords of Georgia. It is true that in my book I have gone rather fully into the political revolt Dr. Felton led, even devoting one chapter to its background. I have not, however, tried to establish the significance and idealism of this movement. Dr. Felton's campaigns were important to my purposes only because they showed how Mrs. Felton worked her way into public affairs and because they furnished lively pictures of her controversies with such worthies as John B. Gordon, Benjamin H. Hill, Joseph Brown, and Alexander Stephens. For the same reason I have not been as concerned with the merits of Mrs. Felton's social crusades as with her aggressive participation in them. Undoubtedly she would have expected her biographer to defend them as stoutly as she did.

I was not, however, interested in Mrs. Felton's causes, but in her: first, as a robust character whose pronounced virtues and prejudices sustained her through a strenuous and, at times, tragic life; and, second, as a type of Southern liberal who, for all his professions of faith, cannot cut himself loose from his regional roots. In trying to make clear this view I have had to deal critically—although I hope not unkindly—with some of Mrs. Felton's ideas and activities. Not that this explanation would appease her. Criticism and hostility were always synonymous in her lexicon.

I have many to thank for help and encouragement. Dr. George H. Boyd, Dean Emeritus of the University of Georgia Graduate School, Dr. Gerald B. Huff, his successor, and Dr. Edwin M. Everett, Head of the English Department, approved a teaching schedule that allowed time for research and writing. Their confidence in my project was as welcome as their assistance. The University Center in Georgia and the Graduate School furnished financial aid for travel, typing, and the purchase of material.

Others have been equally generous in making available needed information. Mrs. Lillian Felton of Cartersville placed on deposit at the University of Georgia Library valuable papers of her late husband's grandmother. Dr. James Z. Rabun of Emory University kindly allowed me to go through his extensive files on Alexander Stephens for Felton information. Mr. Sumter Kelley of Atlanta located for my use a copy of Mrs. Felton's will, and Miss Carol Hart, formerly of the University of Georgia Library, obtained the loan of two ante-bellum catalogues of the Georgia Female College from Mrs. Louise McHenry Hickey of Madison, Georgia. The late Honorable Walter George explained his help in getting Mrs. Felton sworn into the Senate, and William Bates, a former student of mine, copied stories from Washington newspapers about that tense ceremony. Mr. and Mrs. Francis Vaughn of Cartersville and Frank Daniel of the Atlanta *Journal,* friends of Mrs. Felton, have made me better acquainted with her. Either Mr. John Bonner or Mrs. William Tate of the University of Georgia Library was always available when I lost my way in the large *Felton Collection.* I am especially grateful to Mr. William M. Henderson, a great-nephew of Mrs. Felton and a professor in the University of Georgia Law School, for making me a copy of a letter from Charles Latimer to his son during the Civil War, and for allowing the reproduction of daguerreotypes of Mrs. Felton and her sister and of her parents.

The style and organization of my book have been made more presentable through the help of colleagues and friends: Professors Edwin M. Everett, Robert H. West, Edd W. Parks, and Marion Montgomery of the English Department; Professor Kenneth Coleman of the History Department; and Professor Francis B. Simkins of Longwood College, Farmville, Virginia. Mrs. Kathryn DeBaillou passed judgment on some of the later chapters, and Mrs. Conn Harris West showed her fortitude and friendship by reading the entire manuscript and suggesting many helpful changes.

The dedication expresses inadequately my gratitude to Miriam Coffin Talmadge.

JOHN E. TALMADGE

English Department
University of Georgia
Athens, Georgia

1
. . . . .
. . .
.

Growing Up in Georgia's Golden Age

TEN miles south of Decatur, Georgia, on the Covington Road, a bronze marker once stood. It has disappeared since World War II, with the coming of filling stations, motels, and bungalows. The marker carried the following inscription:

Birthplace of Rebecca Latimer
MRS. WILLIAM H. FELTON
Born 1835
Died 1930
First Woman Member of the Senate of
The United States, Educator, Author,
Pioneer in Temperance Movement and
Advocate of Woman's Rights,
W. P. A.   1936   U. D. C.[1]

Rebecca Felton would have been displeased with such indifference to her memorial. She had worked hard for the honors mentioned on it.

Her birth had stirred quite a bit of excitement at Latimer Tavern, since she was the first child born to Charles Latimer and Eleanor Swift Latimer. Rebecca Ann was strong and red-faced, and able to take all the milk allowed her—attributes one would expect in a baby with ninety-four active years ahead of her.[2]

In 1835 the Decatur-Covington Road ran through a peaceful, lonely countryside. The deep forests, recently cleared of Cherokee Indians, had been levelled here and there to make rolling farms of rich bottom lands. Sturdy, one-story farmhouses stood on some of the hills. The people in the yards or driving along the road were dressed in broadcloth, homespun, or deerskin. It was a different world from the middle Georgia of today, except that the men and

1

women in it exhibited characteristics found still in their descendants: stubborn individualism, assertiveness, and local pride.

They were the first or second generation of settlers from Maryland, Virginia, and North Carolina, who had come steadily into Georgia after the Revolutionary War. Stopping first in Wilkes and Oglethorpe counties, they had later moved on into the newer counties to the west. Determinedly they wrested the political leadership of the state from the coastal section and elected a series of progressive-minded Governors: George Gilmer, John Forsyth, and Wilson Lumpkin.

These executives disagreed with each other on national issues, but stood united on one objective: their rich state must be developed, and developed according to the desires of its people. Each of them pushed the Federal Government aside and hurried the removal of the Creek and Cherokee Indians from the state. When Abolitionist pamphlets began to appear in Georgia, Gilmer promptly passed a law against teaching Negroes to read and write. In 1835 Lumpkin was pushing the construction of a state-owned railroad which would connect the Tennessee border with private lines running out of Macon and Augusta. Under the leadership of such determined men, Georgia seemed headed for prosperity and self government.[3]

The world into which Rebecca Ann was born had a place for women, but a rather limited one. They were supposed to look forward to being wives and mothers, a full-time occupation then, either in a mansion or a cabin. At marriage a husband took over his wife's property; he took charge of her conduct, too, for Georgia had not yet repealed a law allowing a husband to beat an offending wife with a stick of prescribed circumference. A minimum of formal education was considered necessary in training girls for their life's work, but there were signs that Georgia might soon provide more education for its women. In 1825 a bill to finance such opportunities passed the House, but was defeated in the Senate. Meanwhile some churches were establishing academies for girls, and the Methodists were actually planning a woman's college in Macon.[4]

In ante-bellum Georgia there were unmarried women who managed their property, and there were undoubtedly married ones who resented the law depriving them of this economic right. Rebecca's paternal grandmother sold her Maryland farm before moving to Georgia with her husband. On the other side of the family,

Grandmother Swift once wrote her daughter complaining angrily that a female relative's "negro man is advertised to pay her husband's debts." Rebecca was descended from strong-minded women.[5]

Men, however, and not women, were to exert the greatest influence on the course of Rebecca's life. Her father was the first of these. It is doubtful that Charles Latimer had advanced ideas on the rights of women. More likely he gave his daughter that concern and affection he had been prepared to give to a son. But in any event, his relationship with her was unusual for that day.

Charles Latimer was a man of great energy and strong character. As a small boy he had come to Georgia with his parents, who settled in Warren County. In the early 1820s he had moved with his brother, William, Jr., to the newly formed county of DeKalb. The Latimer brothers had cleared some farm land near the Covington-Decatur Road and opened a general store and tavern. In 1832 a post office was established in their store, with William as the first postmaster. Two years later when William moved to Houston County, Charles took over their several enterprises, and prospered.[6]

As occupied as he was with the farm, tavern, and post office Rebecca's father found time for less practical interests: he played the violin, helped to establish a neighborhood school, and read closely such Whig newspapers as the Milledgeville *Southern Recorder,* and the Augusta *Chronicle and Sentinel.* Rebecca learned early to respect the power of the press. When the editor of the *Recorder* visited her father, she was puzzled that such a small man could have so much sense in his head.[7]

Latimer was fiercely partisan in his politics. His daughter always remembered the morning after the Polk-Clay Presidential race when she watched a man lead their best horse from the stables. Mrs. Latimer tried to explain to her weeping daughter that it might have been worse. "He went wild," she said, "and might have staked all he had on the election." But then, Mrs. Latimer had come from a family of Democrats and could not understand that her daughter, a true Whig like her father, was weeping more for the lost race than the lost horse. That night Rebecca watched angrily while some Democrats put a coffin on the porch of a Whig neighbor.[8]

Georgians have always been noted for their stubbornness, but Charles Latimer seems to have been unusually difficult to move.

A DeKalb grand jury once had to threaten him with the law if
he persisted in refusing to unblock a river ford on his property.[9] He set high standards for his children and was determined that they should be maintained. When his only son Charley
went to the Civil War, the father wrote him instructions for
becoming a proper soldier:

> I would further impress on your mind the importance of
> attending to your duties as a soldier. You have voluntarily
> taken upon yourself those duties at too early an age. Hence
> the importance of studying and attending to them, and at-
> tending to them punctually and cheerfully.

He went on to emphasize, however, that attention to military duties was no excuse for neglecting the accomplishments of
peace. Charley was told not only to write home regularly, but
"to take more pains in writing and it will improve you." [10]
The father's own writing was usually rather labored and
stilted, but when angered he was capable of biting, colorful
prose. During a prolonged argument with the Atlanta *Intelli-
gencer,* he wrote a friend that he had been forced again "to
come in contact with that Skunk's nest." The quarrel had not
been of his choosing, but he supposed that he could not ". . .
pass through a life of fifty or sixty years without coming in
contact with a snarling Curr who must be kicked even at the
risk of dirty shoes."[11]
In Rebecca's memories of childhood this sturdy, affectionate
man was the principal figure: reading aloud in a clear voice,
playing his violin to her accompaniment on the guitar or piano,
laughing at her for a tom-boy when she galloped up on her fat
pony. Hand in hand they walked to school together on her first
day. He was with her, too, when trouble came. He appeared immediately that horrible afternoon when she found a drunken
man hanging on their front gate shouting the most awful things.
She was not surprised when the man became quiet and went stumbling away.[12]
Eleanor Swift Latimer did not have the intellectual capacity
or leisure to share the common interests of her husband and
daughter. But she was a woman of spirit, able to hold her own
in a family of strong characters. Her letters to Rebecca are
bright with homely wit. Mary, the second daughter, was too
busy "with love scraps" to pay attention to her schooling.
Charley was studying "geomitry" and feeling "quite large about

it." Her careless husband was "no hand to carry keys." Even
if her tastes had been more cultural, the mother would have
had little time to give to music, books, and newspapers. She had
a large house to manage, several Negro slaves to supervise, two
daughters, and a son to rear. Rebecca must be trained to take
over one day the same routine. The daughter served an appren-
ticeship in each household department: cooking, cleaning, sewing,
even working in the garden. Her work must pass inspection too.
If her stitches for the slaves' clothes were too long, they must be
ripped out and done over. There would be no riding of the pony
or playing the piano until the job was finished properly. There
is no indication that the daughter felt frustrated or imposed
upon by this strict discipline. Her mother's letters reveal the affection that existed between them. Across one envelope Rebecca
wrote "From my precious mother." [13]

With attentive parents, good health, and the freedom of a large
plantation, Rebecca enjoyed a secure and happy childhood. There
were the fat pony and the big shaggy dog. In the endless woods
she gathered wild strawberries in the spring, chestnuts and chin-
quapins in the fall. There was a twisting brook for her flutter
mills, and tall trees with inviting bird nests. In the black, crumbly
earth of her own garden plot, she raised vegetables and proudly
saw them appear on the family table. And all around her were
kindly, fun-loving Negroes to praise and pet her and make her
feel important.[14]

Her father's store was always a mysterious, eventful place.
She loved to wander up and down the aisles examining the
wonderful strange things that came from so far away: the coun-
ters piled high with pretty dress goods, the shelves loaded with
tins of coffee and tea, packages of spices, and boxes and bottles
containing things she had never heard of. And the unbearable
joy of Christmas when the wagons returned from Augusta, bringing this time not only their usual freight, but also candy, fruit,
and firecrackers. People were always coming and going in the
store: farmers' wives riding up in buggies to be gallantly as-
sisted to the ground by her father and his clerk; men arriving
to stay longer and talk more, either on the front porch benches
or on kegs and boxes around the comfortable stove. Once her
father sent her home when a Whig and a Democrat got too loud
in their dispute.[15]

And even the dullest day was always brought to life by the

coming of the stagecoach. Far across the hill a horn would
suddenly sound, bringing everyone out of doors and her to the
roadside where she would dance in the excitement of waiting.
There it was, thundering down the road in a sweeping gallop,
bringing people and news from the world beyond the plantation.
One day it came filled with important-looking men. Later she
learned that they were engineers who would live at their tavern
while working on the new railroad everyone was talking about.[16]

In the evenings she listened eagerly while the men told her
father of the progress and difficulties of their work. Then one
day down the Covington Road came an unbelievable sight: a
huge railroad engine on a flat wagon drawn by sixteen mules!
It was the "Florida" on its way from Madison to the little village of Terminus where the tracks of the new railroad began.
December 24, 1842, brought an experience that almost made her
forget the next day was Christmas. Decked in her best, she was
taken by her parents to Terminus, now called Marthasville,
where a train stood puffing and waiting. Clinging to the hands
of her parents, she climbed aboard and watched fearfully through
the window as the train raced at a tremendous speed to Marietta, ten miles away.[17]

She was learning, however, that she could not expect each
day to bring new and exciting adventures. There were things
that one had to do, such as go to school. Undoubtedly she had
already heard her father talk about how fine it was to get an
education. He had decided that the spasmodic, incompetent teaching offered in the usual "field" school was not adequate for his
children. When Rebecca was five, he provided most of the money
for building "a nice, new-framed, weather-boarded" school
house on his own land. He hired a capable teacher, the young
Reverend Francis Haygood, and enrolled his small daughter to
make the requisite number of pupils.[18]

Faithfully small Rebecca marched down the road every morning, a speller under her arm, and a lunch bag in her hand, containing such delicacies as cornbread "plugged" and filled with
molasses. When the afternoon sun shone across her desk, she
would sometimes fall asleep and wake to find her face covered
with the teacher's big handkerchief. But she stayed awake
enough to compete fiercely for the spelling prize, and, to her
father's delight, shared it with a much older pupil.[19]

Latimer hoped that the Reverend Haygood would make a long
stay at the school, especially after he married one of his older

pupils, to Rebecca's great delight. But after a year he moved on, to be followed by a series of less able teachers. One night the small building burned, and Latimer made a rather drastic decision. Boarding the coach with his eight-year-old daughter, he travelled to Covington and on to nearby Oxford. There he enrolled her in a school conducted by a Miss Hayes for the daughters of Emory College professors and Methodist ministers. Rebecca boarded and slept at the house of a Reverend Simmons, and was allowed to come home on occasional week-ends. It made her feel quite grown up to take the trip alone on the coach.[20]

Little is known about Rebecca's two years in the small village dedicated to old-fashioned learning and religion. Competitive by nature, she won a pound of candy for "repeating the multiplication table back and forth without missing a figure." At the school concert she was highly praised for her piano rendition of "The Blue Bells of Scotland." The applause may have been spontaneous. Rebecca had been studying piano under Professor Guttenberger, a blind German musician, who not only improved her technical skill, but inspired her with a real love of music.[21]

Her education at Miss Hayes' was terminated by another decision of her father's. Mary, born in 1840, was almost ready for school, and now there was a boy, Charles, Jr., to think about. Latimer could not be forever sending his children away to school. Resigning his postmastership, he sold his holdings on the Covington Road and bought a house in Decatur, county seat of DeKalb County. There was a fine school there, conducted by the Reverend John S. Wilson, a Presbyterian minister and former member of the State Educational Commission.[22]

Rebecca found the Reverend Wilson a bit too stern a moralist for her tastes. He immediately informed his girl pupils that they could choose between dancing and attending his school. Angrily Rebecca hurried home to her father. He allowed her to dance. He wouldn't let any teacher tell her what she could and couldn't do outside of school. But when education was at stake, the stubborn Latimer was willing to compromise. He reminded his daughter that later on "there would be time aplenty to educate your heels." She agreed.[23]

There were still plenty of pleasures for her besides dancing: picnics to Stone Mountain, trips to Marthasville, now as large as Decatur, and weekends at their new plantation on South River, where Latimer had built a handsome two-story house with white columns and an upstairs porch. In Decatur she joined the "Wash-

ingtonians," a junior temperance society, and sang emotional
songs about the evils of drink. And there was always her piano
waiting in the parlor, and the abundance of sheet music her
father provided. On the back of "Will You Come to My Mountain Home," she wrote proudly: "R. Latimer May 1848. Learned
in one day after nine hours' practice. Rebecca age 13." [24]

Unfortunately she had to learn, too, that life could be cruel
and tragic. At the South River Plantation she saw a neighborhood boy leave for the Mexican War, and she recalled the stories
of General Santa Anna's brutality. Then there was the day when
a Negro drowned near their house and the body was brought
up into the yard. At her Decatur school she heard whispers about
a girl pupil who was going to have a baby without having a
husband. Rebecca, however, was far too healthy-minded to brood
over unpleasant things.[25]

She was growing into a lovely girl. A miniature of her in her
teens shows a bright face, regular features, a firm, sensitive
mouth, and intelligent, dark eyes. People always seemed to remember her eyes. Her parents allowed her to be a bridesmaid in
two weddings and to attend a Christmas party in Marthasville—
whose name had been changed again, this time to Atlanta. Egg-
nog was served at the party, but mindful of her Washingtonian
pledge, she had only a glass of syllabub. The next morning she
sat on a fence and argued that country life was better than
city life with two lively young brothers, Evan and Albert
Howell. She was beginning to feel like a lady.[26]

Such diversions during holidays were harmless, but Charles
Latimer had been wondering whether his intelligent daughter
ought not to take advantage of the advanced education now ob-
tainable in Georgia. Their own church, the Methodist, had an excellent female college in Madison. Rebecca could stay with kin-
folk there. He was delighted when she consented readily to go.

The curriculum of the Madison Female College offered a rather
formidable array of courses. The juniors, Rebecca's class, studied
logic, moral philosophy, geometry, natural philosophy, physiol-
ogy, and composition. The seniors went on to mental philosophy,
trigonometry, chemistry, astronomy, zoology, and geology. Of
course, there was instruction offered in more feminine fields
such as music, voice, and "Oil Painting, Water Colors and Mono-
chromatics." And it may have been, as a newspaper editor of
that day said, that the courses were not taught as extensively
as in male institutions. Nevertheless, it was hardly a program

calculated to attract the traditional Southern belle of fiction.[27]

Although the young ladies all roomed in private homes, carefully chosen, they lived under the strict regulations of the college. They must attend prayers or divine service twice a day; must not leave school or their boarding-houses without permission; must receive no gentleman visitors except those certified by their families; and must attend no parties or dances. In brief, as the catalogue emphasized, the trustees wanted their graduates to be not only well educated, but "of pure morals and unblemished character." [28]

Rebecca lived with her mother's sister Mrs. Robert S. Douglas. It is doubtful that she was disturbed by the curriculum or the rules; she had come for work and self-improvement. Notations and dates written on her sheet music show that she progressed on the piano to operas, and that she played in several school recitals. Her sketch book of pencil drawings reveals a competence probably attained by serious effort. Only one of her written compositions has been found, a theme entitled "The Spirit of Improvement." The style is self-conscious and ornate, but the grammar is correct and the sentences are clear.

> In no respect is improvement more apparent than in the intellectual world. After a slumber of ages the mind of man has awakened to a realization of its power. This is especially true of the Anglo-Saxon race, for the mental powers of the Eastern nations are still folded in the Lethean slumber of ages.[29]

In her senior year she went through what was probably her only religious experience. The Academy—faculty and students— was caught up in the fervor of a local religious revival. Rebecca found it impossible to concentrate on her books. Had her interest in music and education caused her to neglect the things of the spirit? She had a long talk with one of her professors. When he advised her to "seek the better part," she joined the church of her parents, and pledged herself never to indulge in dancing and card-playing. Soon she was back at her books again, but she kept her vows.[30]

At the close of the year she was told that she would share first honor with another girl. She was to deliver the class valedictory, although she was the youngest in her class. How proud her father would be of her.

2

. . . . .
. . .
.

A Hill Country Wife

IN ante-bellum Georgia, commencements at men's colleges were large imposing affairs, prolonged by the earnest orations of students and visiting dignitaries. At Franklin College in Athens, state politicians would gather to make alliances and plans for coming campaigns. Female academies and colleges modelled their commencements on those at Athens and Oxford but could offer fewer, tamer speeches and less imposing visitors. On the whole, Georgia males of that day did not take women's graduations too seriously. A contemporary humorist had one of his rural characters attend a Wesleyan commencement at Macon and comment that if "wimmin" kept getting so much education, they were going to "turn the world upside down with their smartness." [1] Nor were the young ladies allowed to suppose that their diplomas would alter their status in Georgia society. A speaker warned the graduating class at LaGrange College that a woman could not speak "what she pleased" because her husband must answer for her words "either by fight or by law." [2]

In spite of this prevailing attitude of male superiority, Rebecca probably found her graduation impressive and serious. Charles and Eleanor Latimer were surely there to meet their daughter's teachers and friends. Perhaps they shook hands with the principal speaker, Dr. William Felton of Cass County in northwest Georgia. The exercises extended over two days, with prayers, a sermon, speeches, and readings. One young graduate became so nervous when she faced the audience that she could not speak a word. Later in the program she was introduced again, and, fortunately, this time performed admirably. [3]

Rebecca's speech was delivered on schedule. She had chosen a

10

rather profound subject: "Poetry—Its Practical Nature and Moral Tendency." Strangely, she preserved no copy, but years later she said that she warned her audience to have nothing to do with the Byron craze. Evidently she also touched on more moving aspects of her subject, if the Augusta *Chronicle's* account is to be believed. According to that paper, "Miss Rebecca Latimer read in a clear and beautifully-modulated voice," moving the audience with the "freshness of her religious emotions and her genuine enthusiasm." Before she ended, "strong men wept under the power of sentiments at once so strong and natural." The journalism of that day was inclined to be as extravagant as its oratory, but the young speaker was probably pleased with the report of her first speech—especially since it appeared in one of her father's favorite newspapers.[4]

When Dr. Felton was introduced the audience saw a tall, serious-looking man in his early thirties. His face was far from handsome, but there was a definite nobility about his high forehead and strong, irregular features. Good Methodists in the audience probably knew that he was a minister of their church, a medical doctor who had given up his profession, and a member of the state legislature. A few may even have known that he had recently lost his young wife and had been left with a small daughter. If any had heard him speak, they anticipated a learned, eloquent address.[5]

As was customary, the speaker began by praising the faculty, the graduates, and, especially, the young ladies who had performed so admirably on the program. They had all proved that Georgia and its churches had done well to provide a fuller education for the girls of the state. No country could reach true greatness, he said, without educated mothers. They, above all other influences, could raise public morals and purify a nation's literature. And only that literature with moral intent could endure. Poetry like Lord Byron's was destined for speedy oblivion. The speaker and the valedictorian were in agreement as to the demerits of that poet.[6]

Dr. Felton declared that it was Christian homes, graced with intelligent, devout wives, that had given America its supremacy over all other nations. A woman's work must, of course, be done within the limits of her home, but he explained how its effect on the world outside was deep and far-reaching. In smoothly-moving sentences, he spoke of man's greatest need.

Man requires a home where the affections are refined, the
passions are schooled, cares are lulled and thought is
strengthened. Mind and virtue are impaired by continual
contact with the throng of pleasure or business. Patriotism
resolves itself into theory unless watched and kindled by the
vestal attendant at home.[7]

Dr. Felton's speech was published in his county paper, the Cassville *Standard,* along with an editorial praising him as one of the
best orators in the state. His old friend Francis Bartow, later to
die on the battlefield of Manassas, read it and wrote that he
found it pleasing in its associations and harmonious in its diction.
Rebecca's committee wrote requesting a copy to print in pamphlet form. Personally she gave ampler evidence of having been
moved by the sentiments of the speaker. She married him on October 11, 1853. The ceremony, in the white-pillared house over-
looking South River, was performed by the Reverend J. H. Echols,
the Madison professor who had counselled her to join the church.
Afterwards the couple left for the Felton farmhouse, three miles
outside Cartersville, a small station on the Western and Atlantic
Railroad.[8]

The groom's father, Captain John Felton, had migrated from
North Carolina to Oglethorpe County in north Georgia. He came
of sturdy, industrious yeomen farmers who took their religion
and public duties seriously. He had served in the War of 1812
and fought in the battle with the Creek Indians at Chalibee, in
western Georgia. Possessing little education, he was determined
that his only son should enjoy its benefits. As a small boy William was taken to hear the orations at Franklin College commencements, and at one of them was deeply impressed by Daniel
Chandler, an Alabama statesman, who pleaded eloquently that
higher education be also offered to Georgia's women.[9]

In 1835 Captain Felton moved to Athens so that his son
could enter Franklin College the following year. William, a true
Felton, worked steadily at his books, but found time to speak
often at the Demosthenian Literary Society and to form a close
friendship with Benjamin Harvey Hill, a handsome, brilliant
fellow student from LaGrange, Georgia. Like Rebecca, young
Felton graduated at the head of his class, but, unlike her, he
refused the honor of valedictorian. In 1842 he entered the Medical College of Augusta, where he also did well, graduating in
1844. Returning to Athens, he began his practice and married
Ann Carlton, member of a prominent local family. Plagued since

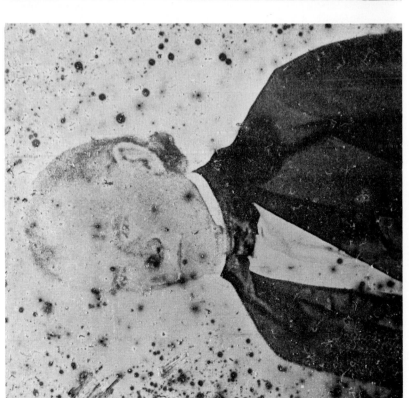

CHARLES LATIMER, SR.   ELEANOR SWIFT LATIMER

(Reproduced from daguerreotypes made about 1860)

REBECCA LATIMER FELTON (LEFT) AND HER SISTER
MARY LATIMER MCLENDON
(Reproduced from a cameo made in the 1850's)

WILLIAM H. FELTON HOME NEAR CARTERSVILLE

MR. AND MRS. WILLIAM H. FELTON

MRS. FELTON IN HER LAST YEARS

" 'BRER' CANDLER TRIES TO 'JUMP' ON THE UNIVERSITY—BUT—
MRS. FELTON DISAPPROVES AND CHASTISES HIM."—*Pandora*, 1893

childhood with a nervous ailment, he was soon forced to give up the strenuous life of a physician for a more healthful occupation. In 1847 Captain John Felton bought a large tract of land near Cartersville, in the new county of Cass, where he and his son moved to farm the rich soil of the Etowah Valley.[10]

Evidently farming improved William's health, for he became active in religious and public affairs. Devout by nature, he entered the Methodist ministry during his first year in Cass County. Although he never held a regular pastorate, he continued active in his office. In 1851 he ran for the state legislature, perhaps to take his mind off a recent sorrow—Ann Carlton Felton had died shortly after the birth of her namesake. He was elected, but served only one term. As a maiden member he was conscientious but hardly distinguished, serving as chairman of the committee on the lunatic asylum and as a member of the committee on banks. He supported the passage of the important bill which repealed an act of 1849 allowing an unrestricted domestic slave trade. Possibly he did not stand for re-election because he was too busy paying court to Miss Latimer.[11]

The section of the state to which Dr. Felton brought his second wife was not far removed from the frontier. Life on one of its hill farms lacked many of the comforts and pleasures found on a large middle Georgia plantation. The people of the Piedmont Region were primarily concerned with "livin' at home and eatin' in the kitchen." The winters were bleak, and neighbors lived a considerable distance away. More interested in land than in books, these small farmers usually had in their parlor cabinets a Bible, a treatise on home-doctoring (probably the most used book in the house), and some odd volumes brought from their old homes nearer the coast. Even the owner of slaves claimed no higher social position, but worked in the fields side by side with his Negroes. Security and leisurely living were still to be won.[12]

Rebecca probably found life in the Felton home rather austere. The one-story farmhouse on the Tennessee River was clean and well built but small and rude compared with the mansion above South River. The Feltons respected learning and her husband was well-read, but she missed the lively sound of Charles Latimer's fiddle, the wit of her mother, the gaiety of sister Mary. Dr. Felton, she complained later, never perpetrated a joke and never understood one. She was missed at her old home, too. Her parents wrote how lonely they were without her.[13]

What impelled Rebecca, when little more than a child, to break

away from a devoted family circle and go with her sober, older
husband into this sterner life? Primarily, she had found a man
well suited to her temperament—one, in fact, not unlike her beloved father. William Felton was less gregarious and worldly than
Charles Latimer, but he had the same respect for education and
the same concern with religion; and he, too, saw nothing un-
desirable in a woman who could share and voice such interests.
And Rebecca, for all her wit and gaiety, also looked on life as
a serious affair in which she, too, must prove her worth. She was
undoubtedly impressed by Dr. Felton's commencement speech,
and when she came to know him better—however that came
about—she decided that she could be happy as his wife. In all prob-
ability she chose wisely.

She found Cass County not entirely void of intellectual and
cultural activities. Nearby Cassville, the county seat, was proud
of its two colleges: Cassville Female College, established by the
Methodists, and Cherokee Baptist College for men. The Cassville *Standard* might not be as large or as widely circulated as
the Augusta *Chronicle* or Milledgeville *Southern Recorder,* but it
was admittedly the best newspaper in Cherokee Georgia. There
were even visiting lecturers, among whom was a "female itinerant"
who came to speak on woman's rights. The *Standard,* however,
did not think the lady met with much approval, judging by the
smallness of her audience.[14]

Neighbors called on the young bride—good, friendly people like
the John A. Erwins and the John Howards—anxious to make her
feel at home in her new surroundings. Many were members of
her own Methodist church, and deeply concerned with the religious and moral conditions of their community. A law had been
passed banning the sale of intoxicants within the limits of Cassville, so as to remove temptation from the young men studying
there. Of course, most of the people she met were Democrats,
and she had been taught to think poorly of that political faith,
but then, they did belong to the Union branch of the party
which had often voted with the Whigs on state questions.[15]

She could hardly have escaped homesickness, but she learned
early that work was the best medicine for a troubled mind. And
there was work aplenty to do. She took over the rearing of her
small step-daughter, and when her mother-in-law died, she became the woman of the house and the farm. Fortunately, she
had been trained for her job by an excellent teacher, her own

mother, who had emphasized that work must be done efficiently and on time. Babies arrived at regular intervals: John Latimer in 1854, Mary Eleanor, named for her sister and mother, in 1856; and William Harrell, Jr., in 1859. A new and intensified life began for her, a period she would often recall fondly and sadly. Long afterwards she wrote: "For eight or ten years my life was so absorbed in my children that it was cloister-like, months elapsing sometimes when my feet were never outside the front gate." [16]

Death came for the first time in 1857 to take the only daughter she would ever have. It is likely that a mother with so much vitality and healthy optimism bore her loss bravely, although there are no family letters to substantiate such an assumption. Perhaps she found some consolation in her music; the dates on her sheets show that she bought several pieces during that year. There was still Johnny to care for, and probably there would be more children. Life on a farm was usually too eventful to leave time for brooding. Sudden accidents happened, such as the day Johnny was badly bitten by a dog, and there were emergencies like the "black frost" which drove a group of Baptists into the Felton home for overnight shelter. Occasionally she made the hundred-mile trip to South River—but only occasionally, and for short stays.[17]

Undoubtedly she was proud that her husband and father-in-law were prospering. She had a deep respect for money as an evidence of industry and economical management. In 1860 John Felton's real estate was valued at $12,000 and his total assets at $25,000. William's real estate was valued at $5,000 and his total assets at $14,000. Between them they owned fifty slaves, twenty-eight of whom were listed as prime field hands. The Feltons had done well in Cass County.[18]

In 1860 she could not have known that her life had spanned what one historian has called "Georgia's Golden Age, the era of its relatively greatest wealth and importance within the union." The hard-working immigrants from Virginia and North Carolina had built a prosperous economy. Georgia was producing over seven hundred thousand bales of cotton a year, and was leading the South in textile manufacturing. It had greater railroads than any other Southern state except Virginia. In politics it was represented in Washington by such nationally known statesmen as Howell Cobb, Alexander Stephens, and Robert Toombs. Down at Milledgeville a line of strong, resourceful governors was being continued by a thin, granite-faced man named Joseph Emerson Brown. It was indeed a state to take pride in.[19]

And yet, as 1860 drew to a close, Rebecca Felton was bound to have felt that those days of peace and plenty might be almost over. The Southern states seemed headed towards a crisis with a Federal government that was growing more determined that the Union must be preserved. Some Georgians were declaring that there was no solution short of secession. The fiery Toombs had said as much in a speech at Cartersville.[20] Then South Carolina seceded, and Joe Brown called for a convention in January. Cass County would stand for the Union, but how would the state go? Like many another Georgian, she waited anxiously.

3

·····
···
·

War and a Railroad

THE roar of cannon in Rome, Georgia, echoed over the hills, and cheering crowds paraded its streets. Word had finally come from the convention in Milledgeville: Georgia had seceded! Twenty-five miles away in her home by the W & A tracks, Rebecca Felton heard rumblings on the night air and knew their meaning. A chilling fear came over her, and her mind was "filled with forebodings as to the future." [1]

Her many accounts of the war were written long after the deep suffering that its closing years brought her. It was easy, therefore, for her to imagine later that the despondency felt that night was a clear premonition of things to come. Naturally she was depressed by the firing of those cannons. Her Whig father had taught her to love the Union. Also, she feared the coming of war, even if Dr. Felton was physically unfit and her sons only young boys. Her heart grew heavy a few days later when she saw seven-year-old Johnny wearing the blue cockade of secession. It is not so certain how her husband felt about the decision made at Milledgeville. After the war she said he had been a secessionist, but in view of his long record as a Union Democrat, it seems more likely that he merely felt bound to accept the will of his state. [2]

It was the attitude of many other north Georgia Unionists. Cass County, which had voted heavily against secession, now stirred with military preparations. Several companies were raised of men eager to go immediately to the front, and the Inferior Court authorized a $20,000 bond issue to equip volunteers and help feed their families. Before long the excitement of parades and rallies was sobered by rumors of impending battles. Then one bright July morning the Cartersville churches were crowded

for prayer. Local boys were leaving for a little town in Virginia
called Manassas, where the war was beginning. Mrs. Felton never
forgot the scene that day at the railroad station:

> There was a war cloud in the very air. The feeling of
> anxiety was portentous. The hot July sun looked down upon
> us here with the streets full of anxious men and weeping
> wives and children. As the train rolled in sight, the tears,
> embracings and entreaties that filled the air. . . . When the
> whistle blew . . . such a wail went up to Heaven from those
> desolate wives and children as I can never forget.[3]

Weeping also, she went down the line of cars, shaking hands
with the men and boys she knew, promising to look after their
families. Any day now she might hear that Charley, her sixteen-
year-old brother, had boarded such a train.[4]

She and the Doctor joined in the war effort of their community. He gave up the idea of entering the army as a chaplain, possibly because of his health, but he did some local service
with a Home Guard company. At a nearby military camp he
attended the sick, and as the war went on, he cultivated his
farm more intensively to raise food for the expanding Confederate
armies. In what time she could spare from her work at home,
she nursed her husband's soldier patients and was long remembered by one for her "ministrations" to him and his comrades.
Like many another Southern woman she found that her problems
and work increased daily. She made military shirts from treas-
ured dresses, blankets from carpets, and knitted socks from a
dwindling supply of wool. As the Federal blockade pinched more
tightly, she found substitutes for coffee, tea, and sugar, and
boiled the earth of her smokehouse for salt. Fortunately she had
never resented hard work.[5]

But she worked now with a troubled mind. Charley Latimer
was in Virginia, and his father could not always be at the iso-
lated house on South River. The war brought other dangers besides battles. Her mother wrote, "I am the only white person on
the place tonight." [6] Of course the fighting was still far from
Cartersville, but, whether Mrs. Felton realized it or not, the two
iron rails in front of her house would some day draw the enemy
like a magnet. For it was over the W & A that the Confederate
Army in middle Tennessee got much of its food and munitions.

One quiet April morning in 1862 the northbound train went
by the Cartersville station without stopping, to the indignation of

several people waiting to board it. If Mrs. Felton saw it pass her house, she probably paid no attention. A short while afterwards, however, she may have been startled to see the engine "Yonah" from the Etowah Mines go thundering by, its coalcar filled with armed men. Later she undoubtedly heard that a band of Yankees in civilian clothes had stolen the engine "General" and three cars at Big Shanty Station and headed north to destroy behind them the Confederate supply line. Fortunately they had been closely pursued and captured near the Tennessee border. But the war had come to Cartersville, if only for a brief visit. That night the Doctor and others guarded the Etowah Bridge.[7]

A year later the Yankees struck again at the W & A. Colonel Abel Straight with sixteen hundred horsemen rode out of Tennessee through north Alabama towards Rome. His mission was to destroy the arsenal there and cut the railroad tracks somewhere near Cartersville. Fortunately for the hungry Confederates in Tennessee, General Bedford Forrest was soon snapping at Straight's heels like a well-trained bear dog. At Cedar Bluff, near Rome, Forrest brought the Federals to bay and bluffed them into surrendering to his six hundred men. A second drive at the precious rails had been forestalled, but a far mightier one was already in the making.[8]

When Vicksburg fell in July, 1863, many of the Federal troops that had besieged that river stronghold were hurried into Tennessee to swell General W. S. Rosecrans' army closing on Chattanooga. General Braxton Bragg's Confederates withdrew from the city into northwest Georgia, followed by the huge forces of their enemies. Cartersville stirred uneasily, even though there were rumors of reinforcements to come from Virginia. Refugees began to pass the Felton house, headed south.[9]

On September 17, the tension of unbearable waiting snapped like a tight string. The big battle had begun, along a little creek called Chickamauga, the first major battle on Georgia soil. As the hot morning wore on, the people of Cartersville gathered at the railroad station to get any news that might come over the telegraph. Suddenly the high shriek of a locomotive pierced the dead air, and a long train was seen laboring up from the south. The tops and doors of the freight cars were crowded with dirty, sunburned men. Never mind how they looked. They had come. Lee's men. From the Army of Virginia. Veterans of Manassas . . . Fredericksburg . . . Gettysburg. The Yankees were in for some real fighting now. All that day and into the night, trains glided through the town. There was a collision outside of Cartersville, and Mrs. Felton saw the dead and injured that were brought into the village.[10]

Again the waiting for two days, with tension as oppressive as the heavy heat. Then the heart-lifting news—a great victory, *finally* a victory in Tennessee. The Yankee army had been cut in two and driven pell-mell back into Chattanooga. In the midst of the rejoicing a call went out for all women to hurry immediately to the railroad station. The freight cars were returning, filled now with broken men bound for the Atlanta hospitals. The great victory had been dearly paid for.[11]

To the end of her long life Mrs. Felton would never forget what she saw that day. The cars were packed with bloody, filthy men, lying almost on top of one another, gasping with pain and thirst. Frantically she worked with the other women until the train began to move: swabbing out throats too inflamed to swallow, wiping the feverish face of a boy whose own mother would not have known him, taking faint messages for women far away. Climbing down from the car, she noticed dull-eyed prisoners in soiled blue uniforms seated on its top. Train after train arrived loaded with human suffering. In one car she found a young boy with a deep body wound. She begged him to let her take him to her home. She could nurse him there. She wanted so to make him live. The soldier could only shake his head. When he suddenly began to call for his mother in Texas, Mrs. Felton could control herself no longer. As she wept bitterly, she felt the dying boy's hand close over hers. War would forever mean to her those stifling charnel cars in the Cartersville station.[12]

As the autumn passed she realized gradually that the high price for Chickamauga had been paid largely in vain. The incredible Bragg sent Longstreet to Knoxville and left the Federals in Chattanooga unmolested. Reinforcements and supplies came in time to raise the siege. Mrs. Felton begged her husband to take them away, out of the obvious path of invasion. He assured her that there was still time, and hope. In early December she became seriously ill, and did not hear the fearful news which was brought to their door by bandaged, hungry men. Bragg's army had been shattered at Missionary Ridge, and what was left of it had fallen back to Dalton, fifty miles north of Cartersville. When she was better, the Doctor told her he was going to middle Georgia to find a place where they could live until the war moved elsewhere. Near Macon he rented a large farm about four miles outside the little village of Clinton on the Monticello Road. The only house on the place would not be very comfortable, but they would be safe there.[13]

In March the Feltons left for Macon, shortly before General William Sherman launched his huge veteran army down the route of the W & A. At the end of her wearying journey, Mrs. Felton saw a scene that must have taxed her sturdy courage: a plank shack in the midst of a lonely pine grove. It was to be their home— the Lord only knew for how long. Inside she walked through un-plastered, unsealed rooms, and felt the winter air seeping under the clumsy window shutters. In July the place would be as hot as a brick-kiln. Well, they must make it do, and be thankful they had left the Yankees so far behind.[14]

Through the spring and into the summer she cooked, mended clothes, and looked after the three children, while the Doctor and the slaves worked the alien soil. Yes, July was hot, but it was pleasant that evening sitting on the front porch talking with some visiting neighbors. Of course the news in the paper didn't sound good. Sherman had probably taken Cartersville by now. But Joe Johnston would stop him soon, and anyway, he'd never take Atlanta. She became a bit irritated when one of their Negro girls came hurrying up to the porch stuttering with fear. On her way home from Macon a white gentleman had told her the Yankees would be there that night. Angrily Mrs. Felton sent the girl to the quarters. People ought not to tease the poor silly things. The guests agreed.[15]

But the white man, whoever he was, had not been teasing. Even while the little group rocked on the Felton porch, a column of blue-coated horsemen was riding down the Monticello Road with orders to join another column at or near Clinton. The detachments made up a boldly planned raid under General George Stoneman, to destroy Macon and move on to release the thousands of Federal prisoners suffering at Andersonville fifty miles further south.[16]

When the neighbors left, the Feltons tried to get some sleep in the sweltering heat. Just before dawn Mrs. Felton dropped off only to be awakened by talking on the front porch. Slipping on a wrapper she hurried to the door and peeped out. A man in a *blue* uniform was questioning Dr. Felton! Now she could make out in the dim light that the yard was swarming with men and horses.

Yankees—a hundred miles south of Atlanta—here in these lonely woods. It seemed almost as if they had been seeking her during the past four months and had finally found her.[17]

All the next day she watched stonily while great, bearded men emptied the smokehouse, shot her chickens, even stripped the early fruit trees. Another group rode up, drunk on peach brandy. She saw officers slipping in and out of the slave cabins. Late that afternoon firing broke out in the direction of Macon, and their visitors began to mount and ride away, leaving their camp-fires burning in the meadow. Throughout the night the Feltons sat on their porch watching the fires fade into bright embers. It was good to hear the next afternoon that most of the raiders were captured. But she could feel safe no longer. Others would come.[18]

The news from Atlanta increased her apprehension. John B. Hood, who took over the Confederate Army from Johnston, launched two saving attacks and was beaten back into the city's fortifications. Thank God her parents had left there and gone to Crawfordville, near Augusta. In early September came the inevitable announcement that Atlanta had fallen. In which direction would Sherman strike now? Perhaps they ought to move further south. She wrote her uncle in Perry asking him to find them a house.[19]

Before her uncle could reply, an epidemic of measles, a frightening disease in those days, struck the Felton farm. Without sleep or rest she nursed the small sufferers, white and black. Willie died, but she could not leave the others long enough to give way to her grief. One poor Negro woman returned from burying a child to find another one dead. "We did nothing," Mrs. Felton wrote years later, "but wait on the dying and dig seven graves in less than two weeks." [20]

Her uncle in Perry wrote urging them to come to his house immediately. But by then, she was preparing to go alone in the opposite direction. Word had come that her mother was dangerously ill and calling for Rebecca. To reach Crawfordville, she must travel across the route which, according to newspapers, Sherman was likely to take any day now. She might be cut off from her family. The Yankees might come through Crawfordville, headed for Augusta. But she was going. The Doctor would have to stay with Annie and Johnny.[21]

She nursed her sick mother on into November, even though she knew that the Yankees had left Atlanta and were marching

to the sea. Then came the news she had expected every hour:
Sherman was moving their way and might arrive at any time.
She sat silent, but the woman on the bed spoke: "Try to get
back to your husband and son. I am better." The weeping
daughter caught the train for Augusta, only to find there would
be no train from there to Macon until the next morning. In
the midst of the confusion and panic, Dr. Felton appeared—almost miraculously—with the two children. How good to see his
strong, quiet face, to hug the children. They would get home now.
Fortunately for her strained nerves, she did not know it would
be almost Christmas before she saw the refugee shack again.
Next morning the Macon train stopped at Tennille. Black columns of smoke were rising in the direction of the Oconee River
bridge. Sherman was moving fast. Back in Augusta the Feltons
boarded a train for Savannah. They could have returned to
Crawfordville, but all they had was in those far-off pine woods.
They would circle the advancing Yankees and get back to Macon
from the south.[22]

The horrors of that journey lived on in her memory. Dreary
autumn rains beat on the car roof, but inside the air was stifling and foul. They were seldom able to secure more than one
seat for the four of them. Food was almost unobtainable: a
handful of greasy potatoes when the train stopped near a farmhouse; a few stale rolls in Savannah; odds and ends at railroad
stations. Once the train, crawling through the night south of
Savannah, passed a long line of flat cars on a siding. By the
eerie light of pine torches, she saw that the cars were littered
with living skeletons in shreds of blue uniforms. They were Federal prisoners being transferred from Andersonville to more secure prisons. At the next depot she saw a dead Negro on the
platform—"the quivers of dying flesh had hardly subsided in his
stalwart frame." He had been impudent to a guard on the prison
train.[23]

At last they rested in Quitman, near the Florida border. Mrs.
Felton and the children stayed there with friends until the Doctor returned to the shack and sent word that it was safe for
them to come. He met them in Macon. Some of the slaves had refused to follow the Yankees, he reported, but most of their food
had disappeared. When Mrs. Felton entered their dilapidated
house, she found a wounded Confederate on one of the beds. She
could not escape the war.[24]

During the next few months unwelcome callers of all sorts

came to the Feltons' door: Confederate commissary officers demanding food and forage; embittered, hungry deserters in grey and
butternut; liberated Negroes, rebellious in their sudden freedom.
One night a group of them turned the Feltons' slave quarters
into a hell of drunkenness and knife-fighting. And then—with
peace expected any hour—a young Confederate staff officer came
galloping madly out of the woods one afternoon. A large force
of the enemy was approaching from Columbus, followed by a mob
of unruly whites and Negroes. Macon would be surrendered,
and civilians, especially women, should leave immediately. Young
Annie burst into tears, but Mrs. Felton shook her head: "I can
run no further. I have nowhere to go." So they stayed through
another night and day of terror. They escaped unharmed, but
little was left them but their miserable home. One day peace
came, so suddenly and quietly that she could hardly realize it
was true.[25]

Even then they could not go home; not yet. Their crops were
in the ground, and the Cartersville farm was barren. Food was
scarce enough where they were. Dr. Felton repaired an old
grist mill and dam on the place so that they could grind their
own corn. June was hot and dry, and the water in the mill pond
grew stagnant. One day Johnny became violently ill. Recogniz-
ing malaria, the Doctor hurried him to a Macon hospital. He
died within five hours.[26]

Later, perhaps years later, Mrs. Felton found the contract her
husband had made for the farm. She wrote a note on the back of it.

> This contract put Dr. Felton in rent possession of the Plant
> farm near Macon, Ga., for a refugee home. My son Willie
> died there. My eldest son was carried from the house at
> 4 p. m. and died before 8 p. m. Oh, the horrors I suffered
> there.[27]

She and Dr. Felton were stricken with the fever, and by the
time she recovered, he was ready to take her home. He had
sold their fine carriage in Macon for a hundred dollars. They
could pay their debts and have money enough for the trip. After
a visit with the Latimers in Crawfordville, they went on to Atlanta where they took the W & A to Cartersville. Through the
train window she looked out on gutted roads, washed fields,
and piles of brick and charred wood heaped around lonely chim-
neys. Sherman had come that way. He had stopped in Cartersville
too. The railroad station had disappeared; many familiar stores

and homes were gone. The Feltons had barely enough money left for a dray to take them and their belongings home. The house was there. A kind neighbor had moved in when he heard Sherman was burning all unoccupied dwellings. In the front yard she saw the rusted springs of a baby carriage.[28]

She demonstrated immediately that she had not been broken by her grief and suffering. A doctor's bill was paid promptly, in spite of his protest that he was in no hurry. Charles Latimer sent her fifty dollars in gold, but she refused to spend a cent of it. They must put that aside for emergencies—must earn the money for current expenses. Such courage in the face of basic needs revealed, more convincingly than words, her determination to go on.[29]

Resolutely she set about helping to find their daily bread. It was difficult work. Northwest Georgia had been the most punished section in the state. After Sherman passed, a bitter guerrilla war broke out between Union and Confederate sympathizers. As late as 1867, the people of Kentucky were sending grain to the hungry in Cartersville. At one point Mrs. Felton became so desperate that she obtained corn by giving her personal note for four dollars to the local Federal commandant. When he left without remembering to collect his note, she was delighted. Perhaps her family sent additional money. More likely Captain Felton, who returned to live with them, had some cash. The legend still persists in Cartersville that he buried a large sum of gold when Sherman approached the town. But however they managed during those first few months, she probably spoke the truth when she boasted that without touching her father's gift, they never lacked bread.[30]

In January, 1866, Dr. and Mrs. Felton opened a school for boys and girls in the local Methodist church. Education in Cartersville had been discontinued during the war. Soon the school had eighty pupils, ranging from six-year-old children to youthful Confederate veterans who kept putting out the grate fire with their tobacco juice. She helped teach the three classes and gave piano lessons. Tuition was not often paid in money; but she was glad to be active, especially at such worthwhile work. For two years she and the Doctor drove back and forth every week day, over the broken, three-mile road.[31]

Other people in Cartersville were working instead of brooding over the things that were gone. Samuel Smith started the Cartersville *Express* and was soon praising his fellow citizens for their efforts to rebuild the railroad station, install street lights, and buy a fire engine. The war had left a spirit of lawlessness in its wake, but the town's better element soon had this largely under control. Announcements of social, cultural, and religious activities began to appear in the *Express*. There were tableaux at the churches, debates at the Lyceum, and meetings of the Temperance Club. A Ladies Aid Society was formed to help care for the widows and orphans of Confederate dead. A number of powerful camp-meetings were held, and Editor Smith was happy to report that "many sons and daughters" had been "born with God." [32]

The two Feltons joined in the revival of community life. He preached at various churches, addressed the Temperance Society, and delivered an eloquent eulogy on Robert E. Lee at a memorial service for the great leader. Mrs. Felton had fewer opportunities to exercise her talents, but she made full use of them. She had sent no men into the Confederate Army, and she expressed a rather low opinion of several of its generals, especially Joseph Wheeler, whose cavalry, she contended, had raided her stables. But these handicaps did not deter her from being elected president of the Ladies Aid Society. At a women's meeting in her Methodist Chuch, she went firmly on record against strong drink, with a derogatory analysis of brandy and its effects. She was incapable of taking a lukewarm stand on any subject.[33]

She was finding less time to give to such meetings. Howard Erwin, her third son, was born in 1869; and Paul Aiken, her last, in 1871. Two of the three gaps in the family circle had been filled. The old pain could be borne more easily now. But in 1873 Paul died, and again she stood by a small open grave. Three little headstones were close to the pile of freshly-turned earth. The two coffins interred in Macon had been brought home with the first money from her school. Only Howard, sickly like his father, was left her.[34]

For the fourth time she had been stricken with the greatest sorrow that comes to women, and again she gave evidence of a will to bear it. A few words on a scrap of paper—perhaps written shortly after the funeral—tell of a determination to hide the depth of her grief. Paul's death, she wrote, had been a grievous affliction, but she had allowed only God to know how dear he was to her. Also, following Paul's obituary in the *Express*, there was a short poem signed with the initial "R." In it she affirmed a faith that she would find and keep her four lost children in another world. Prostrated women rarely try to express their grief in poetry.[35]

Fortunately she had learned that activity is the great panacea for sorrow. She must, therefore, have welcomed, even encouraged, her husband's announcement several months later as an Independent candidate for Congress. Perhaps she could be of some help.

4

Georgia Takes Up Politics Again

ON A chilly morning in 1864 a frightened boy sat on a fence outside Eatonton, Georgia, watching a gigantic procession emerge from the mist over the country road. Joel Chandler Harris, future creator of Uncle Remus, had stolen out for a look at Sherman's dreaded army. It came on in endless streams: thousands of bearded, tough-looking men; cannon after cannon; strong, well-fed horses. They were the enemy—from that different world up north—all those men and guns and horses. No wonder General Johnston and General Hood couldn't stop them. The boy jumped suddenly from the fence and ran back to the plantation home of his friend and employer Joseph Addison Turner. There he found everything strangely quiet and deserted. What had disappeared was the Old South.[1]

As the war closed other Georgians had to face the same hard fact: the South had been completely beaten by a stronger power. The life they had known and enjoyed was ended. Many waited despondently for whatever was to follow. Others, of a more practical mind, began considering how they might fit into the new order of things, which would surely be directed, if not dominated, by the enemy. A few saw their opportunities even that early. War had demonstrated the strength of the North's economy. If the South accepted abolition and began immediately to build its own industries, there would be material benefits for all, especially for those who moved quickly.

Three of Georgia's leading men illustrated these different reactions to the Old South's end. Alexander Stephens, Vice-President of the defeated Confederacy, waited gloomily for the Federals at his Crawfordville home. He appeared to have little hope for the South or for himself. Riding away from Appo-

28

mattox, Lieutenant-General John B. Gordon had no plans for the future. He must have listened attentively, however, as Yankee Congressman Elihu Washborne, also on his way to Richmond, explained that President Abraham Lincoln and other Northern leaders were anxious for the South to be restored to peace and to a place in the nation's economy. War Governor Joseph Brown probably knew what he was going to do, even before the surrender. Released after a short stay in prison, he "went scurrying around Washington and New York trying to find out the North's sentiments towards the South, and incidentally himself." [2] Undoubtedly all three Georgians, even Stephens, expected to have a hand in their state's post-war affairs. They had known fame and high position; retirement would be unbearable.

There were difficult days ahead for local leaders, but there would be political and economic rewards for those who understood the temper of the state. The majority of Georgians were willing to compromise with the victors—up to a point. They understood that they had been defeated, and were not planning guerrilla resistance, as the turncoat Augusta *Chronicle* had feared. They were ready to accept abolition and be restored to the Union. But on certain issues they would not give an inch: they would remain proud that they had worn Confederate grey; they would never consent to political or social equality for the Negro; and they would expect, when they had rejoined the Union, to enjoy all rights guaranteed by the Constitution. [3]

But the people of Georgia were to learn that home rule could not be had again for the asking. For six long years they were forced to fight for it against alien opposition and under confused leadership. Northern adventurers and native opportunists took over the state government, organized the Negro vote, and grew rich on graft and corrupt railroad financing. Twice the Radical Administration in Washington sent troops to back up its puppet government. Those Georgians not disenfranchised were advised by some of their leaders to register and vote, and warned by others to stay away from the polls. And it did seem useless to exercise the right of suffrage. In 1866 when Stephens and Herschel Johnson were elected to the Senate, they were denied their seats. Two years later Gordon, the hard-fighting general, was easily beaten for governor by the illegal tactics of Rufus Bullock, a pre-war immigrant from New York who had ridden out the war in the Confederacy's Quartermaster Corps. Wrong seemed to be comfortably established on the throne. [4]

There were desertions in high places, too. Joe Brown was the first and greatest offender. He joined the Republican Party, supported Ulysses Grant for President, and actually accepted an appointment to the State Supreme Court from the hated Bullock. To some, Brown's conduct did not come as a great surprise. Even before the end of the war, he had showed a tendency to prefer the winning side. But in 1871 the majority of Georgians were astonished and angered to hear that Ben Hill, Dr. Felton's old friend, had accepted the Reconstruction measures of the Radicals. As a Confederate Senator, Hill had supported President Jefferson Davis and the war to the very end, and in 1868, at the famous Bush Arbor Meeting in Atlanta, he had eloquently denounced Brown and his "scalawag" principles. In fairness to Hill it should be pointed out that, unlike Brown, he did not agree to the enfranchisement of the Negro until after the Fourteenth Amendment had become a part of the Constitution. Nevertheless, this change in his position created the widespread impression that he had followed Brown into the camp of the enemy.[5]

But the fight went on, and victory was finally won. The excesses of the Bullock regime hastened its downfall. The more brazen it became in its corruption, the more the opposition increased and hardened. Ex-Confederates, Unionists, and old-line Whigs shelved their differences to unite in the Democratic Party and battle the common foe. Soon there were indications that Bullock's end might not be far off. Conservative Republicans began to vote with the Democrats, and Federal troops no longer arrived in response to the Governor's manufactured reports of brutality towards the Negroes. Then came an infallible sign that the tide had shifted. Joe Brown began to take issue with Bullock's interpretations of the Reconstruction measures, and in 1870 resigned his seat on the State Supreme Court. In October, 1871, Bullock turned over his office to Benjamin Conley, President of the Senate, and fled north, leaving confusion and rejoicing behind him.[6]

The victorious Democrats came out of the long fight with the fixed determination to retain control of their state. It would not be easy. State Republicans controlled rich Federal patronage, and the large Negro population had been enfranchised. The government in Washington was still in the Radicals' hands. To retain power in Georgia, the Democrats must impose strict discipline; they must demand that all members conform to the party line. As the Atlanta *Constitution* warned, "if the true people of

Georgia divided," then they could expect to see the "Radical Party rear its bruised head." Rebellion of any sort within the party could not be tolerated.[7]

But the party must be practical and progressive in its views. It had learned much from fighting the Radicals. The Reconstruction Amendments must be accepted, at least tacitly, so that the Federal government would interfere no longer with the re-established home rule. Such acquiescence was also necessary if Northern capital was to be obtained to build up Southern industry and restore war-wrecked railroads. But it must be understood, certainly among Georgia's Democrats, that the Negro would never be allowed to become a political power in the state. When that dilemma arose, the whites would find ways to solve it without restricting the franchise on the basis of color. Ironically, the Democratic Party reached in 1872 the position which Brown had taken in 1866 and Hill in 1870. Indeed, Hill's argument for this change could serve admirably as a statement of the party's new creed: "Times change; circumstances change; issues change; necessities change; and we should adapt ourselves to them if we expect to prosper." [8]

Carrying out this policy of expediency and progressiveness, the party's delegates to the National Convention endorsed the candidacy of Horace Greeley for President, who had been nominated also by the insurgent Liberal Republicans. Stephens and fiery Robert Toombs denounced this support of a militant Abolitionist, but Georgia was one of that handful of states which gave Greeley their vote. In 1873 the Democratic state legislature decided that Gordon was the practical, forward-looking type of statesman Georgia needed as a senator and chose him over Stephens. But there was a place for little Alec, too; he could have his old Congressional seat from the Eighth District without opposition. The party was powerful enough now to bestow such gifts.[9]

Of course there was nothing that could be done for Joe Brown, even though he had slid back into the Democratic Party by supporting Greeley, the Liberal Republican, instead of Grant. Not that Brown expected anything—yet. Besides, he was busy enough making money from his many enterprises: from the state-owned Western and Atlantic Railroad which he and a group of other businessmen had adroitly leased, from his Dade Coal Mines, Rising Fawn Iron Works, and several large plantations worked with convicts also leased from the state. The Democratic leaders could not welcome him openly back into the party, but they were glad to have him again on their side. They, too, were men of business and might find Brown's friendship useful. Also, he still had political supporters in the state, especially in the Republican counties of the mountains. There would be a political office for him too, in time.[10]

In 1872 the Democrats, or Bourbons, as their enemies preferred to call them, seemed to have the state well in hand. James Smith, a good party man, was Governor; Gordon held one Senate seat; and Thomas Norwood would be replaced by a man more acceptable to the party at the next election. Joe Brown had returned to the fold, and Ben Hill, although a bit rebellious at times, had never left it. People were paying less and less attention to such die-hards as Stephens and Toombs. Gordon had become the man of the hour: a symbol of the state's revered past, and a leader in its progress towards a peaceful, prosperous future.[11]

But single-party control of a state is a vulnerable situation, and before long there were signs that the Bourbons were not likely to continue their rule without opposition. Old differences began to crop up in the heterogeneous organization. There were not enough offices to reward all the faithful, and murmurs were heard about the interference of the State Executive Committee in local issues. These sounds of discontent came loudly from Dr. Felton's Congressional district, soon to be famous as the "Bloody Seventh." It was the district from which revolt might be first expected. A stronghold of Union Democracy before the war, it had troubled more than once the party's majority of State Rightists. It was an area of small farmers and few Negroes; its voters, therefore, could not be easily attracted by promises of industrial development or frightened by warnings of Black supremacy.[12]

The rise of the Independent Movement in the Seventh, however, stemmed from a specific political grievance. Early in 1874 the State Executive Committee indicated that it was going to take a hand in choosing the Seventh District's congressman. First the Atlanta *Constitution*, often a spokesman for the party, reported that General Pierce Young, the incumbent, was said to have been connected with a notorious real estate ring in Washington, D. C. The editor called on the Congressman to answer the charge. Although the *Constitution* later decided that Young had done nothing dishonest, it admitted that some people did not share this belief. Next, the newspaper began to praise the political record of Colonel L. N. Trammell, a former president of the State Senate who lived in the Seventh. If this district decided to send Trammell to Congress, declared the *Constitution,* it would be ably represented. An anonymous letter, also advocating Trammell, was published in the paper and later reprinted and circulated through the Seventh. The Atlanta *Herald,* another Bourbon journal, took up the cry. The party had evidently decided Trammell was to have the office.[13]

There were Democrats in the Seventh, however, who did not seem to appreciate this advice and assistance from Atlanta. "One of the People" wrote to the Cartersville *Standard and Express* warning that the district did not want a candidate hand picked by the Executive Committee, and in the same paper, "Peter Porcupine" ordered the *Constitution* and *Herald* to stay out of the Seventh's politics. The editor of the *Standard and Express* agreed that the people would not stand for the exclusion of better men by orders from party leaders, and the Rome *Commercial* pointed out that manipulated conventions were stirring resentment among the state's Democrats.[14]

These warnings must have been taken lightly, however, by some of the district's delegates who met on September 2, to nominate a Congressional candidate. When on the seventeenth ballot Trammell had gained a bare majority over Young, the convention set aside the requirements for a two-thirds majority and declared him its nominee. Such high-handed methods were sharply criticized by the newspapers of Cartersville, Rome, and Marietta. But open rebellion against the party was another matter, and these editors proceeded to place Trammell's name on their mastheads. The Marietta *Journal's* endorsement was rather unenthusiastic: there had to be political parties, said the editor, so his paper would support the party and its nominee.[15]

But political leaders and newspaper editors do not always represent public opinion. A month before the Calhoun Convention, ruffled Democrats had persuaded Dr. Felton to stand as an Independent against the party's nominee. On August 3, he announced his candidacy in the recently-established Cartersville *Sentinel.* Undoubtedly he had been approached much earlier. In March a letter-writer to the Rome *Courier* had urged him to run, and a month later the *Standard and Express* warned that an Independent might enter the race.[16] Certainly by June the Doctor was considering the idea, for Nellie Latimer McLendon was writing that she could picture her sister entertaining in her splendid Washington parlors. The Doctor was slow to decide, but once he had announced, he opened immediately one of the most explosive battles ever fought on Georgia's well-worn political fields.[17]

In his announcement the Doctor insisted he was running as a Democrat, but he warned that his campaign would be directed at corruption in the party's entrenched hierarchy. He indicated those groups from which he expected the greatest support. As a farmer, he claimed membership in the "producing class" whose labors, he said, "were only serving to cancel . . . the expenditures of the legislature." He reminded the voters that he had never speculated in the spoils of office, an appeal likely to attract people who instinctively distrusted professional politicians. When he charged that indifference and apathy had kept evil men in many state positions, he could expect response from the sober, God-fearing members of his Methodist denomination. Eloquent and earnest, William Felton was going to prove a formidable opponent.[18]

It is reasonable to believe that Rebecca Felton approved of her husband's decision to stand for Congress, and that she planned, from the first, to help in his campaign. She was deeply ambitious, both for her family and for herself. From her Whig father she had inherited an interest in politics and a conviction that the Democratic Party was far from a sacred institution. The excitement of the contest would take her mind from that shack in the Macon woods, from the four small graves on the hill outside Cartersville. She knew, of course, that no Southern lady was expected to concern herself with politics, but she knew also that times were changing, and that women in other sections were beginning to play a part in this change.

Her husband needed any help she could give. The forces against him seemed unbeatable. Except for two small weeklies, the Cartersville *Sentinel* and the Cedartown *Record*, the press of the Seventh District had come out obediently for Trammell. In Atlanta the *Constitution* and the *Herald*, with large circulations in northwest Georgia, had already established a stake in the contest. The powerful State Executive Committee was determined to elect regular Democrats from each of Georgia's nine Congressional districts. Undoubtedly it would send popular orators to every county in the Seventh. The war cry of the Democrats could already be heard: Dr. Felton was standing against the party that had redeemed Georgia from the Negroes and the Radicals. He must be put down.

5

. . . . .
. . .
.

A Georgia Lady Enters Politics

FROM speaker's platform and editorial page the Bourbons opened an abusive attack upon the Independent candidate, calculated to discredit him immediately with those groups from whom he expected support. Trammell, it was pointed out, had been "raised between the plow-handles," while Dr. Felton, far from being a tiller of the soil, was an owner of large estates. He was charged with mixing politics and religion exactly like those debauched Yankee preachers who had brought on the Civil War. But the most consistent accusation was one designed to stir a prejudice latent in the minds of most Georgians. Dr. Felton was not a true Southerner. Where was he when such gallant Democrats as Colonel Trammell were fighting in Confederate grey? What had he done to help drive the Radicals from the state? One letter-writer to the press volunteered to tell what he was doing *now*: soliciting votes from Negroes and Republicans. In his acceptance speech Trammell insisted that the most important question for Georgians to decide was whether there should be forced social equality in the Southern states between whites and blacks. This was the issue on which the Bourbons intended to fight the campaign.[1]

The attacks on Dr. Felton were studded with a variety of uncomplimentary terms. He was called a "self-nominated candidate," "a clerical demagogue," "the old Democratic Pharisee." A lively reporter on the Atlanta *Herald* (perhaps brash young Henry Grady) ridiculed his "reckless coat and breeches," and insisted that his rude, untrained eloquence stamped him as a man innocent of culture. One letter-writer even advocated that the Independent candidate be hustled roughly out of the race.[2]

The Bourbon editors warned constantly of the dangers in bolting the party. Split the Democratic vote and a Republican might well be elected. If Felton won, declared the *Constitution,* the Seventh District would learn, too late, that an Independent had no power in Congress. Trammell considered that his defeat would be a repudiation of the Lost Cause. Not that the editors entertained for one moment the idea that Dr. Felton would win. Their reports from all counties indicated that he did not have a chance. Murray stood solid against him; Dade would not give him fifty votes. At Spring Place the Independents had already given up. Even Felton had lost heart. He had tried to sneak away from the attack of one Bourbon orator and had come off badly damaged from a debate with another. The Democratic press was doing its best for the party.[3]

Meanwhile Dr. Felton was acting strangely for a man who knew he was defeated. In county after county he was vigorously pressing home two charges against his opponent. One connected Trammell with the infamous bonds of the Brunswick and Albany Railroad. Early in the year a committee from the legislature had investigated the records of that defunct railroad. Charles L. Frost, its president, had admitted giving H. I. Kimball, a Radical promoter, sixty-five one-thousand-dollar gold bonds which were paid to L. N. and W. T. Trammell for their efforts to get state endorsement of the road's securities. Dr. Felton offered the testimony as evidence of what Trammell had done for his state during Reconstruction. Hurriedly Trammell produced a contract, signed by Kimball, which hired him as one of the road's attorneys for only five thousand dollars. But Dr. Felton had made his point. The Democratic candidate had admitted his connection with the Radicals.[4]

Against Felton's second charge the Bourbons could offer even weaker defense. Questionable methods had undoubtedly been used at Calhoun to nominate Trammell, and the Democratic editors had been unable to conceal their awareness of this fact. In speech after speech Dr. Felton condemned the "Calhoun cesspool." Several delegates, he charged, had been tricked into giving Trammell a bare majority by agreeing to cast a complimentary vote for him on the seventeenth ballot. The Bourbon *Standard and Express* had unintentionally supported this charge when it bragged that Trammell's friends brought the convention to a close sooner than was expected. A newspaper friendly to Felton named three delegates who had disregarded their instructions not to vote

for Trammell, and declared that another delegate had switched
to the nominee after getting a wire from Joe Brown. At least
it seemed certain that the convention had not gone off in complete harmony.[5]

The Doctor's accusations were warmly backed by three small
newspapers: the Cartersville *Sentinel,* the Cedartown *Record,*
and the Atlanta *News,* the last edited by the brilliant Alexander
St. Clair Abrams, bitter foe of Joe Brown. Probably even more
helpful was a series of anonymous letters which began to appear
alongside these papers' editorials. "Fair Play," "Etowah," and
"Un-Trammelled" belabored the Bourbon candidate unmerci-
fully. He was called "Farmer Trammell," "the ring-master of
the Brunswick and Albany," "the horse" which the "Calhoun
Jockey Club" had been forced to enter in spite of the protests
of the jockeys. As the campaign progressed it became increasingly evident that it was not the Independents who were becoming discouraged. The Bourbon Rome *Courier* admitted that
the country parson had forced the powerful Democratic Party
to fight a defensive instead of an offensive battle.[6]

By early October the prospects of their candidate must have
appeared hopeless to the Democratic Executive Committee of
the Seventh District. They proposed to Dr. Felton that if he
would submit his claims to the party, Trammell would withdraw, and the people would be given another opportunity to
express their choice. When the Doctor refused, the committee
had no choice but to let Trammell step down. In a published
statement he explained that he was withdrawing to prevent the
disintegration of the party and the *Standard and Express* insisted that his manly decision was no confession of defeat. The
Herald, however, admitted that the situation in the Seventh was
chaotic.[7]

In Rome a second convention met "in great harmony" and
nominated a second Confederate Colonel—William Dabney of
that city. Rid of the burdensome Trammell, the Democrats closed
ranks and struck hard to save the Seventh. The Rome *Courier,*
which had been lukewarm for Trammell, declared that Dabney's nomination removed any reason for voting against the party.
It was reported that the Negroes were solidly behind Felton.
The *Herald* announced that they had organized a band in Rome
to serenade the Doctor, and the *Constitution* followed with a
story that the notorious Negro Crumley had spoken strongly in

Cartersville for the Independent candidate. The chairman of
the Executive Committee appeared in the District to boost Dabney
and the Bourbon newspapers promised that Ben Hill, former
United States Senator H. V. M. Miller, and General Gordon were
on the way.[8]

Unperturbed by the shift in opponents, Dr. Felton continued almost single-handedly his condemnation of the Democratic
Party's methods. Dabney, he pointed out, had been put forward
by the same men who had picked Trammell and then summarily
withdrawn him. The Bourbon speakers were finding the preacher
an ugly man to handle. At Spring Place he took on three of
them: Trammell, General Young, and Colonel J. W. Johnson.
Cleverly he allowed Trammell and Young to speak before him so
that when his turn came he was able to praise them for their
loyalty to a party that had rejected them both. The crowd roared
with laughter. It was the kind of political entertainment that
Georgians relished.[9]

The weary Doctor was far from confident, however, when he
reached home two days before the election. At supper he warned
his wife that the Bourbons might resort to any trickery necessary to win. On election day Mrs. Felton occupied her mind by cutting articles from campaign newspapers and pasting them in her
first scrapbook. When her husband returned late that night he
brought the good news that at least their own county had
gone for them by a huge majority. The next day the Atlanta
papers reported that Dabney had won, and his jubilant followers
in Rome began preparing a victory celebration. And there
were reasons for believing this report. Although Cobb and Bartow had gone for the Doctor, Floyd had swung to Dabney—
possibly because of Gordon's speech there—and Dade, filled with
Joe Brown's enterprises and leased convicts, had given the
Doctor only *five* votes. It looked bad.[10]

During the following day the reported totals of several counties shifted back and forth, but by evening it seemed fairly
certain that the Doctor was leading by sixty-five votes, with
Haralson County only to be heard from. Seated before their fire,
the two Feltons waited, quiet and alone. Suddenly from the direction of town they heard shouting. Hurrying to the door, they
listened to the pounding of horse's hooves in the darkness. Then
a war-whooping friend pulled up at the front steps yelling that
Haralson had gone for the Doctor. Yes, it was certain, by a hun-

dred and twenty-five votes. The warmth of victory spread through
Mrs. Felton's tired body. They had won—against the Democratic
machine, the Atlanta newspapers, Brown, and Gordon. She and
Dr. Felton would go to Washington.[11]

She took to her bed, unable to attend the Cartersville celebration where the Doctor spoke from the porch of the Bartow House
and Joe Brown was hanged in effigy. However, she probably sent
the anonymous telegram which the Atlanta *News* ran, asking
Brown to send some wood for the bonfires. Stung by the impudent
request—and the Felton victory—the ex-Governor answered
in the *Constitution.* He would be glad to supply a few sticks from
the many Democratic celebrations throughout the state if the
Radicals wanted to cheer over their "only . . . victory in Georgia." [12]

Mrs. Felton's activity in her husband's first campaign was
neither evident nor acknowledged. She attended no public rallies
and sent only anonymous letters and articles to the press.
During the campaign no newspaper, friendly or unfriendly, mentioned that a Georgia lady was working busily in the rowdy
political contest, and after the election only the Augusta *Chronicle* commented upon the important part she had played. She
was said to have been her husband's constant counsellor on all
questions; in fact, she had really managed his entire campaign.
A clipping of the article was pasted in her scrapbook, no doubt,
with pride. It was her first recognition won in the masculine
game of politics.[13]

The *Chronicle* did not over-emphasize the importance of her
assistance. If the Doctor had political headquarters, they were in
his farmhouse, and she certainly "managed" everything there
while he was driving and speaking throughout fourteen counties.
For over three months she followed a routine which demanded
physical and emotional endurance: running the farm, writing
daily to her husband, having fresh linen and a brave face ready
on his return. In this first campaign he probably dictated or
wrote most of his letters, but, even so, she must have counselled
him frequently on what to say.[14]

She did handle one exchange of letters without consulting the
Doctor. When the rumor persisted that Gordon, Hill, and Miller were coming to speak against her husband, she wrote each
asking if it was true. Hill and Miller assured her emphatically
that it was not.[15] Gordon replied evasively.

Atlanta, Georgia, October 24, 1874

Mrs. W. H. Felton
Cartersville, Georgia
Dear Madam:

I have yours asking if it is my purpose to make speeches for the mass meeting in the seventh district. In reply I have to say that I have appointments in the second district of long standing and am now preparing to leave for South Georgia to answer them. It is impossible to say now when I will return. I am, Madam, very respectfully your obt. servant.

J. B. Gordon[16]

Exactly one week later Gordon spoke before a huge Dabney rally in Rome, and Mrs. Felton formed an opinion of him which she admitted in her *Memoirs* she "never . . . changed thereafter."[17] Her decision to save his answer may have started her habit of preserving her political correspondence.

By her own admission, she wrote many of the replies to the abuse and misrepresentations by the Doctor's foes. Most of the clippings in her first scrapbook reveal the biting wit and belligerent tone so characteristic of her style. One Bourbon writer was told that if he desired a lively time, he could get it, and another was warned that there were blows to be given as well as received. She probably tried without success to get something into the enemy's papers. Once when the *Constitution* apologized for "mislaying" a letter from Cartersville, a paragraph, immediately appeared in the friendly *News* asking if Trammell owned stock in the *Constitution* as well as the *Herald*.[18]

On two occasions she let the Bourbons know that her husband's political activities were conducted by a partnership. Hearing one day in Cartersville that a carriage-load of Democrats had gone to her house, she turned her buggy and drove rapidly for home. The visitors were just coming down the front steps, but she blocked them at the gate. What were they up to? One bravely explained they had come with the proposition that both candidates withdraw and a new convention be held. The Doctor, he hastened to add, had refused. Mrs. Felton nodded her head. "That was the proper thing for him to do and say." Before she would let them leave, she preached a short sermon on the evils of their ways.[19]

After the campaign, Henry Grady of the *Herald* called to interview the Doctor. She met him at the door. After elaborating on her low opinion of his paper, she announced that she would remain for the interview. Throughout the race she had been the Doctor's partner and she did not propose to be omitted from his councils now. Nor did she remain as a listener only. Before Grady left he decided who "had been helping her husband with the brain work of his campaign."[20]

The following fall she was busy getting ready for the exciting trip to the Capital: finding a home for Pompey, her saddle horse; getting her house in order; packing for the three of them. Realistically she understood that as Independents they could not expect the Democratic Party to sponsor them in Washington's political circles. They must make their own friends. When Ben Hill won the Congressional seat over a recommended candidate in the Ninth District, she wrote Mrs. Hill how pleased she was at the coming opportunity to know her and her husband better. Next she wrote ailing Alec Stephens, offering any help she might give him after they all arrived in the Capital. Before leaving, she made arrangements to send letters from Washington to several Georgia newspapers. Most of them were friendly papers in her district, but even the *Constitution* and *Herald* were willing to employ the services of such an entertaining correspondent.[21]

The trip north in late November was an adventure for the forty-year-old lady who had scarcely been outside her own state. She noticed everything: the sumptuous accommodations of the train; the rich land of Virginia's valley farms; even the road signs advertising "Tutt's Liver Pills" and "Creosote Dye." Every hour carried her nearer to the great Capital where the nation's business was done; where they would be people of some consequence—"Congressman and Mrs. William H. Felton of Georgia." Watching eagerly as the train crossed the Potomac, she saw the dome of the Capitol break through the murky clouds. At the station they took a hack for the National Hotel. It would be their home for nine months. Henry Clay had lived there, the man Dr. Felton was said to resemble. Mr. Stephens would live there when he was well enough to come. It was a part of Washington's history.[22]

Immediately she noticed that an atmosphere of apprehension pervaded the Capital. Grant, still the folk hero of Appomattox to millions, had indifferently allowed his second corrupt administration to rock steadily downhill. But now a Democratic majority in the House was planning investigations which might prove highly revealing. All would go well with their party if its Southern members would only refuse to be drawn into sectional strife, as Senators Gordon and Lucius Lamar of Mississippi had so calmly done. The Democrats were already eyeing 1876, which would be a presidential year.[23]

Mrs. Felton was hardly unpacked before she set out to see Washington. On Thanksgiving Day she attended a Methodist service and was not pleased with what she saw and heard. The preacher delivered a "politico-religious address," the congregation applauded, and whites and Negroes whispered together and sang from the same hymn book. Outside the church she found the crowds staring at "a stout, short man with an elaborately dressed lady, equally short and stout" on his arm. When told that they were the Grants, she was not much impressed. Two days later, she was more moved by the funeral procession of Vice-President Henry Wilson, because she had read his late expression of good will towards the South.[24]

It was a strange new world to the lady from the farmhouse on the Tennessee Road. At her hotel's Christmas dinner she was amazed at the amount and variety of food. Retiring early on December 31, she was awakened by the clanging of cowbells and the explosion of firecrackers. Her annoyance was soothed a little, however, by the sweet music of church bells breaking faintly through the ruder noises. While watching the New Year's Day Parade, she noticed disapprovingly how the dandified men with "roseate" complexions inclined more heavily in their seats as the day wore on. She was glad to hear that nothing stronger than beef tea was served at the President's reception.[25]

The fact of Emancipation was more apparent in Washington than in Cartersville. Evidently she never met Frederick Douglass, the Negro envoy and orator, at a social gathering, but she was indignant to learn that he was invited to White House receptions. Looking down from the House gallery, she counted seven Negro Congressmen from the South, and wondered how they had eaten and slept on the long trip to Washington. She admitted that Blanche K. Bruce of Mississippi, the sole Negro in the Senate, was "decent in his behaviour, and served with credit." His admirable conduct, however, did not lessen her racial antipathy. Her prejudices and loyalties were not readily changed by foreign ways or new experiences.[26]

She was not, of course, cut off in Washington from people who thought and felt largely as she did. There were the warm-

hearted Hills, the genial Blounts from the Sixth District, Milton
Candler from Decatur, her old home. She probably saw little of
the Gordons, although she realized immediately that the handsome, war-scarred Senator was one of the most admired figures
in the Capital.[27]

Gregarious and ambitious, Rebecca Felton had no idea of
moving only within a circle of fellow Georgians. She became acquainted with many Northern Democratic Congressmen: S. S.
Cox of Ohio, Michael Kerr of Pennsylvania, and Samuel Randall
of the same state. Indifferent to party labels, she enjoyed the company of such Republicans as Senator T. W. Ferry of Michigan
and Congressman William ("Pig-Iron") Kelly of New York. She
met and admired David Davis, the liberal Supreme Court Justice whose tremendous paunch fascinated the Blounts' small
daughter Dolly.[28]

Learning quickly the ways of Washington, she welcomed any
opportunity to display her efficiency and connections. In June a
party of Atlantans stopped over in Washington to see the sights.
In a letter to the *Constitution* one of the visitors reported
that "the Hon. W. H. Felton and his lady" had been their es-
corts almost the entire day. At the House of Representatives,
they had found all seats taken, but a note from Mrs. Felton to
her friend Acting Speaker Cox put the Foreign Diplomats' Gallery
at the disposal of her Georgia friends. The grateful writer
agreed with Ben Hill that Mrs. Felton was "our Second Representative from the Seventh." She pasted this clipping in her scrapbook, which was, by then, almost filled.[29]

In August she visited the Philadelphia Centennial and was
greatly impressed. The Art Gallery and Memorial Hall alone, she
thought, would repay a trip from Georgia. In Machinery Hall she
marvelled over a 1400-horse-power Corliss engine. She figured
that the Centennial would give a rich harvest to the city of Philadelphia and was ashamed that the South had only a few booths
and placards in the magnificent exposition. Although a staunch
agrarian in politics, she did not disdain the material benefits from
the country's growing industrialism.[30]

The nine months must have passed quickly. There were so
many exciting things going on, such as Ben Hill's heated debate
with Congressman Blaine on the Republican's Reconstruction
policies. But there were exacting duties for her to perform daily:
answering her husband's mail, keeping the family in clean clothes,
and guarding little Howard's health in the severe Washington

climate. Her numerous clippings from Georgia newspapers show that she was keeping an eye on the home front. Congress would not adjourn until late in the summer, giving the Feltons little time to campaign before the election in November. She intended to come back to Washington.[31]

The Doctor could hardly expect to continue in office unopposed. True, he had proved himself an able, industrious Congressman; and he had voted consistently with the Democrats, helped them to organize the House, and, following the policy of Gordon and Senator Lamar of Mississippi, he had expressed conciliatory views on the Reconstruction Amendments. As a small south Georgia paper put it, he had won the respect of his party and "labored faithfully for his constituents, and indeed for the whole state."[32]

But the Bourbons were not interested in Dr. Felton's record. They wanted to know whether he was ready now to present his claims for renomination to their convention or whether he proposed to stand again as an Independent. Either decision would be risky. Could a convention of Bourbons forget so soon the angry contest two years ago? Would they consider for their candidate a man of such independent views? If he sought the Democratic nomination and was denied, he would cut a sorry figure running as an Independent. On the other hand, if he chose to continue his fight against the party, his opposition might be even more formidable than in 1874. The Bourbons were anxious to stamp out the Seventh District revolt before it spread over the state bringing out candidates in other districts and even in the gubernatorial race. In fact, a rumor was afloat that Dr. Felton might run for governor instead of for Congress. Henry Grady was ridiculing the idea, but the Bourbons were obviously worried.[33]

On August 17 the Feltons were met at the Cartersville station by a band and an enthusiastic crowd. The Doctor spoke again from the balcony of the Bartow House, and received an ovation which even the hostile *Standard and Express* thought must have gratified him. The editor noticed that Mrs. Felton was as enthusiastically received as her husband. Cartersville was proud of its "second representative."[34]

6

. . . . .
. . .
.

Madame Roland of the Seventh

EVEN before Dr. Felton reached home in the summer of 1878, he knew that the Democrats were going to bring out a candidate against him. His friend Ben Hill had tried to get the district leaders to nominate him, with emphatic lack of success.[1] However, the Doctor was determined to make a strong bid for the Democratic vote. In his announcement speech at Rome, and later at Cartersville, he pointed out that he had supported the party in Congress and emphasized that all of his Georgia colleagues wanted him re-elected.[2]

The Atlanta *Commonwealth* pounced upon his words and with an utter disregard for truth, reported him as boasting that Hill and Milt Candler were coming into the Seventh to speak for him. The newspaper demanded that those two Democrats say whether they were planning to support a candidate bent on destroying their party.[3] Frightened by the warning, Candler wrote immediately to Dr. Felton that he would appreciate a public denial of the *Commonwealth* story.[4] The Doctor was not at home when the letter arrived, but Mrs. Felton was, and as she read it, her anger was kindled. Milt Candler could pose as a great friend in Washington, but in Georgia. . .

She wrote Candler that he should have known the Doctor would deny the lie without being asked. She admitted that she and her husband had believed that every one of his colleagues hoped he would be returned to Washington. Perhaps they had assumed too much. But she wanted Candler to know that she would permit no man to put her husband "outside the circle of respectability." Candler could rest easy. The Feltons would do nothing to injure his political prospects.[5]

Determined to show the voters that Dr. Felton did have friends

46

—and more important ones than Milt Candler—she asked Bob Toombs to come and make a speech for him. Toombs sent his regrets. He was coming into the Seventh soon but did not expect to make any political speeches. He did, however, send his best wishes to the Doctor.[6] Next she wrote Ben Hill, asking if he too had deserted them. Hill was hurt by her question. He assured her that he never deserted a friend, but she would certainly understand that as a Democratic nominee he could hardly speak for a man his party was opposing.[7]

Resolutely Mrs. Felton set about giving her husband the help his friends had refused. Of course she must not make speeches, but the Independent weeklies were delighted to publish her letters, provided they were written anonymously. "Bartow," "Plow Handle," and "Feltonite" began to plague the Bourbons at every turn. The people of the Seventh were reminded that Dabney, who had been nominated again, was backed by the same corrupt ringsters who had supported Trammell. Farmers were asked if they were willing for "the slick hat and polished gentry" to control the district. An attack on the Doctor provoked an immediate retaliation. So the Cartersville *Express* said that Dr. Felton had sent a government bulletin to a Negro? What about those campaign circulars that local Negroes were getting at the newspaper's office? [8]

Even before the campaign got under way, the Bourbon editors had worried about the scathing articles that were sure to come. B. F. Sawyer of the Rome *Courier* had written her suggesting that the campaign be conducted fairly and magnanimously. He got no promise from Mrs. Felton. Fairness and magnanimity, she said, would make no impression on that senseless crew that would soon be howling at Dr. Felton. If Sawyer wanted a clean fight let him first do something about those politicians who two years ago had hounded her husband from one end of the district to the other.[9]

For a while Sawyer endured in silence her anonymous thrusts. Then one night in Rome he saw Mrs. Felton and another lady at one of the Doctor's political rallies. Now he had her! If he was supposed to pretend she was taking no part in the campaign, she had no business at such gatherings. In the next issue of the *Courier* he deplored the presence of two ladies at a recent "rough and tumble" rally.[10]

Mrs. Felton struck back swiftly and shrewdly. An indignant gentleman, not she, must answer Sawyer. Dr. O. F. Ford, whose mother had been Mrs. Felton's companion, was more than willing, and the rival Rome *Bulletin* would supply the space. Mrs. Felton gave Dr. Ford the benefit of her journalistic skill in composing the reply. Sawyer's inexcusable behaviour was summed up in the opening paragraph:

> Dastardly beyond expression is the personal attack on a lady visitor, an invited guest whose only offense was her presence and her quiet unobtrusive demeanor. One of the finest stories in French history is the story of how Madame Roland stuck by her husband.[11]

Several anonymous letter writers became interested in the incident. "Saw-Mill Voter" supposed it would be all right for his wife to attend a rally if it was put on by the Bourbons. "Polk County" asked innocently if any Independent editor had attacked Mrs. Dabney.[12] Mrs. Felton supplied a letter on the same subject to the Dalton *Enterprise.* Her original draft must have been a masterpiece, for even after Editor T. E. Hanbury had toned it down, it was still sharp enough to bring a cry of protest from the badgered Sawyer. As might be expected, she did not give up attending political rallies.[13]

Dr. Felton won easily, in spite of Henry Grady's warning that a second Dabney defeat would encourage the Independents to bring out a gubernatorial candidate in 1878. This time Mrs. Felton was included in the congratulations. The local *Express* said she had been a great help to her husband, but the ungracious Atlanta dailies announced their defeat in headlines that read "The Election of Mrs. and Mr. Felton" and "Mrs. Felton and Her Husband Returned." She was undoubtedly pleased with even such uncivil recognition.[14]

*   *   *   *   *

The Feltons were prepared for the excitement they found in Washington. They had already read in the Georgia press that the Presidency had been stolen from Samuel Tilden, the Democratic candidate. The Republicans had won South Carolina, Florida, and Louisiana (where their puppet state governments still held power) by the very simple device of throwing out a sufficient number of Democratic votes. The national returns gave Rutherford B. Hayes a majority of one electoral vote.[15]

The situation in the Capital puzzled Mrs. Felton. Leaders of both parties, who had been filling the papers with threats and accusations, were greeting each other like long-lost friends. It was true that the Democrats fought a motion to set up a five-man commission to pass on conflicting sets of electors, and later protested loudly when the commission decided in favor of the Republicans. Yet within a few days certain Democrats, Hill and Gordon among them, were working with Republicans to have the decision accepted by all. Mrs. Felton was learning rapidly that the political show put on for the public often had little relationship to what went on behind the curtain.[16]

On Inauguration Day she waited tense in the Senate galleries, where she had secured a front-row seat through "feminine strategy." Finally came the great roar from outside. The procession was under way. Was the crack of firearms going to break loose? One newspaper had actually declared that if Hayes reached the Capitol alive, then the people deserved their slavery. Now the dignitaries were coming in . . . Grand Duke Alexis of Russia . . . Sir Edward Thornton, the British Ambassador. What a lovely lady Mrs. Hayes was. There were Grant and Hayes . . . why, they looked like a pair of elderly twins, coming in side by side . . . short, stubby, brown-haired . . . Hayes had the more amiable face . . . maybe he wouldn't look so amiable four years from now. Everything became quiet. The ceremonies were about to begin.[17]

She was tired when it was all over. Outside she had to push her way, step by step, back to the National. Once she heard the cry "stop thief," and then the whack of a policeman's billy on a hard head. Back in her hotel room she was satisfied to see the rest of the goings-on from her hotel window, tightly closed against the bitter weather.[18]

Like her husband, Mrs. Felton was glad that the Inauguration had gone off without any trouble, and that the Republicans had promised to restore Home Rule in those three states which had given them the election. She was careful, however, not to express her feelings too freely. A lot of people at home were saying that Tilden had been cheated and were blaming Gordon and Hill for trading the election to the Republicans. It was easy for her to believe that Gordon was guilty. She had never forgiven him for that devious letter written just before he appeared in Rome to speak against Dr. Felton. When Joe Brown, over the psuedonym of "Citizen," wrote a series of letters to the *Constitution* accusing Gordon of selling the Presidency, she clipped them for her scrapbook. They might be useful some day. Apparently she had no curiosity about the part their friend Ben Hill might have played in this deal.[19]

Her friendships were as wholehearted as her hatreds. Mr. Stephens was her idol. She nursed him through a critical attack of pneumonia, sitting by his bed for hours and listening to his delirious cries for his dead half-brother Linton. When he recovered she kept a motherly eye on him. After breakfast she would stop by his room to help with his correspondence, read the newspapers to him, ask his opinion about men and measures. When he had rested in the afternoon, she would come down again to hear what had gone on at the Capitol that day. In fine weather she drove with him past historic sites made famous by men he had known intimately. She attended his evening parties, although she would not take a hand at his favorite game of whist. She was even uncritical when black Alec Kent brought out a bottle of "Jeffersonian democracy." Her tolerance was a tribute to the little man's charm.[20]

In the summer of 1877 Stephens visited the Feltons in Cartersville. She would never forget that evening on her back porch when he and Sam Jones, a local evangelist, swapped stories in the warm Southern darkness. When he went on to nearby Catoosa Springs, she sent him parcels of home-cooked food. She worried constantly about his health even though Richard Malcolm Johnston, their mutual friend, assured her that Mr. Stephens had been threatening to die for forty years.[21]

But he in turn was good to her in time of trouble. In the spring of 1878 Howard was stricken with typhoid. She and the Doctor watched anxiously for days, praying that this, their last child, might not be taken from them as the others had been taken. She watched alone that long afternoon when the Doctor left resolutely to go and register his vote against the Silver Bill. Mr. Stephens came continually to ask and to offer advice on medicine. She could be sure of at least one friend.[22]

Howard's long recuperation kept her in the hotel, but it gave her the opportunity to make plans for the coming campaign. She tried to buy the Cartersville *Express,* but gave up the idea when its editor, Charlie Willingham, came over enthusiastically to Independentism. In retaliation certain Bourbon creditors foreclosed on the paper, but the Feltons promptly started the *Free-Press* and made him their editor.[23] News from Georgia was encouraging. Emory Speer was confident of beating the Democratic candidate in the Ninth District, and Mr. Stephens was warning the Eighth District Democrats that he was going to run again even if their convention refused to nominate him. Independent candidates were offering for the legislature. The movement was obviously gaining momentum.[24] Encouraged by these signs the Doctor announced for re-election even before he left Washington.[25]

Ben Hill tried again to persuade leaders in the Seventh that the Doctor was one of the staunchest Democrats in Congress and deserved their nomination. They were not interested.[26] Already they had a campaign planned that promised to stamp out Independentism in the district. They were going to nominate Judge George N. Lester, an authentic Confederate Veteran who had lost an arm in battle. Surely the true Georgians of the Seventh would follow him rather than a man who had never worn a grey uniform.

The contest exploded in an angry battle. During the morning of July 11 people poured into Cartersville. Packed trains arrived at the depot, and wagons and buggies crowded the streets. The courthouse could never hold such a crowd; a platform was hurriedly erected in a nearby grove. The two Feltons drove up about noon. The Doctor got out and sat down under a tree, while Mrs. Felton made herself comfortable in the buggy. People nearby noticed a big scrapbook in her lap. She had brought the ammunition. There was going to be a fight.[27]

Lester spoke first. He must have learned that his opponents had been making certain investigations, for he denied, before being accused, that he had taken a fee from Joe Brown to help lobby his Western and Atlantic lease through the legislature. He denied also that he had voted for a Republican against Cartersville's Pierce Young in the Congressional race of 1872. Then he moved to the attack. Felton, he shouted, had stayed at home while his neighbors had fought and died on bloody battlefields; had stayed at home, making money, while loyal Democrats drove the Radicals from his state; now, and only now, when Georgia was safe and prosperous, had he come forth to attack the men who had fought the war and afterwards won the uphill fight for home rule. As Lester grew more excited, his stump of an arm "went flying through the air." The crowd saw and roared its approval.[28]

Dr. Felton listened quietly. When his turn came he walked over to the buggy, took some papers from his wife, and leisurely mounted the platform. His first words were ominous. His opponent had begun the attack; he would answer in kind.[29]

It was a merciless answer. For over two hours Dr. Felton paraded Lester's iniquities. He *had* accepted a fee from Brown; the Doctor had the proof. He had squandered State money as Commissioner of Immigration, and he was holding onto his judgeship while soliciting votes from men who might appear, any day, in his court expecting justice. Turning towards the enraged Colonel, the Doctor calmly accused him of trying to draw attention from his record by waving his empty sleeve. As the attack grew more vicious, Mrs. Felton heard Henry Grady mutter "My God, he's killed him too dead to skin." The crowd was on its feet, shouting now for Felton. This campaign was going to be a rough one.[30]

Throughout the blistering summer and into the fall the extravagant debate continued, in crowded courtrooms with the thermometer over one hundred, in pine groves as stifling as the inside of an oven. Rebecca Felton listened quiet and hard-eyed. She heard speakers denounce her husband as a Radical, a disgrace to his clerical calling, a traitor to the South. She heard Lester call him an unmitigated liar to his face, and taunt him with "leaving no tracks at Manassas or Chickamauga." As the Doctor tried to explain his war-time service, she heard the cries of "hospital rat" go up around her.[31]

When the stage was properly set, Lieutenant-General John B. Gordon appeared to put on the final act in the Confederate show. Again and again she watched him march to the front of the stage, his fine head held high, his scarred face alive with the joy of battle. She sat silent while the crowd rose in reverence for the Hero of Appomattox . . . sat silent while he lifted Lester's empty sleeve and smiled down at the tumult. Her hatred of the Bourbons became centered on him. He, not Lester, was the enemy.[32]

The Bourbon newspapers kept her anger at a white heat. Dr. Felton was accused of turning a weary Confederate soldier from his door. He had not lifted a hand against Bullock and the Radicals. He was encouraging his Negro supporters in their impudence and rebellion. The Rome *Courier* even circulated a rumor that the Doctor's daughter had married a man with Negro blood.[33]

Mrs. Felton struck back with story for story. Lester also had refused shelter to a Confederate—and refused it while he was a Senator drawing nine dollars in gold a day. Perhaps the Democrats would be interested in a piece of news that indicated what their candidate had done during Reconstruction? He had felt so indebted to Bullock for political favors that he had written a letter of sympathy to the Governor just before he fled the state. The Negroes knew Lester had been a Radical. One had recently said in Rome that he was for Lester because he had supported Bullock. Gratuitously she offered some information about Lester's friend Gordon. He had defrauded the public—and his fellow-Veterans—through his textbook company and insurance agency, both of which had failed because of his questionable management. He had betrayed Tilden and sold out to Hayes. Joe Brown had accused him of this in the *Constitution*. He was still hand in glove with the Republicans. A member of that party had said he could never get Hayes' ear because Gordon's arm was always around the President's shoulder. The picture she gave of Gordon differed radically from the one found so often in the *Constitution*.[34]

By moving rapidly she got her first signed letter into a newspaper. The *Constitution* published an article signed "Citizen," asking the Doctor several questions and demanding answers. She wrote Evan Howell, the paper's editor, that since Dr. Felton was away from home, she, as his "private secretary," was enclosing a reply to "Citizen." When several days passed without her letter appearing in the paper, she wrote again to Howell accusing him of turning it over to "Citizen." It was published the following day.[35]

She was undoubtedly disappointed that both "Citizen" and the *Constitution* refused to argue with her. The newspaper accused the Doctor of not having the courage to sign his own letters, and "Citizen" pompously ordered her to stand aside and uncover her husband. Nor would they reply to several Independent editors who rushed to her defense, even though one promised "Citizen" two beatings, one for insulting Mrs. Felton, and another for insulting Southern womanhood. The *Constitution* was content to refer slyly now and then to "Mrs. Felton's husband's private secretary" and to "Mrs. Felton's husband." [36]

During the campaign she did write a personal letter that would, within a few months, give her a greater opportunity to display her controversial skill. When Jesse Holtzclaw, a Seventh District Republican, announced against Dr. Felton, she wrote Senator Thomas Ferry of that party's National Committee, warning him that unless Holtzclaw was withdrawn, a Bourbon would be elected. Shortly afterwards Holtzclaw dropped from the race, probably by party orders.[37]

As election day approached, tempers began to flare on both sides. At Marietta a mob boarded Dr. Felton's train, shouting in-

sulting epithets. A duel between the Mayor of Cartersville and
Charlie Willingham's son was barely averted. Two small girls
were soundly spanked by their Feltonite father when, bribed
by a waggish cousin, they solicited votes for Judge Lester from
their perch on the front fence.[38]

The Bourbons fought until the closing of the polls, but the
Seventh gave Dr. Felton his greatest victory. The *Constitution,*
Gordon, and the Confederate flag could not prevail against the
Doctor's Congressional record, his stormy eloquence, and his
wife's busy pen.

Reading the *Constitution's* account of the election, she came
upon Gordon's explanation of the defeat in the Seventh. The Independents, he charged, had penned up a number of Negroes and
voted them at polls where the election was close. She pasted the
item in her scrapbook. With Lester beaten, she could now give
more attention to Gordon.[39]

7

The General and The Lady

REBECCA Felton was a stout hater. Anyone who fell out of her favor could expect to read immediately in some newspaper a discussion of his shortcomings. She fought with many prominent Georgians, but with none so long and wholeheartedly as with John B. Gordon. There was something almost heroic in her hatred for him. Even after his death, she admitted readily that she had many reasons to avoid and dislike him while he was alive.[1] Her fights with Governor Alfred H. Colquitt and Joe Brown were far briefer and less spectacular. Gordon, alone of the three, opposed her husband openly and determinedly. Colquitt stayed out of Seventh District politics, and Brown, when it suited his purposes, fought the Doctor from behind the scenes. Gordon alone took the stump, and she never forgave him.

What undoubtedly angered Mrs. Felton more than his intrusion in their local fights was the tactics he used. He came as the Confederate hero to expose a man who had not supported the Southern Cause. The war he gloried in had brought her only loss and suffering. She could never put from her mind the picture of Gordon smiling triumphantly from the platform while the "Rebel yell" echoed around him. She was willing to believe that "because someone had scratched his face with a bayonet, he tiptoed to show how he saved his country by fighting the Yankees." [2]

As a practical business woman she was contemptuous of Gordon's failures as a lumberman, insurance agent, and book publisher. She could respect shrewd, successful Joe Brown even while she fought him politically, but she saw Gordon, at best, as a charlatan with limited capabilities. She never trusted him after his evasive letter about speaking against the Doctor in 1874, but the Lester campaign turned her into a relentless enemy who would harry him to the end of his political career—and beyond.

Gordon would hardly have found Mrs. Felton an attractive woman even if their political interests had never collided. In his Southern code a lady was supposed to rear her children, grace her home, and leave the affairs of the world in her husband's hands. And even if one was imprudent enough to enter politics, a gentleman must continue to treat her with that courtesy due her sex. To Gordon's credit it must be said that he tried to ignore Mrs. Felton's outspoken enmity. But she was a difficult person to ignore.

He might conceivably have found it easier to fight her if her looks and manners had been those of the professional feminist. But despite her activities in the masculine game of politics, she appeared a gracious, handsome lady. The hostile Augusta *Chronicle* declared that "for a political woman she had somehow retained her womanhood to a wonderful degree"; and even the *Constitution* admitted that "she was not like those stalwart females who strut across the rostrum and magnify their unwomanliness." [3]

She would not let her opponents forget she was a woman. With a complete lack of logic, she would abuse some unlucky man and then complain loudly if he did not answer her with the traditional politeness of a gentleman. Admittedly she took an unfair advantage in such arguments, and to an extent took it consciously, but to stop there would be to stop short of the full explanation. Rebecca Felton was a complex person. The loss of her several children and her war-time suffering had developed within her a deep antagonism towards men—almost the feeling that they were instinctively hostile to women. In any debate with a man she would suspect, sooner or later, that he was trying to impose his masculine superiority upon her.

Fate could not have harassed Gordon with a more formidable opponent: a lady who insisted on being considered a lady even while she was employing all the bare-knuckled tactics of a belligerent man. And she was so steadfast in her hatred!

Although the Feltons had beaten Gordon soundly in the 1878 election, she immediately set out to make him sorry he had taken any part in it. First she tried to persuade Senator John Young Brown of Kentucky that he ought to tell the public about Gordon's part in selling the presidency to Hayes. She warned that Gordon's denial of this charge was making Brown appear to be the main culprit. Brown refused her bait, insisting that he knew nothing dishonorable about his Georgia colleague.[4] Failing to prove that Gordon had sold the election, she next sought evidence that he had tried to buy it. She wrote Amos Akermann, a prominent Georgia Republican, asking if their Senator had not used bribery in his efforts to obtain South Carolina's vote for Tilden. Akermann admitted that some of Gordon's activities did look questionable, but he could add nothing to what the New York *Tribune* had carried on the subject. He did, however, offer some advice. Even if bribery was proved against Gordon, most Southern Democrats would consider it only a patriotic effort to save the state from the thieving Republicans.[5]

The advice was wasted on Mrs. Felton. She could never understand the emotional appeal that the Democratic Party had for Southerners. In January of 1879 she launched a series of letters in the *Free-Press,* accusing Gordon of those sins for which she had just failed to find conclusive proof. He was charged with having a finger in the pie when the Democrats tried to buy South Carolina. Four months later, according to "Bartow," he was just as busy meddling with John Young Brown to get Hayes seated. For good measure a new Gordon iniquity was given currency: he was said to have failed to pay back a loan borrowed from an Episcopal bishop shortly after the war.[6] As the serial exposé increased in vehemence, the Macon *Ledger* commented, in a bit of an understatement, that the *Free-Press* was awfully out with General Gordon.[7]

Up in Washington Gordon had been reading "Bartow," as had Anderson W. Reese, correspondent of the Macon *Telegraph* and a member of what Joe Brown had called "Gordon's puffing brigade." Asked by Reese if he had read the offensive letters, the Senator lost for a moment his chivalric restraint. Yes, he had read them, and they were ". . . so utterly false, malicious and contemptible that he could not stoop to notice them even if they had been written by one of his own sex." [8]

Probably the sympathetic journalist suggested to Gordon that a little research on Mrs. Felton might also produce some newspaper copy. Wasn't there a rumor that during the Lester campaign she had written Senator Ferry for Republican help? Gordon asked Ferry for the letter. The Michigan Senator couldn't remember receiving it, but he had been passing all "political" letters on to Congressman Jay Hubbell of his state. Gordon tried Hubbell, who suggested that George Gorham, Secretary of the Republican Executive Committee, might have the letter.[9] Meanwhile Reese had grown too impatient to wait any longer for evidence. A dispatch, over his initials, appeared in the *Telegraph,* declaring that during the last election someone from the Seventh District had written the Republican Executive Committee "imploring in piteously pathetic tones material help for Dr. Felton." Reese said he had not seen the letter, but Ferry, Hubbell, and Gorham had all told him how eloquently the writer pleaded for money. He would not give the writer's name, but slyly suggested that it was that of "the controlling spirit of the Independent canvass for Congress in the past three elections." [10]

Irritated by Reese's subterfuge, the Augusta *Chronicle* demanded that he say whether or not he meant Mrs. Felton. Eagerly the lady in question volunteered to supply the answer if the *Chronicle* would give her sufficient space. Considerable space was required for her accompanying letter. She admitted promptly that she had urged Ferry to force Holtzclaw from the race, but she had not asked for money—not one cent. Let her accusers produce the letter. She pushed Reese aside as a "mere servitor doing General Gordon's dirty work in the newspapers." Gordon was the man she was after. Angered by his failure to beat her husband, he had put Reese up to attacking her—a sly, malicious trick but exactly what one should expect from a man with his unsavory record. She reviewed this record for the *Chronicle* readers, repeating with even greater positiveness all the charges she had been making in the *Free-Press.* In closing she declared that it was a sad day when sensational newspaper mendicants were permitted to assail a woman because her husband had opposed public plunderers. [11]

The *Constitution,* defender of all things Bourbon, cautiously rebuked the plain-spoken lady. It regretted that she had chosen to attack such a good and patriotic man and suggested that she, not Gordon, should produce the "friendly, harmless letter." [12] Unwittingly the editor made a suggestion which Mrs. Felton eagerly seized upon. She wrote back that the letter had been found and was in her hands. That very morning Congressman Hubbell had brought it to the table where she and the Doctor were having breakfast with Milton Candler and several other Georgians. She had showed it to the company and later to Alec Stephens. Let the *Constitution* ask either of those two good Democrats what she had written. [13] Unable to ignore the challenge, the paper sent its Washington correspondent to Candler, who admitted a bit grudgingly that there had been no request made for money. [14]

But by then Reese had made his second blunder. He had sent another article to his paper stating that an ambassador of Dr. Felton had failed to wheedle or bully Gorham into giving up the letter.[15] When Candler's interview appeared, Reese tried to make a joke of the whole affair by asking why Mrs. Felton didn't publish some of her attacks on Gordon and him in the Radical Washington *Republican*. Journalism in that day was not always distinguished by its objective reporting.[16]

Gordon wisely took the argument into his own hands and sent a long piece to the *Chronicle*. Apparently he did not find it necessary to mention Reese or the Ferry letter. Emphasizing that nothing he said was applicable to Mrs. Felton, he denounced the Doctor as the real author of the calumnies and then denied in detail each one of them.[17] Bowed out of the controversy, Mrs. Felton was forced to let the Doctor reply.[18] Gordon, however, refused to continue the fruitless dispute.

The Bourbon press considered that Mrs. Felton's signed attacks had deprived her of a lady's immunity from criticism, and proceeded to lecture her sternly on her improper conduct. She was told that she had used poor taste, put herself in an unenviable position, and should leave politics to men folks. One editor hoped that she would not continue her political debut, and another asked innocently which Felton was the Congressman and which the wife?[19] Angrily the Independent newspapers replied to those ungentlemanly remarks. The Democratic editors were told that they should "bow to a lady who loves her husband" and that a whipping was too good for a man who suggested Mrs. Felton might have lied.[20] She was urged "to lam it to them" and assured that the Independent press would stand by her.[21]

She was far from embarrassed by the controversy she had stirred. It had enabled her, she claimed, to expose Gordon as an underhanded vindictive politician. But she had not been as successful as she believed. Reese had certainly revealed himself as an unscrupulous journalist, and Gordon had worked with him to uncover the letter to Ferry. But Mrs. Felton could furnish no proof that Gordon had prompted Reese's inaccurate articles. As for her other accusations against the popular Senator, it was largely her word against his, and his supporters had no trouble deciding whom to believe.

The Bourbons were already getting a bad enough press to satisfy even her. Since the preceding year Governor Alfred Colquitt had been squirming under a continuous attack from Ben

Hill. The Northeastern Railroad had hired Hill to secure endorsement for its bonds, yet when Colquitt had signed the securities, he permitted J. W. Murphy, a clerk in his State Department, to collect the lobbyist fee. Corruption in the Treasury and Wild Life Departments had also become so apparent that the legislature was planning an investigation of them. In March of 1879 a murder on the floor of the State Capitol brought the unpopular convict lease system—and Senator Gordon—into the headlines. Captain Edward Cox, a sub-lessee of Gordon's, shot down Colonel Robert Alston, who had been authorized by the Senator to sell his lease. Immediately it came out that Alston had completed an investigation of the various convict camps, and was preparing a highly critical report for the legislature. The *Free-Press* boldly charged that Alston had been silenced by the lessees.[22]

During the following winter unfavorable news began to appear also from Washington. The Independent newspapers made much of a widening rift between Stephens and Gordon. Stephens charged that Gordon had failed to get an appropriation for making one of Georgia's rivers navigable, and Gordon issued an angry denial. A second quarrel broke out over the appointment of Census Supervisor in the Seventh District. Stephens supported and Gordon opposed a candidate offered by Dr. Felton. In a committee discussion Gordon shouted at his small opponent. Undoubtedly the *Free-Press* touched up its description of Gordon, trembling with rage, cavorting around the old patriot.[23]

But on May 20 news began to break which threatened to shake loose the Bourbons' hold upon Georgia. The *Constitution* announced, as a bolt from the blue, that Gordon had resigned from the Senate! The next day the second bolt struck: Colquitt had appointed Joe Brown to serve out the balance of the term! Then the full story came to light. Victor Newcomb, Vice-President of the Louisville and Nashville Railroad, was giving Gordon a $14,000 job.[24] This was the same Newcomb who a month earlier had persuaded Brown to put the Western and Atlantic into a vast combine that would link Georgia's ports with the Mississippi Valley. The pieces of the puzzle were falling neatly into place.[25]

An angry uproar swept the state. How dare Colquitt appoint Brown! an ex-Scalawag-supporter of Ulysses Grant—Bullock's henchman. Why couldn't Gordon serve out the few weeks left in the session so that his successor could be *elected* in the fall. It was a "regular bargain sale."[26] Gordon had turned over his Senate seat in exchange for a high-salaried job which Brown had procured. In Columbus, drums shrouded in crape summoned citizens to an indignation meeting. Ex-Governor James Smith suggested that Hill resign also, so that Colquitt could appoint Rufus Bullock to that seat, and Toombs declared that he could beat Colquitt in the next election "with a black Negro." [27]

Stoutly the Bourbon Triumvirate denied the trade. Brown claimed that he had urged Colquitt to make Gordon reconsider, and the late Senator said he had resigned without knowing who would succeed him. Colquitt insisted he had appointed the best man available, but later he did not deny Gordon's statement that Brown's political strength in the troublesome mountain districts made him a desirable choice.[28]

Gordon had more trouble explaining his own part in the transfer—especially when he did not report immediately to his new job. He explained the delay by saying that he had resigned to go with an Oregon railroad which needed his services immediately; but that Newcomb had later offered a position that would enable him to live in Georgia. Although Gordon did not say so, it was evident that Newcomb was not highly concerned about when his new employee began work. Aided by his friend Grady, Gordon now gave a variety of reasons for giving up his political career: he had accomplished his mission of restoring home rule to the South; he could not live on a senator's salary; he wanted to enjoy a more leisurely life with his family.[29]

Mrs. Felton believed none of them. She publicized a story in the Athens *Southern Watchman,* which was ignored by Gordon. A week before the resignation was written, Grady, on his way home from Washington, had revealed the whole story to Athens friends. It was beyond her how anyone could doubt that there had been a bargain. She could hardly wait to help turn the Bourbons out of office. Nor would she neglect Gordon in his fat job. Now she could prove to the people of Georgia that she had been right about him.[30]

8

. . . . .
. . .
.

Joe Brown Lends a Hand

IN THE summer of 1880 Mrs. Felton and the Independents
were a little hasty in assuming that the Bourbons faced certain
defeat in the coming elections. The scandals of the Colquitt administration had not proved as damaging as she had expected. Although the legislature dismissed the Comptroller-General and
impeached but acquitted the State Treasurer, it exonerated the
Governor of any dishonesty. Hill stopped grumbling about the
Murphy fee, and the court decided that Alston's killing had no
connection with his investigation but was the outcome of a quarrel about the sale of Gordon's lease. Although Cox was obviously
the aggressor, Alston had fired first and wounded his man. The
judge, therefore, refused to impose the death penalty and sentenced Cox to life imprisonment. He was given a clerical job at
Joe Brown's well-run Dade County Camp.[1]

Nor did the Bourbons act like beaten men. Colquitt took the
stump to defend his administration and Senatorial appointment. Gordon followed, evidently still not pressed to take over
his duties with the L. & N. Up in Washington Brown used the
few weeks left in the session to demonstrate his legislative abilities. He obtained an appropriation for Brunswick's harbor, helped
to strike out a clause in the Census Bill depriving Georgia of one
Congressman, and spoke eloquently against a bill denying Mexican War pensions to Confederate Veterans. The Democratic
machine and Grady's *Constitution* were also busy. By the beginning of the summer the Bourbons were gaining back some of
the ground lost in the spring.[2]

Mrs. Felton also went into action. Her *Free-Press* kept up a
continuous fire, calling on Colquitt to resign before a party convention repudiated him, asking Gordon why he wasn't working

at his railroad job.[3] The *Free-Press* offered an explanation of Gordon's resignation. Immediately after the Alston killing, Cox had told Brown something which enabled him to force Gordon out of the Senate.[4]

Mrs. Felton's paper was surprisingly easy on Brown. It called him a better man than his predecessor and practically absolved him of any guilt in the "bargain sale." [5] When a Bourbon editor asked Willingham why he was so kind to Brown, he replied that he only attacked those who attacked the *Free-Press*.[6] Subsequent events indicate that Mrs. Felton may have ordered the paper not to antagonize Brown. She realized that he still had considerable strength in the Seventh, and her husband was coming up for re-election in the fall.

In fact, she was beginning to worry about this contest. The Bourbons were acting strangely. By late June they had still not promoted a candidate to oppose the Doctor, and had not attacked him once. She wrote Stephens, asking whether her husband should announce his campaign or wait until the enemy showed his hand. Always cautious, Stephens replied that the Doctor should wait, and if asked whether he planned to run again, he should say that he would always serve his people when they called upon him. Stephens suggested that the Bourbons might be planning to let Dr. Felton run unopposed this year. He thought that Colquitt had indicated this when he recently appointed the Doctor to the State University's Board of Visitors. Stephens' advice was to watch and wait—difficult advice for Mrs. Felton to take.[7]

Soon she had other worries besides the Bourbons' failure to open the fight. Her husband's support was not coming forward. She wrote Ben Hill that Dr. Felton needed help and asked him to see Brown. Hill replied that he would go immediately, and that he believed Brown was the Doctor's friend.[8] Very likely a proposition made by Hill and Brown came as the result of her letter. In her *Memoirs* she wrote that in the summer of 1880, Hill, after a conference with Brown, told Dr. Felton "if he would agree to run no more after 1880 . . . all opposition would be withdrawn." According to her, Dr. Felton indignantly refused.[9] Hill's proposal must have come around July 16, for on that date the *Constitution* suggested that the Democrats might restore peace in the Seventh by offering the nomination to Dr. Felton.

In July the Doctor announced his candidacy, but the Democrats remained silent. Perhaps they wanted no trouble in the Seventh until they could get Colquitt safely renominated. However, at a drawn-out convention during early August, the Governor obtained a large majority vote, but not the two-thirds necessary for a nomination. A small, determined opposition, spurred on by young Tom Watson from the Tenth District, refused to be stampeded. The Democrats were forced to run Colquitt as a "suggested candidate." [10] The minority wanted to nominate Dr. Felton, but Mrs. Felton persuaded him that the race would be too great a strain on his health and pocketbook. Maybe conditions in the Seventh had convinced her that the Independents were not so strong in the state as she had supposed. Ex-Senator Thomas Norwood, a man of little political strength, agreed to oppose Colquitt. [11]

By the middle of August the Doctor was so discouraged by the hostility of his constituents that he sought Brown's help. A cryptic letter from the ex-Governor does not explain why the Doctor's supporters were deserting him, but it does make plain that the desertion was increasing. [12]

Brown wrote that there had been "some difficulty in the way of the matter I named to you yesterday." A certain man "spoken of at Rome" would, however, "be down tonight or in the morning." Dr. Felton must come to Atlanta that night so that the three of them could meet the next day at the house of Mrs. Felton's father. The Doctor was warned that the opposition against him was growing, and unless something was done immediately the Republicans were going to drop him. Brown realized his danger in working with an enemy of the Democratic Party, and in trying to get him Republican support. Dr. Felton was told to exercise the greatest secrecy in sending back a message by the bearer of the letter, and to bring it with him to Atlanta. Mrs. Felton thought it best to make a copy before the Doctor returned it. [13]

Brown did not take this studied risk out of friendship for the Feltons. He was watching carefully the races for the legislature that would decide whether he returned to the Senate. He wrote Mrs. Felton that he knew her power in the Seventh and hoped she would support his candidates. [14] Later, when some of them were beaten, he wrote again, asking if she would bring the proper pressure to bear on their successful opponents. His instructions to burn or destroy the second letter were not carried out. [15]

In spite of Brown's help, Mrs. Felton continued to worry. The Democrats nominated young Judson Clements, a political unknown, to oppose the Doctor. Their newspapers appeared to take little interest in the contest, and Clements spoke only with the utmost respect of his opponent.[16] She couldn't make it out. Were the Bourbons merely running a token candidate? The *Constitution* and Colquitt were ignoring the Seventh; Brown was working, behind the scene, for the Feltons; she had even heard that Gordon had said he wanted to be friends with the Doctor. But perhaps it was all a trick, even Brown's friendly concern. She wrote Stephens, asking him what they should do.

Stephens admitted that he did not like the situation. If he could talk with certain men in the Seventh, he might be able to advise her, but he was not in physical condition for such a trip. She must be careful whom she trusted. He believed that Brown was the Doctor's friend; he didn't know about Colquitt. On no account was she to put any confidence in Gordon, even if he professed friendship. The Doctor must decide for himself, and then act.[17]

The campaign dragged on, with no burning issues or unfair attacks to bring forth her scathing letters. Faithfully she accompanied the Doctor on his speaking tours, enduring the long uncomfortable buggy rides in the scorching autumn sunshine or through quick fierce deluges of rain. Clements refused to debate the Doctor. Apparently he was well pleased with the way things were going. As election day approached, the *Free-Press* warned the Independents that unless they turned out and voted, the Bourbons might recapture the Seventh. It was all to no avail. Dr. Felton's majority in Bartow was heavily reduced, and he lost the large counties of Floyd and Cobb. Jubilantly the Cartersville *Express* announced "Felton's Fall," along with an epitaph, "Here lies Etowah Bill." [18]

It is difficult to determine why Dr. Felton lost the strange election of 1880. The contest is clouded with a mystery that might be explained if the Feltons' letters to Brown, Stephens, and Hill were available. None of the several explanations offered then and later are entirely convincing.

Ben Hill believed that Dr. Felton beat himself by continuing to attack the Democratic Party after it ceased to attack him.[19] In view of the quiet campaign conducted by both candidates, one is forced to conclude that Hill was still hurt by the Doctor's refusal to compromise with the Democrats. Dr. William Roberts thinks that many Independents left Felton because some of his views were becoming too close to those of the old line Republicans. This conjecture may be true even though it conflicts with Brown's warning that the district's Republicans were turning against the Doctor.[20]

The *Free-Press,* undoubtedly speaking for Mrs. Felton, accused the Bourbons of deliberately planning an un-aggressive campaign that lulled the Doctor into defeat. It was a "still-hunt," the paper said, which created the impression that no great effort would be made against him.[21] Mrs. Felton's letter to Stephens certainly reveals that she was worried about the Bourbons' apparent indifference to the Seventh District contest. And there can be no doubt that she—and the Doctor—must have felt helpless with so little to attack.

She was convinced, also, that Brown was a party to the Bourbons' strategy. The issue of the *Free-Press* that announced Dr. Felton's defeat called upon the legislature not to return Brown to the Senate. The paper recalled, rather belatedly, that he had betrayed his state during Reconstruction, and warned that he would betray anyone when it suited his convenience. It also published a letter from "Bartow" charging that Brown had defeated Felton.[22] In a later letter to Stephens, Mrs. Felton stated that Brown had led them to believe he was working for the Doctor, but now she had conclusive proof "of his fiendish hate and treachery." [23] Whether her accusations were true or not, she was, unfortunately, in no position to publish her copy of Brown's letter to Dr. Felton.

Reading the election returns in the *Constitution,* she came upon a piece by Carey Styles, an ex-editor of the paper. Highly pleased with the results in the Seventh, he assured his readers that Dr. Felton was the most disappointed man in the state, and that there was not a woman "who didn't feel happier than Mrs. Felton." When she read it to her husband, he trembled with indignation.

"Possess your soul in peace," she told him. "When I've finished with the dirty dog, he'll tuck his tail and scurry under the house."

She was glad to have someone to attack; glad to be able to let the enemy know that she and the Doctor were not broken by their unfair defeat. She composed her letter to the *Constitution* carefully. After repeating innocently what Styles had written, she suddenly lashed him with a single blistering stroke:

> I will tell Colonel Styles I have a proper appreciation of his interest in my unhappiness, but I prefer to interview Mrs.

Styles (a lady in every sense of the word, I understand) before it is decided who is the unhappiest woman in Georgia.[24]

It was fortunate that she could get this relief. One by one the
elections went in favor of the enemy. Colquitt beat Norwood by
a huge majority. The Democrats captured all of Georgia's Congressional seats, except in the Ninth where Speer (a dubious Independent in her opinion) had won. The legislature elected was
sure to return Brown to the Senate. But the wily old statesman
took no chances. The night before it was decided, he assured a
large Atlanta audience that what he had accomplished during
his three weeks in the Senate was only a sample of what he
could do in a full term. The legislature gave him a one hundred
and sixteen to forty-eight victory over General Alexander Lawton.[25]

It seemed incredible. In May the people of the state were
calling for the Bourbons' heads. In October and November they
were electing them to any office they desired. Colquitt was exonerated and Brown, the ex-Scalawag, was restored to political
office by the Democratic Party. Except for a few die-hards like
the Feltons, the voters would remember the "bargain sale" as a
rather questionable means to a desirable end. Perhaps B. F. Frobel
was right when he commented to Stephens that Brown's victory
had demonstrated that the people of Georgia were concerned
only with material prosperity and whatever caused it.[26] Unknown
to Frobel, Stephens had already taken care that he was not going
to be counted an enemy by the all-powerful Brown. In October
he had written the Senatorial candidate that he would do nothing
to oppose his election.[27]

The unregenerate Feltons left for Washington in December.
Gone was the pleasure and excitement of past trips. She steeled
herself for the sympathetic greetings of their Georgia colleagues,
lesser men who would not be returning home when the new
Congressmen arrived in March. Bravely she took up their official
life, but she no longer had heart for the Congressional debates, the
visits of old friends, even the long evenings with Mr. Stephens. It
would all be over so soon. Of course Dr. Felton assured her that
they would be back in 1882. And apparently he planned to be.
In an interview with a Washington paper he announced, rather
significantly, that he was going to continue his fight even if he had
to join the Republican Party.[28] She was still depressed, however,
when the time came to say their good-byes. Friends who met

them at the Cartersville station noticed that she looked pale and tired.[29]

Never given to brooding, she was soon busy about the house and farm: quilting, making soap, looking after the chickens and the vegetable garden. Articles and letters on her favorite subjects began to appear in the *Free-Press*: convict lease, corrupt railroads, and Senator Gordon. But her thoughts were on Washington and the news from there.[30]

It came mostly from Mr. Stephens. He was so good about writing. He assured her that everyone in Washington missed them, down to the hotel chambermaid and black Alec, his valet. His whist parties, made up mostly of ladies, were still his greatest pleasure. A troublesome growth had appeared on his face. But he preferred not to write about politics, declaring that he had never had less interest in them. In turn, she wrote him everything that was on her mind, from her grief over the death of a pet chicken to her latest suspicion of Gordon. She was pleased when Stephens praised her racy style. A steady stream of letters passed between the Cartersville farmhouse and the National Hotel. One day he got a letter from the Doctor, and reading it too hurriedly he assumed it was from her and answered accordingly. He was terribly embarrassed. She sent him a pair of woolen socks which he prized highly because she had knitted them. At Christmas he was delighted with the two photographs of her, but wished she had autographed them.[31]

Stephens may have forsworn politics, but as 1881 drew to a close it became increasingly apparent that she had not. She insisted on discussing the situation in Georgia, and even began to suggest that he take a more active part in it. Whether he knew it or not—and he probably did—another rebellion of the state's anti-Bourbon forces was coming to a head. Mrs. Felton intended to play a larger part in this one. In late December the *Free-Press* carried a warning that the Independents would be heard from in the next elections and that better times were just ahead.[32]

9

· · · · ·
·   ·   ·
·

Little Alec Makes New Friends

BY 1881 A NEW WORD had come into the vocabulary of Georgia's Democrats: "Mahoneism." It had been coined to name a dangerous alliance of anti-Bourbon groups that was spreading through the South. In 1879 General William Mahone, a scrawny Confederate brigadier, had united Virginia's Independents and white Republicans, captured control of the state's government, and won a seat in the United States Senate. There were signs that a similar movement was taking shape in Georgia. General James Longstreet, an active Republican in Louisiana politics since the war, had returned to the state in 1880. Longstreet's defection to the Republicans had not endeared him to his fellow-Georgians; but he commanded rich Federal patronage, and when he began to visit Dr. Felton in 1881, the Bourbons waited fearfully for the new revolt to break.[1]

It came on December 28, when Dr. Felton gave an interview to the Atlanta correspondent of the Chicago *Tribune*. Mahone's victory, said the Doctor, had showed that the Bourbons could be beaten and that a coalition of Independents and white Republicans would not restore the Negro to political power. Clearly Dr. Felton was declaring total war on Georgia's Democratic Party, for he did not hesitate to praise the partisan administration of President Chester Arthur. The following day he called a meeting at Atlanta's Markham House. The Independents present were headed by Dr. H. V. M. Miller and Judge John S. Hook; the Republicans by Henry S. Farrow and James Atkins. The *Constitution* warned the faithful that the "Coalition" had at last come into the open.[2]

Up in Washington Ben Hill became alarmed at developments in Georgia, and wrote to Dr. Felton. Earnestly he begged his friend to have nothing to do with a movement that was bent on "africanizing" the state. If Dr. Felton joined it, he would stamp himself not only as a Republican, but a Radical Republican.[3] When the Doctor passed the letter to his wife, she read it and shook her head.

"Look out for an atrocious attack on you," she warned. "This is the *avant courier* of what is coming in print." [4]

Sure enough, in the *Constitution* of January 7, Grady reported from Washington Hill's opinion of the new movement. Hill denounced the Coalition rather than Dr. Felton, but he did link his friend with a scheme to stir up the race issue so that "spoilsmen may be kept in place and public plunderers protected in their greed."

Ironically, when their copy of the *Constitution* arrived, Mrs. Felton was writing a friendly letter to Mrs. Hill. It was never finished. Immediately she helped to compose a reply to the *Constitution* condemning all the past sins of Mrs. Hill's husband, sins which, until then, had apparently not disturbed the Feltons. He was called a corrupt lobbyist; charged for the first time with selling the presidency to Hayes, and denounced for arguing with Colquitt over the Murphy fee, even though the *Free-Press* had warmly supported him in that controversy. His entire career was said to have been distinguished for violence and animosity. On January 19 the *Constitution* carried Hill's answer. It was not worthy of him either. He suggested that political defeat had probably unhinged the Doctor's mind. Thus ended a friendship begun years before in the halls of Franklin College.[5]

The *Constitution* pointed out that Hill's stand was additional proof that the leading men of Georgia wanted no part of the Coalition. Brown, ex-Governor James Smith, and Independent Congressman Emory Speer were all against it. The paper was not so sure about Stephens but had heard that he planned to stick with the Democratic Party in the coming elections.[6] The *Constitution* had pointed to an obvious weakness of the Coalition. Except for Dr. Felton, it had attracted no promising candidates, and even he had refused to run for Governor.[7] Perhaps he had taken the advice of James Atkins to "name the man for Governor" and enter the next Senatorial race.[8] But the problem remained: who was the man for Governor?

The man the Coalition needed was Alec Stephens. He alone could win the support of both insurgent groups and at the same time draw those votes needed from the Democrats and Negroes. And he might consent. Although he had remained a Democrat in name, he had frequently acted independently of the party. In 1878 he had warned that if he was not re-nominated, he would run against the Democratic candidate. Even before the Markham meeting the Coalitionists had made overtures to him. In the fall of 1881 Mrs. Felton and Judge Hook had written him about "the same subject," but he had told both that he did not think the people were concerned at the time with anything in the way of politics.[9] Then Longstreet, working through a mutual friend, had tried and apparently failed to convince him that he had no political future in the Democratic Party.[10]

Mrs. Felton was determined to redeem her old friend from the party of Gordon, Brown, and Colquitt. At first she tried to interest him in the Senate. Everyone knew that Ben Hill's chance of living through his term was growing dimmer. In the summer of 1881 a malignant growth had been removed from his tongue, and although back in office, he had obviously not been cured. Without mentioning Hill's illness Mrs. Felton made Stephens a definite proposal: he should plan to run for the Senate in 1882 and persuade John Stephens, his nephew, to run for Governor. She got a discouraging reply. When Gordon beat him for the Senate in 1872, he had resolved never to stand again for that office. He was afraid his nephew lacked the experience and reputation that a gubernatorial candidate should have. Again the Old Commoner declared that he was weary of politics.[11]

Mrs. Felton refused to give up. When the Hill controversy erupted, she was afraid its violence might make it even more difficult to bring Stephens into the Coalition. He had always tried to stay out of heated arguments. She was vastly relieved when he wrote that Hill's attack on the Doctor seemed "not only un-politic & indiscreet but eminently unjust." [12] Unduly encouraged by his comments, she replied immediately, urging him not to give up politics when there was so much fun ahead. As for herself, she declared that she had never felt so war-like since the Hill fusillade.[13] When two weeks passed without an answer she let William Hiddell, a mutual friend, know that she was hurt by Mr. Stephens' silence. Forced to write, Stephens wrote bluntly. He explained that he had not written sooner because when his friends quarrelled, he preferred to keep silent. But what was even more disturbing, he let her know that he had reservations

about the Coalition: he could not sanction a political organization that put Federal patronage in the hands of irresponsible
Republicans.[14]

At this point she might have left him in peace if she could have
been sure that he would continue his independent Congressional
career. But a fearful warning came that the Bourbons also had
plans for Stephens. On March 2 a letter from Henry Farrow appeared in the *Constitution* reporting that Colquitt on a recent
visit to Washington had offered Stephens the Democratic nomination for Governor. It would be a clever piece of strategy if the
Bourbons could bring it off. With Stephens as their gubernatorial
candidate, they could kill any hopes of the Independents for that
office and, at the same time, sidetrack Colquitt's most dangerous
competitor for Hill's seat when it became vacant.

Although Stephens claimed that Colquitt had only made "a
friendly call," and the Governor later explained that he had only
said he hoped Stephens might succeed him, Mrs. Felton was troubled.[15] She knew that Joe Brown was always at Stephens' ear,
"like a serpent." [16] She watched the *Constitution* closely for developments. On March 10 came unexpected—perhaps welcome—
news. F. H. Richardson, the paper's Washington correspondent,
announced that Stephens was retiring at the end of the Congressional term. She wrote Stephens asking if it was true. He replied that it was, although he didn't know where Richardson had
got his information. Almost petulantly he added that when he
was last elected, he had planned for this to be his final term.[17]

She was probably not convinced. Whenever he stood for an office he tried to make it appear that the people had persuaded him
to run. But she dropped the subject of politics for the present, and
their letters discussed Hill's sad condition, Mr. Stephens' own poor
health, and the weather in Washington and Cartersville.[18] Then
disturbing items began to appear in the newspapers. Stephens
had dined with Brown. Stephens had praised Brown's speech on
the tariff. Brown had warned Stephens that it was sometimes
dangerous for elderly men to retire. The danger signals became
brighter. Stephens was said to have admitted that no man has a
right to decline a call of the people, and the *Constitution* was
asking if Stephens had changed his mind. From Washington
Richardson reported Stephens' admission that Georgians of all
parties were begging him to run, and if his health continued
good, he might do so. Rather impatiently the *Constitution* trans-

lated this to mean that Stephens was in the race. It warned him, however, that he could not expect to be the candidate of both parties.[19]

Mrs. Felton got back into the fight. The Bourbons were not going to capture Stephens if she could help it. She wrote asking whether he had read the *Constitution's* bullying article, and what he was going to do. Stephens replied that he had read it. Yes, he was willing to run, but only if there were "unmistakable demonstrations" that the people wanted him to save them from the horrible effects of division.[20] It was obvious that the *Constitution* had been right; Stephens wanted to carry the standards of both parties.

Richardson called again, this time with some embarrassing questions. Would Mr. Stephens accept the nomination of the Coalition? No, but he would not be "disregardful" of it. Would he accept the Democrats' nomination? Yes, that would be a "sufficient demonstration of public confidence." Still the *Constitution* shook its head. If Mr. Stephens wanted to be the Democratic nominee, he must not compromise with its enemies.[21]

Meanwhile the Coalitionists were also being forced to a decision. General Lucius Gartrell of Atlanta had announced for Governor as an Independent.[22] He could never be elected. They *must* get Stephens, even if it meant sharing him with the enemy. But how was even this to be done? If they nominated him first, he might refuse for fear of alienating the Democrats. On the other hand, if they held back until after the Democratic State Convention, Stephens might accept its nomination with the stipulation that he could not also be the candidate of the Coalition. Dr. Felton called for another meeting at the Markham House on May 15.

On May 12 the two Feltons decided, rather belatedly, that before offering the nomination to Mr. Stephens, it might be well to know whether he would accept it. Determined to get a definite answer, Mrs. Felton wrote asking him whether he wanted the Independents to recommend him for governor. He was told to send a telegram to the Markham House merely saying yes or no. However, by substituting *Independents* for *Coalitionists*, and *recommend* for *nominate*, she made it easier for him to accept.[23]

On Sunday afternoon she and her husband were sitting on the porch when a telegram addressed to him was delivered. He read it to her.

Have sent you an important telegram to the Markham House.
It was submitted to Mr. Stephens.

Emory Speer[24]

The Feltons were puzzled. Why was Emory Speer suddenly
pushing himself into the affairs of the Coalition? And why had
Mr. Stephens allowed Speer to speak for him? He had never cared
particularly for Speer. At any rate, the wire at the Markham
must contain Stephens' answer, and Speer sounded as if it might
be favorable. It was indeed. Speer urged the "Independent Democrats" to "recommend" Stephens. He gave encouraging reasons.

I know positively he will not reject such a recommendation
and that if elected he will be governor of all the people without regard to party.[25]

Dr. Felton had no trouble getting the recommendation. He
wired Speer that Stephens had been endorsed enthusiastically and
unanimously and that he would sweep the state.[26] The *Free-
Press* proudly announced that the Markham meeting had recommended "the incorruptible statesman Alexander Stephens" as
the next Governor.[27]

On May 18 Stephens wrote Mrs. Felton the last letter he
would ever write her. The Independents' candidate did not sound
very elated. He supposed that Dr. Felton and his friends had
done, upon the whole, about the best thing that could have
been done, but he was troubled with forebodings about the
future.[28] He was a little more complimentary in a letter to the
Doctor. He thought that his friend had managed things admirably, and in the best interests of the state.[29] Perhaps the Feltons
were able to persuade themselves that a sprained ankle was responsible for Mr. Stephens' gloomy tone.

His gloom was hardly dispelled by a letter which came from
Evan Howell the following day. Writing as Chairman of the
State Democratic Committee, Howell warned Stephens that if he
wanted to be their candidate, he must repudiate the "nomination"
of the Coalitionists. And he must do it at once. He could
either send for Richardson or write a letter to the *Constitution*.[30]
Stephens did both, immediately. He sent for Richardson, and
they wired a letter to the *Constitution* addressed to C. E. Smith
of Washington, Georgia. Trying desperately not to insult the
Coalitionists any more than he had to, Stephens did not repudiate
their recommendation in so many words. Instead, he denied
that he had sent or authorized a wire accepting their "nomina-

tion" and declared that he would not run for governor against a nominee of the Democratic Party.[31] Even Little Alec had never strained circumlocution so near the breaking point.

Howell must have felt that the letter safely committed his man, for he published it along with an editorial branding Speer as a liar. Dr. Felton rushed to Speer's defense, quoting Stephens' written approval of the Markham recommendation. Speer, however, frightened at the sudden shift in the political tide, hastened to explain that the telegram Mr. Stephens had repudiated was one a Western newspaper reported he had sent, accepting the Coalitionists' nomination. The *Constitution* contemptuously dismissed the whole affair. Mr. Stephens, it said, could not be condemned for getting the endorsement of the Coalition; it was an accident that might happen to any gentleman.[32]

But what had happened was no accident. Stephens had wanted the endorsement of all parties. The Democratic Party, however, was the only one that could assure his election. When it ordered him to stay in line, his desire for office proved stronger than his principles. His obedience gained him the governorship, but he paid for it in humiliation. The Bourbon newspapers accepted him indifferently, and proceeded to campaign for the Party rather than the man. Bill Arp, the *Constitution's* humorist, poked fun at him. The Macon *Telegraph* reported an unfounded rumor that he had told Howell he was in the hands of his friends and would do whatever they said.[33] His sincerest support came from his Independent friends, Hook, Miller, and Willingham. In his own campaign Dr. Felton attacked Stephens more than once, but even he voted for the man he had endorsed.[34]

No one of Stephens' old friends felt the blow of his desertion more deeply than Mrs. Felton. She had been devoted to the complex little man. But she would not subscribe to the excuses that his mind had been weakened by sickness, drugs, and age. He wanted to be governor, she said, and had sold himself to the highest bidder.[35] She would treat him now as she treated all enemies. When he attacked the Doctor before a Macon audience, she sent a letter to the *Telegraph* suggesting that the Devil probably applauded when Brown denounced Radicalism, and Stephens Independentism.[36] With difficulty the Doctor persuaded her not to publish some of Stephens' letters. She sent their author word, however, that the day he carried his campaign into the Seventh District, that day the letters would be sent to a newspaper.[37]

Her warning put Stephens in a quandary. The Democrats

wanted him to speak in the Seventh. It was Gartrell's home district, and he would poll his largest vote there. Stephens decided that before going he had better see what he had written. Hiddell, secretly toadying to both Stephens and the Feltons, tried to get copies for him, but Mrs. Felton refused. It was her "ammunition," and she would not surrender it. The Doctor finally convinced her that it would do no harm to let Stephens see them to refresh his mind. When his mind was refreshed, Stephens decided to stay out of the Seventh.[38]

She gave him one more scare. Reading that he had declared an Independent victory would be degrading to Georgia, she wired immediately asking whether the *Constitution* had quoted him correctly. Apparently he never replied.[39]

The hostility of the Feltons began to annoy him. Dr. Felton was continually pointing out in his speeches the discrepancy between Stephens' past statements and present affiliations. The harassed candidate wrote Hiddell that he had come to look on the Doctor as "one of the lowest, meanest, basest of mankind" and one of his bitterest enemies.[40] Then Dr. Felton, in spite of his admonition to his wife, began to quote from letters "a friend" had received from Stephens. Goaded to the quick, Stephens considered answering him in the press but decided that a letter would only bring on "a mud-slinging contest with the parson and a woman." [41] Perhaps he remembered how Gordon had fared in a similar contest.

Stephens could hardly have been worrying about his election. A Democratic landslide was building up. In October he won over Gartrell by three to one, and the voters elected a legislature certain to choose Colquitt as Hill's successor.

Dr. Felton made a stout fight against Clements, but as the November elections drew nearer, his ranks became thin from desertions. Staunch Independents followed Stephens into Clements' camp. Republicans became disgruntled when the Doctor refused to promise he would help their party organize the next Congress. On the first returns Clements moved into the lead, and taunting telegrams began to come to the Felton house. The defeat was greater than in 1880. This time Speer went down also, in spite of his hold on Mr. Stephens' coattail. Within a few days the legislature went through the formality of electing Colquitt.[42]

The Bourbons had done more than gain another victory. They had extinguished the revolt that had troubled them for eight years. Independentism was dead in Georgia.

The Christmas season brought no cheer to Mrs. Felton. Just a year ago she had been wrapping the two photographs for Mr. Stephens. He had written that he "especially liked the one in plain attire, just as you used to appear when you came to my room."[43] To think that in the same drawer with that letter there were those other letters which had now become written evidence of his duplicity. Yet, try as she might, she could not hate him. She could hate Gordon and Brown. But not him. He had hurt her bitterly but her thoughts kept going back to those earlier years at the old National.

Some Cartersville people were calling at the Governor's Mansion, and her son Howard begged to go along. She consented. Could he take Mr. Stephens a pair of black silk gloves like those he gave him last Christmas? Yes, she would get the gloves. She waited anxiously for him to return. Her first question was what had Mr. Stephens said. Mr. Stephens had praised the gloves, and then had asked "How is Mama?" She could not keep back the tears.[44]

In March she may have been troubled by a short announcement in the *Constitution* that the Governor was quite ill. Two days later a large headline dominated the paper's news page: "Mr. Stephens is dead." Column after column described the scene in the death chamber: his small dog asleep on a rug; black Alec stretched before the fire, worn out with his long watching; family and Bourbon notables around the bed. Others came to gaze silently at the small figure dressed in the familiar dark suit, stiff shirt, and string tie. On his hands were a pair of black silk gloves.[45]

Henry Grady arranged an impressive funeral. He was good at such things. Delegations and military companies from all over the state followed the hearse down Atlanta's streets to the Capitol, where appropriate orations were delivered. Then, with bands playing the Dead March, a huge procession followed the body to Oakland Cemetery, where it would be interred temporarily. An imposing group of pallbearers bore the casket. There was Toombs, of course; Emory Speer and James Smith; the Bourbon Triumvirate: Gordon, Brown, and Colquitt. Finally, to perfect the irony, came Rufus Bullock, now a respectable Atlanta capitalist.[46]

The old, ante-bellum statesman was being honored with a New South funeral.

10

. . . . .
. . .
.

Fighting on the Home Front

IN MARCH of 1883 the *Free-Press* answered the question "What has become of Dr. Felton?" He was on his farm, said Editor Willingham, waiting Cincinnatus-like for his people to call him back to service.[1] Visitors reported they found him looking well and happy.[2] It was fortunate the Doctor could be content in retirement. Georgia seemed satisfied with Bourbon rule.

Peace and solitude were not, however, Mrs. Felton's idea of the good life. Her mind was on Washington and Atlanta, where things were happening. She thought bitterly of the men in public office who had far less ability than the Doctor. It was a shame the Republicans hadn't given him a Federal job. She wrote Longstreet asking what could be done. Within a few months the Atlanta postmastership was offered the Doctor, but he refused. It would stamp him as a Republican, he claimed.[3]

Well, she didn't propose to be forgotten by the outside world. Determined to keep her contact with the press, she found reasons to write to P. W. Alexander of the Macon *Telegraph,* Henry Watterson of the Louisville *Courier-Journal,* and Charles Dana of the New York *Sun.*[4] The day was bound to come when she could put her abilities to greater use than household drudgery. For she had abilities. Hadn't people said she knew more about government than any woman in the country? Hadn't an editor even said it was too bad she couldn't be sent to the legislature?[5]

In 1884 her father's death undoubtedly turned her thoughts for a time from worldly problems.[6] She had not seen much of him in recent years, but the tie between them had remained strong. She could never forget all she owed him: his affection and encouragement, his ambitions for her in those days now so far in the past. Time was indeed going by. She would be fifty in another year, and there were so few things that women could do. Anyway she had come into a substantial inheritance: cash and rich mineral lands in Fannin County. She could make investments of her own now . . . buy farm land too . . .feel more secure . . . more independent.

She enjoyed trading and selling, and she was good at it, but she still missed the excitement of politics—the letters to the papers, the rallies, election day. She wasn't at all sure, however, that the Doctor was strong enough to run any more; not even when a large group called to ask him to stand for the State Legislature. They must talk it over, she told him. A hard campaign would be a strain on his health, and expensive too.[7]

But the Doctor's crusading spirit had been stirred. Corrupt lobbyists, he reminded her, were trying to weaken Georgia's Railroad Commission. Joe Brown's lease of the Western and Atlantic Railroad would end in 1890, and there was already agitation to sell that valuable property to private interests. The Temperance Movement was not making the progress it should. Methodists and Baptists were trying to cut appropriations for the State University, the Doctor's Alma Mater. He was needed in the legislature. He knew it was the sort of argument that would stir her. She agreed. And once the Doctor had announced, she forgot about expense and his health, and worried because he refused to electioneer. Fortunately for the peace of the Felton household, he was not opposed.[8]

During his three terms in the legislature, the Doctor was largely successful with his reforms. When the Maddox Bill curtailing the power of the Railroad Commission passed the Senate, he beat it down in the House. At the end of Brown's lease, the Western and Atlantic was not sold. The Doctor's prison reform bill was beaten, but he furthered the movement which eventually outlawed leasing of convicts. He helped keep the University alive during a critical decade, and he led the Temperance people nearer to their goal of a bone-dry state.[9]

Mrs. Felton made his fights hers. He could never have won so much without her help. No longer did the private secretary merely answer personal and public letters. She helped draft bills and speeches; she even advised on legislative strategy.[10] She attacked his opponents continually in the press. When Charlie Willingham died, she took over the *Free-Press,* changed its name to the *Courant,* and edited it single-handed for a year and a half. It made available for her at all times sufficient space to

present fully their side and to tear down that of the enemy.[11]
Ben Hill had once said that the Seventh District had the services
of two representatives. This was even more true of Bartow County
from 1884 to 1890. The Doctor realized how much he owed her.
Across the back of a legislative bill he wrote: "More that Rebecca
helped to do." [12]

The Bourbons knew also that they had two Feltons to deal
with, but they hesitated to include her in their attacks. In Georgia, ladies must be treated as ladies. Besides, she made a habit
of fighting rather roughly. During the 1887 session of the legislature, however, young E. G. Simmons decided that Mrs. Felton
had been spared long enough. But he would be so subtle in his
ridicule that he could deny, if necessary, any intended insult to
the formidable lady.[13]

On August 4 he got the floor and announced that he wanted to
explain Dr. Felton's proposed reformatory. It was to be a beautiful place, Simmons said: a group of ivy-covered dormitories
built around a court in which a statue of the Doctor would
bear the inscription "The John Howard of Georgia." And there
were indeed many resemblances between the Georgia and the
English reformers—although Simmons hastened to add that Dr.
Felton had, of course, never been put in jail. Howard had married "a plain talker . . . a great writer . . . a great woman for
statistics." He had completely neglected his only son, and had
finally gone crazy on the subject of reform. Simmons moved on
from his malicious comparison to Dr. Felton's bill, but he had not
finished with Mrs. Felton. In closing he prophesied that his opponent was waiting to demolish him with a vicious attack.
But Simmons would meet it calmly.

> When with his stooping form and hallelujah licks he consigns
> me to the tomb, I will go peacefully to my rest with the
> unction in my soul that I died a brave soldier—that I died
> game, killed by *the political she of Georgia.*[14]

Listening in the galleries Mrs. Felton caught each of the
crude innuendoes, and her face grew hot with rage. She was still
trembling when the culminating insult came: "the political she
of Georgia"! She hurried to the stairway. People everywhere
had turned to watch her. If only she could answer him! She was
waiting in the hotel when the Doctor came. He had trouble calm-
ing her. Simmons would be answered, he assured her, in full
measure. She could help with the answer.[15]

On the day of reckoning she was late in reaching the Capitol. The galleries were almost filled, but a kind usher found her a seat on the front row. The Doctor was speaking. Thank goodness he hadn't started on Simmons. He was defending his bill. How old he looked with his great head bowed, and his hands shaking. But his voice rang out clear and strong. The place was packed. Every seat on the floor was filled. Senators were standing along the wall. Several opera glasses were pointed in her direction. Let them look.[16]

Here it came. The Doctor's long finger was pointing at Simmons, and she heard the words she had already read so carefully. "I do not think that man has sensibilities enough to rise above the gutters and slews and scum of a ward politician." Simmons was on his feet trying to interrupt, but Dr. Felton shouted him down. Then the merciless words poured forth again: "A back-biter . . . a ruffian . . . a man who stabs and then runs away." He had defamed "one of the noblest, purest, most intelligent women in Georgia." He did not possess "one thimblefull of her great brain." Simmons had attacked the Doctor's entire household, his loyal wife and his only son. He was too contemptible to be noticed again.

> Hate him? despise him? No sir, no sir. I simply turn him over
> to the intelligence and virtue of Georgia. That is the worst
> fate that can befall him.[17]

A roar of approval broke from the galleries. The floor was more restrained. Tears streamed down Mrs. Felton's face, but she kept her head erect. It was worth it all—the enmity, the abuse, those rankling defeats—to be defended so gloriously. Even the Bourbon press was awed by the Doctor's merciless invective. The *Constitution* hoped that no man would ever have occasion to speak such words again. The following day Simmons offered his explanation, prepared in advance. "She," he pointed out, was a mythical monster in a novel of that name by Rider Haggard, who preyed on mankind for two thousand years. Hadn't Dr. Felton warned that if he was returned to the legislature for a thousand years, he would re-introduce his prison bill until it was passed? The comparison was apt, Simmons argued. He had intended no insult to Mrs. Felton. Dr. Felton paid no attention to the labored excuse, contemptuously reading a newspaper while Simmons spoke.[18]

The row with Simmons was not needed to prove that the Fel-

tons still loved a fight. They had made that clear a year earlier.
Their old enemy Gordon had returned to the state after further
railroad activities which may have left him "a bit out at the
elbow." [19] At any rate, he was available for an appropriate public office, and Henry Grady immediately seized upon him as "a
sure-fire winner" in the coming governor's race.[20] When Gordon
announced his candidacy, the Feltons instinctively came to
the support of his opponent Major A. O. Bacon.[21]

On paper Gordon hardly looked like a certainty. He had
never satisfactorily explained his resignation from the Senate.
In the coming campaign he was certain to be asked some
embarrassing questions about his relations while still in office
with Collis P. Huntington, a notorious promoter of Pacific railroads. Some letters of Huntington had recently come to light
revealing his unscrupulous lobbying tactics. In one of them he referred to Gordon as "one of our men," and in another he wrote
that the Senator was not afraid to go on a trip to the West
Coast as a guest of the Central Pacific. Mrs. Felton had already
showed a keen interest in these letters.[22]

But the astute Grady had no idea of leading from weakness
when he could lead from strength. He was going to parade his
candidate not as a New South statesman but as a Confederate
general. And there was an opportunity coming up to get the campaign marching on the right foot. In early May Ben Hill's monument was to be unveiled in Atlanta, and feeble Jefferson Davis
would be at the ceremony. Grady made the most of his opportunity. Gordon joined Davis in Alabama, travelling to Atlanta
with him, helped the old man on and off trains, and stood
protectingly at his side during the dedication. That night a rowdy
crowd in the Kimball House lobby proclaimed Gordon the next
Governor of Georgia. A few days later he announced his candidacy in the *Constitution*.[23]

Grady's showmanship was irresistible. As he boasted, he almost
made Confederate money good again. Maimed veterans were
called back into service. Gordon was introduced at a Forsyth
rally by an old soldier on crutches, and at Madison by one who
had lost an eye at Chancellorsville. People travelling to his
speakings found one-armed and one-legged sentinels at a cross-
roads giving directions. The *Constitution* dug up touching war
stories of the General's devotion to his men: he had preached to
them between battles; once on the march he had placed a foot-
sore infantryman on his own horse. Ex-Governor James Smith

became so moved he declared that anyone voting against this comrade Gordon "should never assemble again around the graves of our heroes to do them honor." As the show grew more extravagant, Bacon asked whether the Civil War had been fought just for the purpose of giving his opponent "a little boom."[24]

Persistently the two Feltons pointed out that the contest was to choose a governor for the state, not a general for the army. Gordon's political career, they contended, was far more pertinent to the issue. They gave the voters plenty of information on that subject—the Doctor from the platform, his wife through the columns of the press. Several dailies which had fought the Feltons in the past came out against Gordon. It was a new experience for Mrs. Felton to have the *Telegraph,* the *Chronicle,* and the Rome *Courier* asking for her articles. But she was glad to oblige.[25]

Some of her topics were hardly headline news any longer—Gordon's business reverses, the trading of the presidency to Hayes, the "Bargain Sale"—but her sharp colloquial style brought them to life again. Gordon was held up as "a fourth-rate lawyer," an "aforetime textbook salesman," "a political gymnast." His behaviour at Ben Hill's monument was said to have been disgusting. At the close of the ceremony he had jumped up to make a speech, and Grady had had to pull him down by the coattails. When Gordon was reported as saying that honorable men had invested in his textbook company, "Plain Talk" laughingly agreed. He had "sharped" everyone who did business with him, from President Grant to Joe Brown.[26]

As would be expected, she came to the most unflattering conclusions about the Huntington letters. Gordon refused to discuss them with her, but "Virginia" wrote a letter to the *Constitution* giving some "facts" which would clear up everything. While Tom Scott was asking the Government for a $50,000 subsidy to build his Texas and Pacific Railroad, Huntington was already laying the tracks for his Southern Pacific through the same territory, with his own capital. A subsidy to Scott, "Virginia" argued, would have been a useless expenditure of the nation's credit and Gordon had, therefore, persuaded the Senate to refuse it. Huntington's reference to him as "one of our men" had meant nothing more than that Gordon was also in opposition to Scott's scheme. As to the California trip, Huntington had merely wanted members of the Senate to see that he was actually building the needed railroad, and Gordon had agreed to go along to satisfy himself that he was right in voting against Scott. In conclusion, "Virginia" suggested that instead of abusing Gordon, the people ought to vote him a monument for protecting their interests.[27]

Immediately an anonymous letter appeared in the Cartersville *American* questioning the alleged hostility of Gordon and Huntington to government subsidies. "Argus" pointed out that in 1862 Huntington had not only accepted a sizable loan from the Government to build the Central Pacific, but as late as 1877, when Scott was asking for similar help, he had still not paid back one cent of principal or interest. On January 12 of that year Gordon had introduced a bill in the Senate which would permit Huntington to set up a sinking fund for liquidating his debt. But the annual amount to be put into this fund was so small that the Government would not get its money back until after the turn of the century. Five days after the bill was introduced, Huntington was writing his partner David Colton that he could get his bill passed for $200,000. On March 7 he wrote that although the sinking fund bill had not passed, he was still hopeful and that he had stayed in Washington "to fix up the railroad committee." A week later he reported regretfully that one of his men had been taken off the committee, "Gordon of Georgia."[28]

As "Argus" contended, it is difficult to believe that Huntington claimed Gordon as his man only because of their common opposition to Scott. The sinking fund bill, which Gordon was promoting against loud senatorial hostility, would have enabled Huntington to divert the money owed the Government into more remunerative channels, such as the construction of his Southern Pacific, or in continuing the huge dividends on Central Pacific stock of which he owned a considerable block. The *American* prophesied correctly that the *Constitution* would refuse to reply to "Argus." [29]

Although the Bourbons were disinclined to fight with Mrs. Felton, they found her blows too painful to bear in silence. The *Constitution* charged that Bacon was waging a campaign of slander behind the petticoats of a woman. Once it went so far as to point out that these irreverent articles were written by "a member of Dr. Felton's family." [30] Gordon, even more wary than the *Constitution*, directed his attack at the newspaper carrying the "Plain Talk" letters rather than at their author. The issues raised by the *Telegraph*, he complained, took up so much of his time that he could not discuss the policies his administration was going to carry out.[31] Even when the two Feltons broke down his studied indifference he gave vent to his anger without naming either. "If a cannon ball should strike 'Plain Talk,' " he declared, "it would bespatter with blood the slanderer of Ben Hill."[32]

Mrs. Felton's outspoken pieces might delight her allies and irritate her enemies, but they won few votes for Bacon among the Veterans, or among their sons reared in the Confederate tradition. As the *Constitution* boasted, all the newspapers in the state "could not convince the people of Georgia that John B. Gordon ever did a dishonorable thing." [33] Bacon was overwhelmingly beaten. With Colquitt and Brown in the Senate, the Bourbon Triumvirate now held the three highest offices in the state. It was a bitter defeat for the Feltons. Gordon was still the idol of Georgia.

That same year a new revolt was stirring which would alarm the Bourbons more than the Independent movements of '74 and '82. The harassed farmers of Georgia were joining the national Farmers Alliance, an organization formed to fight the urban capitalists. Caught in the grip of an inhuman lien system, the farmer had been sinking steadily in debt to the banker, merchant, and absentee landlord. The situation had become unendurable. Lodges of the Alliance began to spring up throughout the state, and there were indications that the new organization would be no counterpart of the old non-political Grange. In Georgia the movement found a dangerous leader: fiery Tom Watson, who had helped deadlock the gubernatorial convention of 1882.[34]

Brown and Grady, shrewdest of the Bourbons, saw that the rising storm might well sweep the Democrats from power. Shortly before his death in 1889, Grady advised his party to champion some of the farmers' demands so that the rebellion could run its course through traditional channels.[35] But Brown wanted no part of the Alliance. Weakened by age and sickness, he resigned from the Senate shortly before the 1890 elections. Gordon agreed with Grady. Perhaps he was eyeing Brown's seat in the Senate. At any rate, he joined the Alliance, even submitting to the rough horseplay of the initiation.[36]

In the state elections of 1890 other Democrats came out for enough of the Alliance's program to win its support. The farmers apparently swept the state, electing the governor, six of the ten congressmen, two-thirds of the state senate, and four-fifths of the legislature—which in turn immediately chose Gordon to succeed Brown. The *Constitution* heartily approved the election of Watson to Congress from the Tenth District.[37]

The expected reforms did not follow. Once in office those Democrats who had been supported by the Alliance seemed satisfied with the *status quo*. The deluded farmers, incited by Watson, broke from the Democratic ranks and joined the radical Populist Party, which was on the march in the West and South. Bent on maintaining a single party rule in Georgia, the Democrats resorted to the effective tactics of Reconstruction: disenfranchisement, bribery, and intimidation. Both sides herded Negroes to the polls, but the Democrats brought more and voted them more extensively. They won decisively in 1892 and 1894. Watson and R. W. Everett, Congressman from the Feltons' district, were among the Populists swept from office.[38]

Although Dr. Felton had announced his retirement from politics he unwisely allowed himself to be caught up in the excitement of the rebellion. Like Brown, he disapproved of the Alliance, and in 1890, when the Seventh District Democrats dropped Clements for Everett, he agreed to stand for his old Congressional seat as an Independent. Mrs. Felton pleaded with him not to make the hopeless fight, but he could be stubborn too. She could do little to help him; the Democrats refused to engage them in controversy. He was badly beaten, losing Bartow and winning only two of the smaller counties.[39]

Four years later he again overruled her and again took the losing side, this time running as a Populist against John W. Maddox, who had beaten Everett in 1892. By then Dr. Felton had come to believe that Grover Cleveland and the Democrats were a greater danger than the Populists. Also, he had got to know Watson and admired him greatly. About all Mrs. Felton could contribute to her husband's campaign was to keep him from collapsing before it was over. Watson tried to help, but he was having his own troubles in the Tenth. Although the Doctor regained Bartow and won four more counties, the outcome was never in doubt. It was a pathetic end to a worthy career. Like Alec Stephens, Dr. Felton had not known when to retire.[40]

It was then Mrs. Felton made her mistake, as unfortunate as the Doctor's. The election was hardly over before friends throughout the district were writing her of Democratic corruption at the polls, especially in Rome and Marietta. They urged her to demand a Congressional investigation.[41] She wrote Senator

W. P. Frye, a Republican friend of Washington days, asking if she ought to contest the election. He replied that it was a long costly process, with the odds usually favoring the reported winner. But before his reply came, she had decided. She had not wanted the Doctor to run, but she was not going to stand by and see him cheated. She could handle the whole thing. All the Doctor had to do was to inform Maddox that he was calling for a Congressional hearing.[42]

There was plenty for her to do. Local and Washington lawyers had to be hired; investigations made in Rome, Marietta, and several smaller towns; unending testimony taken. She wrote to Republican Senator Henry Lodge, hoping to get his help when the issue reached Congress. At the various hearings in the Seventh she questioned witnesses and presented evidence with a skill that won the praise of General W. W. Dudley, her Washington lawyer. The mounting costs worried her. Of course Congress would make an appropriation for their expenses when the trial was over, but would it be enough? Well, she had decided to fight, and she was not going to stop. It would be worth it all if she could prove how the Democrats had been winning their elections in Georgia all those years.[43]

As the investigation went on the hearings became more abusive and violent. She had to attend one in Rome the same day that another came up in Bartow. Dr. Felton would have to take over the local hearing. Howard must go along to look after him. When she returned from Rome she was infuriated to hear what had happened. A. W. Fite, one of Maddox's lawyers, had marched across the courtroom to where the Doctor was sitting, taunted him, and dared Howard to fight. Her written complaint to the judge produced no results. When it was returned to her she wrote across the back "Lest I forget" before she filed it away.[44]

The Rome hearing, which she attended unescorted, turned out to be an even rowdier affair. She was the only woman in the crowded courtroom. In a local newspaper she had come across some telling evidence which she read aloud to the court. When she had finished, Maddox's lawyer demanded the paper so that he could see whether she had read truthfully. She refused. The judge ordered her to hand it over. Clutching the paper firmly in one hand, she brought her rolled umbrella conspicuously into view and stared hard-eyed at the judge. "I'd like to see you

make Mrs. Felton give it up," said J. W. Davis, one of her lawyers. When the judge finally quieted the laughter, he made no
further demands.[45]

A few moments later the tension snapped without warning.
Maddox's lawyer slapped a Felton witness and the room became
a churning mass of yelling, swinging men. Calmly Mrs. Felton
climbed on to the judge's stand, where she watched the melee
with partisan interest. When peace was restored she was the
first to speak. She informed the judge that the disturbance had
been a disgrace, and she wanted to protest "in the name of the
contestant." That night she wrote her husband she was glad
the fight had taken place; it hadn't hurt their case one bit.[46]

The hearings were finally over and the testimony forwarded
to Washington. It was not as conclusive as she had hoped. Some
of their witnesses had proved reluctant, and she was convinced
that the judges had favored Maddox. Then came the long waiting for Congress to act. The year 1895 went by. Maddox had
served half his term; there would be another election in the
fall. Also, she was worried to learn that Charles Bartlett, Congressman from Georgia's Sixth District, would probably be on
the committee. He was a distant relative but not a friend of the
Doctor. Not once, however, did she consider giving up. This
would be her last chance to whip the Democrats. She was preparing a petition to Congress when a letter arrived from Dudley:
the case was coming up. She left immediately for Washington.
The Doctor would follow in a few days.[47]

She sat next to Dudley at the hearing, the Doctor directly
behind her. It was evident that both sides considered her the
real contestant. Seething with rage she heard Fite charge that
she had falsified evidence. Dudley asked permission for her to
answer. She was given only five minutes at the close of the arguments, but she managed—in spite of an interruption by Bartlett
—to answer the accusation in detail and denounce Fite, Maddox,
and the judges of the Seventh District.[48]

The Feltons left immediately for Cartersville. She wasn't going
to pay hotel bills while they waited for a decision which, for all
Dudley's optimism, she felt would probably be against them.
Sure enough, he wired within a few days that the committee
had voted unanimously for Maddox. It was finally over.[49]

But it was not over. There were still the arguings and bick-
erings that so often follow defeat. She criticized Dudley for a
lack of interest in their case, and he defended himself warmly.

His fees were so high there was little left from the Congressional appropriation for the local lawyers. They complained bitterly.[50]

Even when the bills were finally settled, she had not heard the last of the ill-advised contest. Two years later Maddox charged that she had spent so much of the appropriation on her own expenses that she could not pay the lawyers what she owed them. The Doctor published a statement in the press itemizing every dollar of the appropriation, but her enemies believed the worst. A rankling insult had been added to defeat.[51]

There was no question now about the Doctor's retirement. A loyal supporter wrote him that the men of their generation had sowed the seed and could only hope that the next generation would reap the harvest. By then Dr. Felton was ready to agree.[52]

11

·····
··
·

Walking Alone

THE poet Robert P. Tristram Coffin has said that a newly-married Maine wife always walks a few steps behind her husband. With the passing of the years, however, she gradually moves up, and then they walk together until that day when she goes ahead "to break the force of the wind for an old man." In the same manner Rebecca Felton inevitably became more prominent than her husband. She was first the "private secretary," then the "second representative," and finally the real contestant in the case of Felton versus Maddox.

If Coffin had been writing about the Feltons he would have had to add another stanza to his poem. When the Doctor retired, his wife went on alone. She had come to love the force of the wind. The beginning of her independent career almost coincided with his retirement from the legislature, his last public office. Within a few months she was appointed a Lady Manager of the Chicago Columbian Exposition.[1]

Industrialized America was parading its achievements in huge, spectacular exhibitions. In 1876 Mrs. Felton had been vastly impressed by the Philadelphia Centennial and had surely visited Atlanta's International Cotton and Piedmont Expositions in the eighties. Now Chicago had won the honor of celebrating the country's four hundredth birthday, and was preparing a show that would deserve the name of "World's Fair." The shores of Lake Michigan were being transformed into a city of unworldly beauty. There the products of America's countless activities would be displayed, including those made only by women. Two Lady Managers from each state were to be chosen and put in charge of the women's exhibits. General Lafayette McLaws, one of Georgia's Commissioners to the Exposition, asked

Senator Brown what lady would best represent their state in such a position. He was assured that Mrs. Rebecca Felton was "without a superior in all the qualities that go to constitute a representative lady." McLaws had no difficulty in getting Brown's candidate to accept.[2]

In November she left for Chicago. Conscious of her rural and Southern background, she had resolved not to put up with any slights or condescension from her Northern colleagues. They were distinguished ladies: Mrs. Bertha Palmer, society beauty and ardent feminist, Mrs. John A. Logan, editor of *The Home Magazine,* Mrs. Isabella Beecher Hooker, as dedicated a reformer as her famous half sister Harriett Stowe. Strangely enough, Mrs. Felton immediately passed up an opportunity to quarrel with the formidable Mrs. Hooker. Called unexpectedly to preside over the first meeting, the lady from Georgia announced that in her own work she proposed to know "no South, no North, no East, no West." Perhaps warmed by the generous applause, she refused to take offense when Mrs. Hooker later asked whether her speech really had been impromptu.[3]

Unfortunately Mrs. Felton was not able to maintain this national viewpoint. Waiting in Cartersville the following April for the Board's second meeting, she learned that President Bertha Palmer had not appointed a single Southern lady to the all-important Executive Committee. It was just what she had been expecting—a deliberate snub to her and her section. She was burning for a fight when Phoebe Cousins of Missouri wired that the Executive Committee had dismissed her as Secretary of the Board. Miss Cousins called upon all Southern members to come to her aid.[4] Mrs. Felton was the first to answer the call. She let several members of the committee know that she considered the action infamous.[5] Then she wrote Joe Brown, Charles Dana of the *Sun,* and Frances Willard, President of the W.C.T.U., to intervene for Miss Cousins. Several of her Southern colleagues added their protests. One of the Virginia ladies resigned. Even a New York member joined the revolt, declaring that her state had also been slighted. It began to look as though the first national recognition given women was going to prove their inability to work together.

Miss Willard and Dana tried to calm Mrs. Felton. Brown did write to Mrs. Palmer's husband, a prominent official of the Fair, but only to express a hope that the breach between the militant ladies could be healed.[6] However, it was the Northern members of the Board who quieted Mrs. Felton. She had criticized them bluntly in her letters and expected, no doubt, some indignant replies. Instead the ladies refused, politely but firmly, to believe Mrs. Felton could think such things about them; then they immediately switched to more pleasant topics. Their letters left her helpless to continue the argument.[7]

Mrs. Palmer was more severe, but equally subtle, in handling the Georgia rebel. First she called Mrs. Felton to task for not investigating her charges before she made them. Once the controversy had subsided, however, even Mrs. Felton could not complain that her talents were going unrecognized. Mrs. Palmer made her chairman of the committee for alloting space, praised her extravagantly, and worried needlessly about her health. Mrs. Felton was completely captivated. At Christmas in 1893 she sent Mrs. Palmer a patchwork quilt of over three thousand pieces, made with her own hands.[8]

She got through the fair without any further controversies, although she invited another one when she tried to discuss the Negro question with Isabella Beecher Hooker. Fortunately Mrs. Hooker thought they had more immediate problems at hand.[9] Mrs. Felton did remain sensitive about her plain clothes, especially when she attended formal parties. Writing home about a reception at Mrs. Palmer's, she described herself as one of the sober looking birds among the birds of paradise but she added defiantly that brains were what counted, not clothes.[10] Before the Exposition was over, she came to respect the Northern ladies. As a group they were highly educated and articulate, with advanced ideas on woman's suffrage, temperance, birth control, and other issues. They, in turn, were pleased to find such a belligerent feminist from the backward South. Encouraged by their attention and praise, she left Chicago even more dedicated to her previous causes.

She met important men, too, such as Thomas Palmer, Bertha's millionarie husband, and James Angell, President of the University of Michigan; but, like a good suffragette, she was inclined to criticize their pretensions. She considered Professor George Herbert Palmer of Harvard "the one smart man connected with colleges that seems without conceit."[11]

From 1890 to 1894 she made the long trip to Chicago several times. In that city she travelled to and from the Fair on street cars so crowded she often could not get a seat. It was strenuous work for a woman getting on to sixty, but she wouldn't have given it up for anything. At times she could hardly believe that she was actually helping to run something that people were coming from all over the world to see. And getting paid for it too, six dollars a day and expense money. She couldn't make that in Cartersville.

There were many exciting things to write home: allotting space to a group of handsome young Russians and to "a Cingalese" [sic] as black as one of their Negroes. An Italian Count gave her his card, and "a Jap" gave her his autograph.[12] Chicago delighted her; it was always in a stir. The shop windows were filled with wonderful things, but too high. Everything was too high. Imagine having to pay extra for a fire in her hotel room. At least she had found a restaurant where she could get a fine breakfast for ten cents. The big city made her uneasy at times. The crowds looked so rough, she was glad they kept a detective in the Woman's Building. A man was asphyxiated in her hotel. After that she made doubly sure that her gas light was turned off when she went to bed. You couldn't be too careful about such things.[13]

They were good at home about writing, but she wished they didn't have so much unpleasant news to tell her. It was one thing after another: Howard had the boils; one of her colts was injured; the cook got "uppity" and quit. Her mother had moved in to try to look after things, but she was too old and feeble.[14] Then Dr. Felton became a problem. At first he had urged her to stay in Chicago as long as she kept well and made such a fine salary. But as her trips north continued, he started sending wires to ask if she was sick, and why she didn't write. It did no good to write to him; he still declared he hadn't heard from her. One day she received a wire which read: "Are you planning to reside permanently in Chicago. Answer immediately." Hurt by the Doctor's harsh words, she gave up her place on the Jury of Awards so that she could get home sooner. She did return after the Fair, however, to help write the history of the Woman's Division.[15]

The Doctor's nagging wires may have troubled her last days in Chicago, but they did not kill her enthusiasm for Expositions. Throughout her life she could never resist their appeal, especially when her expenses were paid. Before she left Chicago she accepted a position with the Atlanta Cotton States and International Exposition. As business manager of its Woman's Division she was highly successful in securing exhibits, so successful that

she called down Mrs. Emma Thompson, her chairman, for credit-
ing another Lady Manager with keeping interest alive in their
work.[16] In 1897 Georgia sent her to the Tennessee Centennial to
report on its exhibits, and in 1904 the St. Louis Exposition appointed her a juror of its agricultural awards. At seventy-four
she was hardy enough to chaperon 119 Atlanta school children
to the Jamestown Exposition, and resourceful enough to bring
them all back alive. Age, however, did keep her from the San
Francisco Exposition in 1915.[17]

From 1890 on she was constantly on the go. People in Cartersville grew accustomed to seeing her, bag in hand, waiting on
the W & A platform. She was never away from home too long,
however, to neglect her growing business investments. Like Scarlett O'Hara of *Gone With the Wind,* she was bent on making
money and keeping it. And her reasons were largely those which
drove Scarlett so hard. She too was determined never to suffer
again as she had in the 1860s, and she would have agreed with
Scarlett that people respected you if you had money.

She had immediately put her father's inheritance to work.
First of all she must have farm land, for, as she once said, she
was a natural born farmer. She found it impossible to trade with
the closefisted Sam Jones, but after much dickering she
bought a large tract from Joe Brown.[18] She ran her farms like
a banker, keeping books on her tenants, and suing when one
claimed he could not pay his rent. No detail was too small for
her attention. In selling a cow or a turkey, she bargained just
as intently as she did for the additional land she bought. Every
year the courthouse was enlivened by her fights with the tax-
collector.

With her farms in operation she set about developing another
source of revenue. There were iron and mineral deposits on
some of her land. Many things had to be done before she could
realize anything from them; mineral rights cleared, geologists
consulted, and the Louisville and Nashville persuaded to lay a
spur line. She investigated carefully the man to whom she leased
the rights. It all took time but eventually it brought in a good
income. As busy as she was, she became an agent for an Atlanta
insurance company. More and more she had to keep an eye on the
Doctor's affairs. Fearing that he was going to cash in an insurance policy, she advanced him the money he wanted and took
over payment of the premiums. When he put some land on the

market at too low a price, she bought it and made a nice profit on her own sale.[19]

By 1907 Dr. Felton's palsy had become so severe that he could no longer walk without his wife's arm. She helped him to the polls to vote for the law that made Georgia "bone dry." As they went slowly back to the buggy he said, "I wish you had been allowed to vote it out."[20] He knew how much she had contributed to the final victory. His mind remained clear. That fall he wrote a forceful letter to the *Constitution* advocating Clark Howell for governor. It was the last act of his long political career.[21]

During the winter a serious illness left him a complete invalid. For eighteen months he grew feebler, suffering greatly at times. She nursed him faithfully. Friends who wrote referred to her "care of Dr. Felton," "shut-in life," [22] and "long vigils." [23] On September 29, 1909, he was stricken with an acute attack of indigestion, and they both knew there was no hope. The physician could do little. The heart was gradually slowing down, but there would probably be no more pain.[24]

When the physician had gone promising to return, the man on the bed looked up. "Stay by me," he said. Through that day and into the quiet night she never left him. To take his mind from approaching death she read him a newspaper article on the efficient service that the Western and Atlantic was giving. He had always been so proud of saving the railroad for the state. His face brightened, and then relaxed into that grave calm she knew so well. He slept a little. The rest of the time he lay quietly waiting. Surely his thoughts and the thoughts of the woman waiting with him went back into their long past to the same scenes and people: to the Madison Commencement, the house in the Macon woods, the National Hotel, the Halls of Congress; to their dead children, to Ben Hill, to Little Alec. Just before daylight she saw his lips moving and leaned closer. She could barely hear the words: "My time has come to go to sleep." The coldness of death was soon upon his body.[25]

He was buried from the Sam Jones Tabernacle, local preachers officiating and neighbors carrying his coffin. He would have wanted the simple service, but she felt that a fuller ceremony must follow to honor him appropriately. The next spring she had a monument erected on the courthouse lawn, and consulted Tom Watson about the inscription. In announcing the dedication, she urged all couples whom the Doctor had married, and all families whose dead he had buried to be present. The railroad would not allow reduced rates, but a large crowd came to hear Nat Harris of Macon and Moses Wright of Rome make fitting tributes. She had wanted Watson, but he could not come. Her speech presenting the monument to the county was brief and restrained.[26]

What was the relationship between this earnest, formidable couple? Was it true, as many came to believe, that she dominated his life—planned and directed his career? Corra Harris, the Georgia novelist, evidently thought so. She admitted that Mrs. Felton was the prototype for Susan Walters, the strong-minded feminist of *The Co-Citizens*. In the novel Susan was said to have henpecked her husband, "an elegant, soft, old gentlemen," into running for Congress because she could not run herself; she then proceeded to keep him in office for several terms by exposing the sins of anyone who ran against him. Mrs. Felton was pleased to have it known that Susan was modelled after her. She praised and helped to publicize *The Co-Citizens*. When asked by a reporter whether she had written the Doctor's speeches, she replied that "it wouldn't do much good to deny it." [27]

A man's character is not entirely safe in the hands of feminists, even when one of them is his wife. They are usually too concerned with the interests of their sex to do him justice. In her effort to "interpret" Mrs. Felton, Mrs. Harris did not consider—or did not care—that she was creating an unflattering picture of Dr. Felton. It is even less to Mrs. Felton's credit that she let the picture go unchallenged.

No one could deny that Mrs. Felton helped her husband with his legislative duties, and in every race he ran. He admitted it, generously. Her political advice was always worth considering, and her pen certainly put the fear of Mrs. Felton into his enemies. She was a woman of many talents, and Dr. Felton was fortunate to have her always at his side.

But she did not launch him in politics, elect him to office, and keep him there for three terms. In 1874 the Independents sought him, and did so because they needed the strongest man they could get. He won his first race largely through his ability to handle every speaker that the Bourbons sent against him, sometimes taking on three and four opponents at a time in those rough-and-tumble debates. In the two following campaigns his enemies admitted that their greatest obstacle was his unassailable

Congressional record, a record made on the floor of the House and in the committee room. "A soft, elegant old gentleman" even managed by Rebecca Felton, could not have been elected three times over the opposition of John B. Gordon, Joe Brown, and the Democratic machine.

Her hand is evident in many of his speeches, but it would be hasty to conclude that she wrote them. Lucian Knight is probably nearer the truth when he suggests that she frequently enlivened them with her sharp colloquial phrases.[28] Dr. Felton was a finished speaker before he married his second wife.

It would have been difficult for anyone to dominate him. Stubborn and independent, he maintained his principles through repeated defeats. His biographer believes that if he had compromised with the Democrats he could have remained in Congress until he retired.[29] His fellow-Coalitionists could not persuade him to excuse Stephens' desertion, and yet he calmly but firmly overruled his wife when she refused to give their former friend copies of his letters. He overruled her in 1890 and in 1894 when she did not want him to run. The angry wires to Chicago were not written by a hen-pecked husband.

Nor could she have respected a submissive husband. And she did respect Dr. Felton—even though she did not repudiate the Susan Walters legend. In her *Memoirs* she speaks of "walking for fifty years side by side with a reformer"; of "being his companion in this struggle"; of their "loyal comradeship." Such words undoubtedly expressed her feeling for him. As comrades, they had triumphed and lost together. In spite of her ambitions and self-interests, she had been fortunate in her husband and she knew it.[30]

His death left her the last of those stern fighters from the Bourbon era. Brown and Colquitt had died in 1894, Gordon not until 1904. She had never forgiven Gordon. Two years before he died, she had hoped he would not be re-elected Commander of the United Confederate Veterans.[31] She was living now among a new generation of Georgians with new leaders and new issues, but she was, if possible, more active than ever. There were more opportunities for women now, and she always took advantage of opportunities.

12

·····
·:·
·

Reformer

REFORM crusades, especially those in the interest of women, were highly congenial to Mrs. Felton's temperament. They gave her the opportunity to fight against people in power, to take a high moral stand in the controversy, and to read the praise and attacks that were bound to follow in the press. Above all, they kept her active in public affairs when the Doctor's retirement curtailed her participation in politics. Activity was now even more essential for her. A long stay on the farm left her feeling like a human "cipher."[1]

Her reform work really began in the 1870s with her attack on those Bourbons who leased convicts. Although these early efforts were carried on to discredit Gordon and Brown, they did call attention to the inhuman system. In 1881, however, Mrs. Felton read an article in the *Constitution* which started her on an investigation of what went on in those prison camps. Adaline Maddox, a fifteen-year-old Negress, was sentenced to five years at hard labor for stealing fifty cents. What would happen to that girl confined with criminal men of both races? Mrs. Felton was determined to know.[2]

From Robert Alston's report of prison conditions in 1879 and from other sources, she found out. Negro women and men were housed, sometimes chained, together at night! Illegitimate children were being born in those pens of crime and depravity. She found out more. Prisoners were punished for the most trivial insubordinations. A man was beaten to death for throwing hot coffee on a guard's hog, and a woman was given a hundred and sixteen lashes for cursing. Many convicts had been killed trying to escape. The lessees could not account sometimes for all the prisoners sent them, but bloody, bullet-riddled clothes in the

98

nearby woods could furnish the information. Those who endured their sentences were released in their striped uniforms and frequently shot for fugitives by cautious farmers. The contract of 1879 between the state and the lessees was ignored. Religious services were not held, and medical attention was almost nonexistent. She had been denouncing these camps for years, but she had really not known the barbarity that went on inside them.[3]

They must be abolished. She would shame her state until it closed these "holes of Calcutta."

In her speeches and articles she warned the people of Georgia that the lease system was as firmly clamped upon the state as the Standard Oil monopoly was upon the nation. The lessees held or controlled all important political offices. President Cleveland did not dare make a Federal appointment in Georgia without their approval. She called attention to high-paying jobs given the men expelled from Governor Colquitt's corrupt administration. In an article in the *Forum* she reported that "a United States Senator" and "a newly-elected Executive of the State" were growing rich from trafficking in human beings. These men would have to be removed from office, she insisted, before a more humane system could be attained.[4]

In 1886 she joined the Woman's Christian Temperance Union to bring it into her crusade. Immediately she got its permission to present a memorial to the state legislature demanding that the leasing of convicts be stopped.[5] Her vigorous efforts stirred no immediate action in the legislature, but they did bring approving letters from a prison superintendent in Chicago and from the novelist George Washington Cable.[6]

In 1897 the state finally began to move. A three-man commission was appointed with instructions to see that better living and working conditions were maintained in the camps. Three years later penitentiaries were built at Milledgeville to confine separately the men, women, and younger prisoners.[7] Mrs. Felton accepted this half-loaf but continued to agitate for the state itself to work its prisoners.[8] She scolded the Commission for paying so little attention to its job, even suggesting that it be given a permanent vacation.[9] When the lease system was abolished in 1908, she claimed that all credit must be given to the reforms initiated by the W.C.T.U.[10] It must be admitted she had grounds for considering it a personal victory.

Although Mrs. Felton joined the W.C.T.U. to prod it into her fight for prison reform, she was entirely in accord with its basic purpose. She had been reared in the Methodist Church, of all denominations the most vocal against liquor, and as a child she had joined a temperance club and sung the evils of drink. Her husband and sister were staunch Prohibitionists. She had time and enthusiasm to devote also to this cause.

Before long she was telling the W.C.T.U. how its battle should be fought. Always realistic and politically minded, she pointed out that the sale of liquor could never be stopped by songs and white ribbons or by pledges from people who had never taken a drink. It must be voted out. Of course women couldn't vote, but they could see that their men went to the polls well instructed. She sounded her battle cry at a meeting in 1890 of all the temperance organizations within the state. The W.C.T.U. delegation, spurred on by Mrs. Felton and others, asked its male allies to vote only for political candidates pledged to Prohibition. A Mr. J. Y. Carmichael of Coweta County objected. Temperance was a moral question, he insisted, and must not be pushed into the mire of politics. Immediately Mrs. Felton was on her feet with a sermon for the gentlemen assembled. Their harmonious conventions were accomplishing nothing; if they wanted Prohibition, they must go out in the world and fight for it:

> I have heard you do nothing but pass the same old resolutions applauding sobriety and temperance. What good will that do unless your representatives in Congress will vote, vote, vote for you?

The audience applauded, men as well as women. There would be fighting now with Mrs. Felton taking over, and they were ready to follow her. Even Mr. Carmichael was ready. After the meeting he told everyone that Mrs. Felton had given him the soundest and most deserved spanking he had got since his mother gave him her last one.[11]

Things began to move, slowly, but at least they moved. By 1895 the Legislature was willing to let the W.C.T.U. address a committee that was considering a bill to outlaw barrooms. There was no doubt about who the speaker would be. Mrs. Felton knew politicians. She made an appeal that no legislator would dare to argue against. Speaking as a mother she asked each of them to remember that he had a mother. Wherever liquor was sold, the homes and even the lives of mothers were endangered. Their families were demoralized, and their days and nights filled with terror. Helpless they must watch their sons follow their fathers to drunkards' graves. She put the question bluntly to the committee: were they going to protect the mothers of the state or the bartenders? The committee applauded her politely, but later decided not to recommend the bill. Perhaps they did not think the danger so great as she described it.[12]

Meanwhile she was fighting lustily in the battle the W.C.T.U. was carrying on at the county level. Under the local option bill of 1885 each county could vote out its barrooms. Counties were constantly moving into the dry column and then back into the wet. Others were hesitating.[13] Temperance speakers were needed at crucial spots. Calls came to Mrs. Felton from Madison, Thomasville, Dalton, and Greenville, and she went gladly.

The people who came to hear her were her people: reared like her on evangelical sermons and political oratory, loyal to the same prejudices and beliefs. The sentiments that moved her would move them.[14] She spoke to them, too, about mothers. The greatest joy of a mother, she said, was in her children. But if her husband became a drunkard, that joy was killed forever. Raised in an atmosphere of degradation, her sons acquired their father's habits, and her daughters, like her, became broken in spirit. Had any of her audience ever spent the night in a drunkard's home? / Neither had she—thank God!—but she could describe it. It was like being locked in the cell with a madman. She told of a Georgia farmer crazed by drink who had murdered his wife and four small children . . . of a young man, in the very next county, who had shot his wife and sister-in-law, and when he finally became sober had confessed he had thought he was shooting hogs! If the faithful wife escaped death, she survived only to see her husband punished for other crimes. Mrs. Felton pictured her as listening, with a babe at her breast, while a jury sentenced him to prison or the gallows. Later she could be found pleading in vain for his worthless life at the Governor's knee. Was it any surprise that the women of America were imploring their husbands to banish this evil from the land?

Now she was ready to call for the converted. She refused to believe that the good men before her wanted their country afflicted with such violence and suffering. Then they must take action, and she would tell them what to do. They must not waste time with the drunkard and saloon-keeper; God would decide which of the two must be punished. No, in the coming election they must vote to close these dens of sin. So long as liquor could be had, no home, not even their own, was safe from danger. She wanted them to declare themselves that very night. If any man refused, she would have to assume either that he favored liquor or was afraid of those who sold it. Would every man who was going to vote for the protection of his mother and wife stand up.

She did not hesitate to play upon the prejudices of her small-town audiences. Rich society people, she announced, drank without shame. The men thought that serving wine at their tables would make gentlemen of their sons, and their wives felt they could not entertain without the punch bowl or champagne cup. Mrs. Felton's most caustic comments, however, were saved for those fashionable city preachers who never troubled their congregations with sermons against drinking. Finally, she warned of the fearful menace of drunken Negroes. Whisky was bound to inflame their desires for white women. Although she undoubtedly advanced this argument to win white votes, she may, at the same time, have had the Negro's welfare in mind. For she did believe that he, too, would be benefited by Prohibition. At her temperance lecture in Nashville, Tennessee, she insisted that Negro men and women be given seats.[15]

There was flattering evidence that her appeals were effective. The people of Walton and Morgan counties gave her major credit for closing their saloons.[16] At Madison a farmer came to her lecture just to let her know his low opinion of women who spoke in public. When she finished, he hurried home to tell his six sons that they were going to vote against whisky in the election.[17] Perhaps her most spectacular conversion was made at Thomasville. Months later a man in her audience wrote her that although he was so drunk he had to close one eye to see her, he had never touched a drop since that night. Frances Willard, guiding light of the national W.C.T.U., praised her good work.[18]

She was proud, of course, of her successes as a speaker, but too experienced a politician to suppose that speeches alone could bring in Prohibition. When an election was being held in some county, she could be seen on the streets buttonholing liquor men.[19] As she said, it was a waste of time to talk to people on your side. Through the press she picked fights with the opposition leaders. Her main targets were two clergymen who criticized the W.C.T.U. for entering politics: Bishop Warren Candler of her church and Dr. J. B. Hawthorne of the Baptist.[20] She discredited those systems under which a state or municipality controlled the sale of liquor. Praise of the model dispensary at Athens incensed her. She dubbed it the "striped pig of Georgia" and warned the State University that she was going to advise mothers not to send their sons to a place which countenanced such a compromise with the Devil. In her opinion, whisky sold by a preacher could cause just as much harm as whisky sold by a bartender.[21]

She rejoiced with the other embattled ladies of the W.C.T.U. when Georgia passed its "bone-dry" law in 1908. The battle had been won on the home front. But the fight wasn't over. Those disgusting brown-paper boxes continued to arrive at the Cartersville depot, express-marked from Chattanooga and Jacksonville. Never mind. Other states were following Georgia's noble example: soon there would be enough of them to pass an amendment to the Federal Constitution.[22]

She lived long enough to see National Prohibition become a law in 1919—and lived long enough to see the results.

Just as her work for prison reform carried her into the W.C.T.U., so her fight against liquor convinced her that Prohibition and other reforms could be won more quickly if women were given the vote. It is surprising that she waited so long to take an active part in the Woman's Suffrage Movement. In 1886 she declared that she had no desire to vote, and as late as 1897 she had not joined a suffragette organization or asked publicly that women be enfranchised.[23] Perhaps she was content for a time to be almost the only woman in Georgia to participate, even without the vote, in the man's world of politics. But when the opposition to prison reform and Prohibition continued, and the Suffragette Movement began to make headway in the state, she joined the battle. Although she became active shortly after 1900, it was during the period of 1913 to 1918 that she fought most conspicuously.

In Georgia, opposition to woman's suffrage was far stronger and louder than opposition to Prohibition. The majority of men, including many opposed to liquor, refused even to entertain the notion of a woman at the polls. The churches were against it. Bishop Candler and Dr. Hawthorne, Mrs. Felton's perennial enemies, again stood shoulder to shoulder in their disapproval. Politicians and newspaper editors took the popular side. Most women wanted it known they had no interest in the movement, and the United Daughters of the Confederacy took an aggressive stand against it. Two formidable leaders of that organization, Miss Millie Rutherford of Athens, and Mrs. Walter (Dolly) Lamar of Macon, were not disturbed by the prospect of debating Mrs. Felton, or any one else for that matter. The Georgia Suffragettes could use the talents of the old lady who had fought so long against the all-powerful Bourbons.

Mrs. Felton analyzed the situation shrewdly.[24] Although Southern men had strong feelings against woman's suffrage, they had even stronger feelings against anything smacking of racial equality. In her speeches and newspaper articles she pressed for an answer to one question: in 1869 the men of Georgia had given the Negro the right to vote; were their sons and grandsons going to refuse that same right to white women? The question, she insisted, involved far more than men seemed to realize. The most pressing political problem before America was how to keep power out of the hands of Negroes and aliens. There was only one solution: give women the vote, and the government would remain in safe hands. She offered California as an example: when the women were enfranchised they immediately supported the Governor in passing stricter immigration laws against China and Japan. Impatiently and rather illogically she brushed aside the question as to whether Negro women wouldn't also vote with their men. The white politicians, she said, had learned by experience how to keep down the vote of Negro men; they would use those same tactics with Negro women.

She tried to shame the men of Georgia for their tyrannical attitude. Not until after the Civil War, she said, had a law been repealed permitting a man to beat his wife if he used a stick no bigger than his thumb. (At this point in her speech or article she would ask the men to take a look at that digit.) In antebellum days a husband could spend his wife's inheritance, and frequently did, to pay his gambling debts. Until the close of the nineteenth century he could demand from her employer any money she earned.

Of course she knew men would tell her they would never dream of stooping to such disgraceful things. They were chivalrous Southern gentlemen who sheltered their wives from the wickedness of the world . . . spared them the troubles of business affairs. Well, from what she had seen, Southern chivalry was largely expended during the days of courtship. After the marriage, the husband would explain to the wife that all she had to do was stay at home, do the household drudgery, and raise a family. He would look after everything else. Perhaps the men would like to know who helped look after things for widows and unmarried women. Some shiftless Negro could vote on how much property tax these women owed, and they had to pay whatever they were told to pay. No, Southern chivalry had no appeal for her.

She not only lectured the domineering gentlemen but chastised them for any contradictions. Bishop J. H. McCoy of her own church advised a Wesleyan College graduating class not to seek the vote but to "stay at home, love their husbands, and rock a cradle." Immediately she asked the Bishop to explain why the young ladies needed an education if that was all they were going to do.[25] A Mr. George B. Culpepper made a scurrilous attack in the Macon *News* on the suffragettes. The writer asked if it was correct for him to address them as "Dear Ladies," claiming he had heard that a suffragette was a cross between a man and a woman. In the most abusive language he declared that the only rights these dubious females had were to mind their husbands, bear children, and get to heaven—if they could. The crude outburst would have been better ignored, but that was not Mrs. Felton's way. In a letter to the Macon *News* she paid her respects to Mr. Culpepper's obstetrical theories, sympathized with his wife, and refused to argue with him. The effort, she said, would be as futile as offering a bouquet of rare flowers to a mad bull.[26]

Even men who argued politely got the same rough treatment. J. P. Calloway of the Macon *News* reprinted and commended an editorial from the Richland *News* disagreeing with one of her speeches. Given space by both newspapers for a reply, she denounced them for attacking a grandmother eighty years old. In her letter to Calloway she charged that he had hired the Richland paper to fight her just as cowards had hired "substitutes" during the Civil War to fight their battles. She worked up a thunderous rage against M. R. Brown, editor of the Richland *News*. He had unluckily said that the suffragettes had "fallen from the high pedestal of idealized motherhood and womanhood." Mrs. Felton insisted that he had called her a "fallen woman," and in two heated letters to his paper discussed the lustful desires of "fallen man."[27]

Editor Calloway protested that he was not afraid to argue with her, but whatever he said would never be lacking in respect. He assured her that even in this reply he was writing "with his hat in his hand." Evidently Calloway escaped further punishment, but his colleague did not get off so lightly. In a soothing editorial Brown assured Mrs. Felton that she had mistaken his use of the word "fallen." Back came a second letter on the extramarital activities of men—this one too frank for publication. Poor Brown returned it with the most abject apologies.

> Now Mother Felton, in your feeble age, I fear that you are too easy to take exception and get offended. Let me explain before you cuss me. I do not insinuate that your article is not suitable for print, but I fear local mothers would cuss me just a little for writing about lewd houses and bad women.[28]

It is doubtful that she was pleased by the reference to her "feeble age" but she broke off the controversy. She got no pleasure from fighting with people who wouldn't fight back.

Besides, her hands were rather full at about that time with Miss Rutherford and Mrs. Lamar, who would always stand and fight. In July, 1914, these two ladies met Mrs. Felton, Mrs. Nellie McLendon, and Mrs. Elliott Cheatham in debate before a legislative committee considering a bill to give women the vote. The arguments from both sides were long and earnest; but, on the whole, all of the ladies kept their tempers remarkably well, and the hearing stayed within order. The committee split evenly on the question of whether to bring the bill before the House. Chairman Shelby Myrick's vote went with the opposition, and the bill was lost.[29]

A similar hearing in 1915 produced more exciting entertainment for the committee. Another bill brought out the same teams, except that Mrs. Frances Smith Whiteside had replaced Mrs. McLendon. When the ladies arrived promptly at three p.m. they found the committee occupied with a petition for a new county. Three-thirty passed, and four, but the petitioners droned on, quoting statistics, extolling the advantages of their community. Mrs. Felton got angrier by the minute. A fine example of Southern chivalry. There were already enough counties. Myrick ought to tell them their time was up. She had never forgiven him for that vote last year. It was past four-thirty before he adjourned the discussion and called for a hearing on the woman's suffrage bill.[30]

Each side was told that it had thirty minutes. Mrs. Cheatham spoke for ten minutes. When a few people in the large audience started to clap, Myrick warned them sternly that there would be no applause. Mrs. Smith stayed within her allotted time, and then Miss Rutherford arose and moved to the rostrum. Mrs. Felton got out her pencil and paper; she had been selected for the rebuttal. Miss Rutherford informed the committee that God had said a woman's place was in the home, and there was where the vast majority of Southern women were content to stay. They did not want the vote. Southern men had given them "their hearts, hands, and protection." That was all they wanted. Mrs. Felton began to draw pictures of a large hat—perhaps Miss Rutherford's.[31] She had heard all this before. But why wasn't Miss Rutherford stopping? Her fifteen minutes were up. Mrs. Felton looked at Myrick. He was listening attentively—so were the rest of the committee. Fifteen more minutes passed before Miss Rutherford bowed and resumed her seat, without even getting an annoyed look from the chairman. And now applause was breaking out! Myrick smiled tolerantly. "The lid is off," he announced; "cheer as much as you like." Mrs. Felton noticed that several of the committee availed themselves of the privilege. She could hardly keep her seat.[32]

She had to keep it for a long time. Taking her cue from Miss Rutherford, Mrs. Lamar read for forty-five minutes from a large manuscript. Mrs. Felton fumed in silence. People in the audience began to leave for supper. A committeeman yawned, and another asked, like a school boy, if the chairman would excuse him for a few minutes. When Mrs. Lamar finally stopped and took her applause, Mrs. Felton got up from her hard chair. There was another, and louder, wave of applause. She glared at Myrick, hoping that he would dare to order it stopped.[33]

The committee stayed in their seats during her speech, and it is doubtful that there was any more yawning. One by one she pointed out instances of the chairman's favoritism. He had insulted the ladies of her organization. Then she turned her attention to the two U. D. C. ladies. She wanted to know why they did not stay at home and attend to the "duties" of women instead of running around the country electioneering for offices in their organization. It was no excuse to say that neither of them had children. Each could adopt an orphan and raise it. She also pointed out that one of them hadn't availed herself of some man's "heart, hand, and protection." At the end of fifteen minutes Myrick suggested that her time was up. She would not even answer, going on until she had deliberately taken a little less time than Miss Rutherford. By then the audience had come to life, and gave her an encouraging round of applause. The committee might have voted her the star performer, but it again voted down the bill—this time unanimously.[34]

Perhaps the suffragettes realized that they were not going to convert the legislators, or perhaps, after the following April, they devoted some of their abounding energies to America's war effort. In either event, their movement in Georgia subsided somewhat, as did Mrs. Felton's controversies.

She and her fellow-workers must, however, have watched with delight the steady progress of their cause in other states. By 1918 a majority in Congress was ready to pass the Nineteenth Amendment, and she and Mrs. McLendon travelled to Washington to be present on the historic occasion. It was a strange feeling to know that after forty-five years in politics, she could cast her vote. Outside the Capitol, she told Washington reporters that she preferred a national law, after all, because it had more "stickability." [35] She was worried, nevertheless, about whether her state was going to ratify the amendment. On returning home she was irritated to learn that the legislature was hurriedly assembling so that it could be the first state to refuse ratification. Angrily she reminded its members that they were about to go against the wishes of their beloved Woodrow Wilson, whose war measures they had approved so slavishly. When they persisted in their stubbornness, she warned them that the women of Georgia had long memories.[36] She, at least, never forgave them. They had made it evident to all that the long efforts of the Georgia suffragettes had been in vain.

The fourth major movement that attracted Mrs. Felton was in the complex and confused field of education. By 1890 there was little opposition in Georgia to education itself. Almost everyone had come to believe that its benefits were indisputable. There was, however, no unanimity as to which system could best assure these benefits. The national faith in a more secular education was making headway in Georgia, but the Methodists and Baptists were fighting back with demands that the state reduce its appropriations to the University in Athens. The first efforts for co-education were encountering the same opposition that blocked woman's suffrage. Many Georgians believed that only the secondary schools should be given tax money, while a few contended that the money given was not being wisely spent. As the economic philosophy of the New South took hold, there were louder requests for more vocational training. On all these questions Mrs.

Felton had strong views—especially on the question of co-education.

Both she and her husband took the side of the State University against the denominational colleges. Their main opponent was pugnacious Warren Candler, President of Emory College. During the 1880s and 90s he continued to remind the tax-payers that although many of them were sending their sons to church colleges, they were still forced to help pay the expenses of the University. He advocated diverting a part of the University's appropriation to the public school system which prepared boys for all colleges within the state—an idea calculated to win the support of fathers whose sons would not go to any college. Finally he asked that the state exempt from taxes the endowments of church colleges. Did not the income from this money, like taxes, go to the education of Georgia boys? These were compelling arguments.[37]

While the Doctor answered Candler in the legislature, Mrs. Felton attacked him lustily in the *Constitution*. She maintained that the University was not a rich boys' college; in fact, it made higher education available to the poor of Georgia by means of those very taxes that Candler objected to. And speaking of taxes, she added, what about the way the Methodist church collected money for Emory? The assessment "levied under Candler's dictation" upon each church was the equivalent of a tax upon the property of its members. The penalty for non-payment was "social and church ostracism." She advised President Candler to stop trifling with words and admit that he had fastened this scheme of extortion upon their church.[38]

Candler replied that he had not trifled with words, and, what was more important, that he had not "trifled with facts." He asked her to name one Methodist who had suffered social or church ostracism for failing to contribute to Emory. By her own admission, she had never given a cent. Had she been punished for her refusal? He was unable to agree with her that there was no difference between the state's collecting money by fi. fa.s and a preacher asking for a voluntary contribution. The truth of the matter was, said Candler, that Mrs. Felton was not upset about how Emory got its money. She was angry because he opposed woman's suffrage. Well, he hoped it was still not a crime in Georgia for anyone to differ with Mrs. Felton.[39]

Candler could usually hold his own in controversy with Mrs. Felton. Without descending to personal comments and abusive language, he could match her in cutting satire, and he never allowed her extravagant charges to pass unchallenged. He probably had her grudging respect.

It is impossible to determine how much she helped the University during those crucial years when it was beset by churchmen and public-school advocates. Undoubtedly she won some support for it in rural areas, where it badly needed support. At any rate its faculty and students were grateful for her efforts. Chancellor Walter B. Hill and Professor Henry White became her warm friends, and the student body voted her its thanks. Editor Harry Hodgson dedicated the *Pandora,* the University year book, to her, and, for good measure, threw in a cartoon of her spanking Dr. Candler. The artist left no doubt that she was enjoying the task.[40]

Mrs. Felton maintained a stern friendship for the University throughout her life, spanking it too whenever it failed to mind her. Irritated by the students' craze for athletics and dancing, she wrote an article to the press advising them to leave off educating their arms and feet and to pay some attention to their heads.[41] The same year the *Pandora* was dedicated to her, she denounced the trustees, a bit hastily, for refusing to allow girls from the State Normal School to receive awards in the University Chapel. Her blistering letter to the *Journal* was published before she learned that the Trustees, after considerable debate, had decided not to exclude the young ladies.[42] As early as 1894 she demanded that the University become co-educational. When the student newspaper took issue with her, she declared that the boys reminded her of stubborn oxen who wouldn't eat but wouldn't let anyone else near the manger.[43] Fortunately, the University had admitted women before the 1921 commencement at which she was given an honorary degree; otherwise she would probably have enlivened the ceremony with some remarks on that subject.

Nor did she hesitate to criticize Georgia's public school system. She pointed out that the state was spending more and more money on schools which many boys and girls were either not attending or attending irregularly. In a speech before the legislature in 1901, she called for a compulsory school law. The purpose of education, she said, was to produce better men and women. Education in Georgia could never accomplish this objective, no matter how much money was spent, unless the boys and girls were made to attend classes. She offered the Negroes as an example.

They were staying away from the schools provided by white tax payers, and, as a result, crime among that race was steadily increasing. A larger percentage of white students was enrolled, but many of them were kept at home whenever they were needed on the farm. She warned the Legislature that if this waste of good tax money continued, Georgia was going to wake up some morning and find itself bankrupt.[44]

Mrs. Felton undoubtedly had her own high taxes in mind when she criticized the public school system; just as she defended the University more heatedly because Warren Candler attacked it. There can be no doubt, however, of the sincerity and unselfishness of her efforts to make vocational training available to the poor white girls of Georgia. Her crusade was not prompted by personal interests and animosities; and it afforded her few controversies and little publicity. For years she worked to convince the public of this need, and helped mightily in the founding and operating of one of the vocational schools that was finally established.

Her most eloquent plea for these underprivileged girls was made before a U. D. C. convention in 1891. She described graphically the hard, helpless lot of the daughters and granddaughters of those men who had made up the rank and file of the Confederate armies. The assembled ladies were told that they could honor their dead heroes far more appropriately by looking after their descendants than by building expensive monuments to their memory. Determined to stir her audience to action Mrs. Felton told of seeing a young Negress studying Greek on a train which was passing through a cotton field where white girls were laboring. She pointed out that Northern philanthropists were endowing schools in the South for Negro girls. If the poorer white girls were to get a comparable education, the richer Southerners would have to provide the money.[45]

When Southern money was not forthcoming, Mrs. Felton tried and failed to interest Andrew Carnegie in her project.[46] In 1913, however, Mrs. Russell Sage of New York gave six thousand dollars to help her establish a training school for the girls of Georgia. The State appropriated additional money, and Atlanta donated the land. The first building erected was named the Felton-Sage Cottage. In 1915 the Georgia Training School for Girls enrolled its first students. Mrs. Felton was elected and re-elected a trustee, serving faithfully until her death. She remained convinced that the school carried on the noblest educational work in Georgia. It was fitting that her most altruistic crusade should have produced such worthy results.[47]

She was always proud of her stormy career as a reformer. In her old age she loved to recall how she had gone to the rostrum to plead her causes in days when women did not attend public meetings unaccompanied by men. She claimed that she heard more than one man say, "If that woman was my wife, I'd rope and tie her." [48] More likely these remarks were reported to her by other listeners. Men did not usually speak disrespectfully of Mrs. Felton without first making sure that she was out of hearing.

13

. . . . .
. . .
.

Sectionalist

REBECCA Felton prided herself on being a progressive, but except on the woman question she was in basic agreement with the thinking of her section. For all her feminism, she was a Southerner, with the prejudices and loyalties of her people. Her participation in the man's field of politics must not obscure the fact that she fought with the older agrarian wing of the Democratic Party. Certainly her views on the Negro, religion, and economics were the views of the South—often the very dogmatic views of its rural areas.

Her attitude towards the Negro was so extreme that it calls for explanation. In some ways it was the traditional Southern attitude: she praised him for his loyalty during the Civil War, accepted his emancipation, and advocated his rights to elementary education and the opportunity to work at menial labor.[1] But she could never think of him as merely a member of an inferior race: he was a ravenous beast at heart, capable at a given opportunity of violating any white woman. It is difficult to account for the depth of Mrs. Felton's abhorrence. During the 1890s there had been several brutal attacks upon women in her neighborhood, and one night she had listened to the ominous tread of a mob pursuing its victim.[2] But many a Southern woman had lived close to such horrors. A possible explanation is that her antipathy for the Negro was accentuated by her strange antagonism towards all men. More than one of her firmest convictions were warped by this persistent hostility. But whatever the cause, there can be no doubt of her feeling on the Negro problem. It was revealed in some of her most intemperate statements.

During the summer of 1897 she had been reading in the newspapers of several attacks upon white women and had easily

become convinced that public apathy was encouraging the out-
rages. Eagerly she seized upon an opportunity to release her pent-
up indignation. The State Agricultural Society wanted her to
speak at its annual meeting on the problems of farm wives, and
the secretary hoped that she could infuse new life into the organization.[3] She certainly tried. The gravest problem facing farm
wives, she told her audience, was the danger from Negro rapists.
It was time the men of Georgia took a hand in protecting their
wives and daughters. If religion and the law could not put a
stop to this fearful crime, then they must lynch these "ravening
beasts a thousand times a week if necessary." [4]

The Georgia newspapers played up her speech in front-page
headlines, but their editors hesitated either to applaud or criticize
her proposed remedy. Up in Boston, however, the staid *Transcript*
was properly horrified and proceeded to read Mrs. Felton a
scathing lecture. The theme of its editorial was that the lady's
inhuman sentiments had made clear that there were other wild
beasts in Georgia besides the Negro. The Macon *Telegraph* was
perfectly willing to do battle with the *Transcript,* but decided it
could do more for the cause by giving Mrs. Felton space to launch
the counterattack. Bluntly she charged the Northern newspapers
with encouraging those crimes that made lynching necessary.
Their maudlin sympathy for the Southern Negro had made him
restless and unruly. If Boston wanted mixed marriages, that was
its business but it might as well understand that in the South a
Negro who laid hands on a white woman was going to die. Of
course she had rather see the brute hanged legally, but if he confessed to a mob, then he stood condemned by civilization, with
the possible exception of Boston.[5]

In Wilmington, North Carolina, A. L. Manley, Negro editor of
the *Record,* read Mrs. Felton's speech, but, for some reason, waited
a year before taking exception to it. In his editorial he agreed with
her that the poorer classes of Southern men were careless in
protecting their women, but he insisted that these women were
no more averse to clandestine meetings with colored men than
were white men with colored women. These meetings eventually
attracted attention and brought on a lynching. Manley advised
Mrs. Felton to begin at the fountainhead if she wanted to purify
the stream.[6]

In almost any other Southern city the editorial would have
also attracted the sort of attention that ended in lynching, but
in Wilmington a corrupt Republican administration was giving

adequate police protection to its Negro supporters. The white editors of the State, however, took care that this impudence was not overlooked or forgotten. It was well remembered in Wilmington when the local Democrats regained power in November of 1898. A large mob made a call at the *Record's* office, but Manley had fled to the friendlier atmosphere of New Jersey. Frustrated, the mob burned the building and opened a race riot in which at least eleven Negroes were killed.[7]

Anxious to get as many headlines as possible out of the Wilmington trouble, the Atlanta *Journal* wired Mrs. Felton that Northern newspapers were saying her "lynching" speech had caused the riots. She obliged with a letter that was given the caption: "Lynch 1000 Weekly Declares Mrs. Felton." The only change in her original statement was to advocate dispensing with a legal trial, even when it was possible, for a proved Negro rapist. It was an unwritten law in Georgia, she declared, that he must die without benefit of clergy, judge, or jury. Warmed to the fight, she sent another letter to the *Journal* a few days later attacking Miss Elizabeth Grannis, a white woman who had attended a meeting of the New York Negroes protesting the Wilmington killings.[8]

Strangely enough the Northern newspapers seemed inclined to make little of the North Carolina disturbance. The New York *Tribune* even suggested that the scandalous Wilmington administration was largely responsible.[9] But Mrs. Felton had not heard the last of her lawless advice. A month later in Nashville her old enemy Dr. J. B. Hawthorne preached a sermon during the Christmas season on "Christianity and Mob Law." Hawthorne declared that when Mrs. Felton advocated hanging a thousand Negroes, she represented "humanity verging towards the animal and the fiend." [10] Infuriated, she wrote a letter to the *Constitution* denouncing Hawthorne as a craven and a coward who attacked women from the safety of his pulpit. Without giving the source of her figures she announced proudly that lynching in Georgia had decreased fifty per cent since her speech. She urged the public to pay no attention to Hawthorne; he was only a "slick-haired, slick-tongued Pecksniffian blatherskite." [11] In his reply he attempted to justify his sermon by protesting that he had only tried to correct the impression Mrs. Felton's speech must have made in the North. Unwittingly he left her a wide opening, and she struck swiftly. Hawthorne was playing up to the South's enemies, she said, in the hope that they would offer him a high-salaried job. There was no further reply.[12]

If lynching was decreasing in Georgia, as Mrs. Felton claimed, this healthy trend did not continue. On the night of April 12, 1899, Alfred Crandall, a farmer living near Newnan, was brutally murdered by Sam Horse, a local Negro. According to Mrs. Crandall, the Negro then raped her by the body of her dead husband. Middle Georgia became alive with mobs of grim-faced men. The newspapers omitted no details of the gory crime and spurred on the searchers by publicizing the large rewards offered for Horse's capture. Each day they announced that he was about to be taken.[13]

But when a week passed with the Negro still at large, the editors were forced to shorten their reports from the hunt and move them to inside pages. The *Constitution,* to keep the story alive, ran a symposium in which prominent men and women suggested ways to stop such inhuman crimes. As something of an authority on that subject, Mrs. Felton offered her solution. It was the one she had given in her recent speech: lynch the black fiends by the thousands until the Negro understood that there was a standard punishment for rape and he could not escape it. She urged Horse's pursuers to forget the reward offered for his capture and to shoot him on sight as they would a mad dog. If he was spared for trial, Mrs. Crandall would have to tell in court the shameful outrage she had suffered. Hadn't she been tortured enough?[14]

On Saturday night, April 22, Horse was finally taken and lodged in the Newnan jail. The following morning, while some Georgians were in church and others reading the *Constitution,* a mob broke into the jail and hurried the Negro to the outskirts of town. There he was emasculated and then burned alive. When the fire subsided, men pulled grisly souvenirs from the coals.[15]

The Northern newspapers fulminated against the savage execution: it was called a "stench to the nostrils of the nation," a deed "worthy of Yahoos," punishment "beyond the cruelty of an Apache." Some Southern papers, such as those in Richmond and Savannah, joined the outcry, but the majority stood sullenly together in refusing to condemn the lynchers.[16] A single voice spoke out in the Atlanta press against the inhuman outrage. A brave lady begged the South, "in the name of humanity, civilization and Christianity," to stop these barbarous reprisals.[17] Mrs. Felton made no public comments.

Three years later, however, when a reverberation of the Horse lynching was heard in Georgia, she found plenty to say.

An article appeared in the *Atlantic Monthly* entitled "The Negro: Another View" by Andrew Sledd, who announced himself a Southerner. The writer blamed both North and South for the Negro's tragic plight: the North had tried to push him into a racial equality for which he was not fit; and the South had denied him the protection of the law to which he was entitled. Sledd used the Horse killing as an example of the South's brutal attitude. The ghastly scene came alive in the article: the holiday spirit of the mob, the Negro's death agony, the souvenir hunters. Sledd condemned it as an act of "the purest savagery." [18]

The *Atlantic* had a small circulation in Georgia, and the article might have passed unchallenged if an Atlanta man had not sent it to Mrs. Felton with the suggestion that she make an appropriate reply.[19] Her letter to the *Constitution* carried Sledd's views— or rather, her interpretation of them—to a far larger audience. If she had known he was a professor at Emory College she would have found him even more reprehensible; but she did know he was a Southerner, and she had a stock treatment for such "traitors." He was a "sniveling ink-slinger," she said, who had betrayed his section for the silver of a partisan magazine. He had sneered at the South in the hope that some Boston negrophile would give him a high-salaried job. Angrily she pointed out that he had been glib enough about Horse's suffering but had not even mentioned what happened to Mrs. Crandall. If he was still in the South she advised him to head north before his love of the Negroes earned him the tar and feather treatment.[20]

Mrs Felton's mail became heavy with letters telling who Sledd was and thanking her for exposing him. Indignation mounted in the neighborhood of Emory. The citizens of adjoining Covington sent her a hearty endorsement signed with many names. Stirred by this applause and the pertinent information about Sledd, she sent the endorsement and another tirade to the *Journal.* Editor Jack Cohen thanked her but decided that she had already covered the subject rather fully in the *Constitution.*[21]

Sledd published a short letter in the *Constitution* protesting that Mrs. Felton had used only those statements in his article that suited her purpose. He refused, however, to get into a controversy. In the summer he resigned from Emory and later accepted the presidency of the University of Florida. In 1915 Emory made restitution by appointing him Professor of Greek and Latin Literature.[22]

It should be pointed out that Mrs. Felton's incendiary appeals for lynching were made during a period when racial feeling ran high in the South. From 1890 on into the first of the twentieth century there was an alarming outburst of Negro violence and white reprisals, both of which were probably brought on by the white man's efforts to curtail the political and social advances made by the Negro. Unquestionably Mrs. Felton was influenced by the temper of those times. By 1913 she had apparently grown more moderate. Once in a benign mood, she went so far as to say that it was better to allow a thousand murderers to escape than to lynch one innocent person. It is doubtful, however, that she had changed her mind about the proper punishment for Negro rape. That same year she warned a Northern critic that as long as that crime prevailed in the South, lynching would continue.[23]

She stood as firmly for the religion of rural Georgia as she did for its racial feeling. Since joining the Methodist church as a girl she had never questioned its doctrines of an Almighty Providence, the divinity of Christ, and a personal immortality. She dismissed the theory of evolution with the trite witticism that she had rather be descended from Adam than from a ring-tailed monkey. When a friend invited her to a lecture by agnostic Robert Ingersoll, she refused. Her faith, she said, was too precious to take any chances with it.[24]

Like most Southern Methodists she opposed reunion with the Northern branch of her church. The National Conference, she argued, wouldn't be above sending Negro preachers and presiding elders to the white churches of the South. Hadn't a delegate to a Northern Baptist conference boasted that he was "part Indian, part white, and more nigger"? She shared the apathy of the rural churches for foreign missions, contending that there were enough heathen closer to home. Instinctively hostile to Catholicism, she subscribed to the popular notion that the Pope was plotting to gain political control of the United States.[25]

How did a woman of such orthodox and conventional beliefs come to fight so persistently with the preachers and bishops of her church? First, because the opposition of certain clergy to the woman's rights movement angered her so that she welcomed any opportunity to attack them. Second, because her distaste for strong central government and urban ways made it easy for her to believe that the bishops were autocratic and that the city preachers were more interested in salaries and easy jobs than in saving souls. With this viewpoint, she had no difficulty in finding much to criticize in her church.

One of the briskest of these controversies was with Bishop Warren Candler and the Baptist Dr. Hawthorne on the momentous question of whether Jay Gould, the notorious Wall Street baron, had gone to Hell. When the incorrigible capitalist died, both preachers declared publicly that his new abode was not as comfortable as his earthly one had been. Mrs. Felton became highly interested in their announcement. Under the caption "Jay Gould's Whereabouts" she wrote an anonymous letter in which she asked if someone had come up from Hell to tell the two clergymen of Gould's arrival. She was also curious to know if John D. Rockefeller was going to the same place. Of course he had given money to church colleges, but he was even richer than Gould. She begged Candler and Hawthorne to pardon her for these bothersome questions—she knew they hadn't much patience with women —but a lot of people wanted to hear more about the other world. When her letter reached Editor Clark Howell of the *Constitution*, he immediately saw the possibility of a warm argument and wrote begging her to let him run it over her signature. News had been dull of late, he said. She consented.[26]

The news columns of the *Constitution* came to life. Candler and Hawthorne replied immediately, offering Gould's unscrupulous career as proof of his whereabouts. But by then Mrs. Felton had lost all interest in the deceased; she wanted to discuss the money Hawthorne had got from endorsing a patent medicine, and Candler's methods of increasing Emory's endowment. Hawthorne decided that he could not indulge in a controversy with an angry woman and several Emory officials replied for Candler, urging the public to pay no attention to the misguided statements of "our erring sister." The *Constitution* declared Mrs. Felton the winner and bragged of the number of papers sold during the comic-opera debate.[27]

In 1897 she raised a more promising issue that gave the entire North Georgia Conference some bad moments. It all began with an anonymous article she wrote for the *American Outlook,* a Methodist paper published in Nashville, entitled "The Future of Methodism." [27] The future of Methodism was, apparently, far from hopeful. She quoted "one of the brainiest" preachers in Georgia on the reasons for the sad spiritual condition of the church. The unnamed clergyman declared that the bishops were ruling with tyrannical power, giving the best appointments to their toadies and punishing their enemies with small-salaried pastorates in rural areas. The immorality of the city clergy was said to be beyond belief: they fawned upon their rich parishioners, lived worldly lives, and even refused to pay their debts. Instead of preaching against drinking and gambling, they chose such safe targets as Christian Science. Unless the church underwent a spiritual rebirth, the brainy gentleman believed it was headed for certain dissolution.[28]

The article provoked a highly successful altercation. Walker Lewis, pastor of Atlanta's First Methodist Church, took it as a personal attack. He had recently delivered an eloquent sermon against Christian Science. Immediately he wrote the *Outlook* demanding the author's name. Editor B. F. Haynes was willing to shield Mrs. Felton, but that was the last thing she wanted. She published a letter in the *Outlook* admitting that she had written the article, and promising to take care of any critics. Wanting no row with Mrs. Felton, Lewis insisted that the real culprit was the preacher she had quoted. Immediately the Reverend Clement C. Carey of Cedartown, an aggressive ally of Mrs. Felton, indicated that he was the guilty party by declaring publicly that he agreed with four-fifths of what she had said. Lewis decided that he had his man. He announced that he would bring both Carey and the offensive article before the annual meeting of the Conference and demand an investigation.[29]

Mrs. Felton and Carey were delighted. She could not attend the meeting—unless summoned later—but he must see that the article was read before the entire delegation.[30] The leaders of the Conference, however, skillfully sidetracked the issue. Lewis' motion for an investigation was quickly referred to a safe committee for consideration. After appropriate deliberation the committee decided that since the charges had been made against no specific person, they could not be investigated. Bishop Candler got in a rebuke for Mrs. Felton by moving that in the future such general accusations should not be considered. The motion passed except for a loud "No" from Carey. A resolution to censure his approval of the letter lost by a substantial margin. The Conference then turned to less explosive matters.[31]

Although the issue had been blocked short of the floor, Mrs. Felton took care that it was brought to the public's attention. When the Conference adjourned, she wrote a long letter to the *Journal* giving the history of the controversy, from her own viewpoint, and accusing Candler of refusing to investigate her charges because he knew they were true. Claiming a complete victory, she dismissed her clerical opponents as being unworthy of further notice.[32]

A year later she pushed the investigation of a far graver charge which threatened the integrity of the entire Methodist Church South. During the Civil War the Church's publishing house in Nashville had been destroyed by Union troops. After repeated failures to obtain an indemnity from the Federal Government, the Church had placed its claim in the hands of E. B. Stahlman, a resourceful lobbyist. In 1898, when a bill to pay the indemnity reached the Senate, the question was asked whether Stahlman was to receive a large fee from the money appropriated. Senator Bate of Tennessee answered that he had asked Messrs. Barbee and Smith, book agents for the Church, and had been assured Stahlman would not be paid one cent. The Senate passed the bill for an indemnity of $288,000.[33]

Shortly afterwards Mrs. Felton learned that the General Conference had approved the payment of 35% of the indemnity, or $100,800, to Stahlman for his services. She wrote a letter to the press exposing the fee, and got her friend Senator Henry Cabot Lodge to demand a Senate investigation, which revealed that her accusations were true. To her surprise and indignation the Senate did not demand that the indemnity be returned, and the Church, after some debate, voted to keep it. Declaring that she had done all she could, she washed her hands of the whole business with the warning that ill-gotten money would burn all it touched.[34]

At times Mrs. Felton's friends wondered if she was going to leave the Church.[35] There is no evidence that she ever considered such a step. Her cordial dislike of certain bishops and preachers could not alienate her affection for the Church she had worhipped in for fifty years. She continued to believe that the rank-and-file Methodists were as honest and God-fearing as any people in America. But she would always hold some of their clergy in less esteem.

Mrs. Felton had less inclination to argue with the leaders of the Southern business world. Their views were too nearly hers. She fought the Bourbons in politics, but she approved of the industrial expansion they were promoting in the state. In the midst of her political battles with Joe Brown, she concluded business deals with him. Her economic opinions were as conservative as his own. She favored the capitalistic system and a modest tariff on

products that could be manufactured in the South. She had made
money and she intended to keep it—and make more.[36]

There is no doubt that wealthier Georgians had profited from
the New South economy; the question was whether the laboring
class had benefited. The textile industry was a case in point. After
the war large mills had sprung up in Atlanta, Augusta, Columbus, and Macon. Their operators had found an abundance of
cheap labor. Farmers were eager to exchange the uncertain yield
of their washed acres for a small, steady salary. There was employment for the entire family, too—wives, children, even grandparents. Of course the hours were long, the company-provided
houses were cheap affairs, and groceries at the mill commissary
ran terribly high. But life on a Georgia farm apparently seemed
harder in retrospect, for the workers remained at their looms.[37]

There were reformers, however, who were not so satisfied with
conditions in these Southern mills, and with their use of child
labor. In February, 1891, *Century* magazine published an article
by Claire DeGraffenreid of Washington, D. C., on "The Georgia
Cracker and the Cotton Mills." It was a dismal picture Miss De-
Graffenreid drew. The mill worker was described as a shallow,
shiftless fellow, content to keep his family in a house no better
than a pigsty. The morals of the women were said to be deplorable,
and the children, raised without education or religious training,
could look forward to nothing but the grim labor they had already begun. Although the writer placed the blame mainly on the
mill owners, she did admit that the war, reconstruction, climate,
and diet had all helped to bring about the degeneration of a once
hardy, energetic people.[38]

The mill owners of Georgia could hardly ignore this attack.
The state legislature had begun to show an unfriendly interest
in their employment of children. Perhaps Mrs. Felton would answer the troublesome Miss DeGraffenreid. J. F. Hanson, President
of Macon's Bibb Manufacturing Company urged her to reply, offering information he had used at a legislative hearing.[39] Other
owners invited her to visit their plants and see for herself how
the employees lived and worked.[40] She consented, and after a tour
of several mills she wrote a long article which, to her indignation,
was refused first by the *Century,* and next by *Harper's.* The
Constitution and the *Chronicle,* however, would publish it and
also her scathing criticism of the *Century* for refusing to present
the other side.[41]

Mrs. Felton's defense of the mills took the form of a personal attack upon Miss DeGraffenreid. She was accused of being one of those Northerners who hold up everything in the South to derision. Her report of flagrant immorality among the mill wives was called untrue and contemptible. Mrs. Felton declared that these women were as loyal and industrious as women in any walk of life. If the workers were not complaining, why should Miss DeGraffenreid complain? Her attack on the mill owners was called equally unfair. These men had given homes and employment to some of the neediest people in Georgia. According to Mrs. Felton, the operators did not want child labor in their mills. They allowed it because they could not refuse orphans or children with helpless parents the opportunity to earn their bread. If Miss DeGraffenreid had really visited Georgia mills, as she claimed, then Mrs. Felton could only conclude that she had deliberately issued her report to injure a commendable industry and its hard-working employees.[42]

How could the two ladies have inspected the same industry and come up with such contradictory findings? It is impossible to dismiss as irrelevant the fact that Mrs. Felton was invited to the mills to get information for the defense, and her tours were arranged by the owners. Also, both investigators probably took up the question with prejudiced minds. Perhaps the opinions of another Georgia woman came nearer to the truth. In 1903 Miss Mary Bacon of Athens also published an article in the Atlanta *Journal* on the same subject. Like Mrs. Felton she believed that the mill owners had given the poor of Georgia a more remunerative work than they could get by farming. But she agreed with Miss DeGraffenreid that their living conditions were shameful, and that the state should put an end to child labor. Miss Bacon's quiet analysis sounds far more convincing than the extreme views of the two excited controversialists.[43]

Mrs. Felton's support of the mill owners earned the praise of the Georgia Industrial Association. At one of its annual meetings it commended her "temperate, conservative, and very able presentation of the child labor situation." [44] It should be pointed out that the workers too approved of her attack on their detractor. The women at the Roswell Mill showed their appreciation by raising sixty dollars to help pay for an appropriate monument at her grave.[45]

Like the Roswell women, Mrs. Felton did not take kindly to the criticism of her state by outsiders. Perhaps she considered herself adequate to detect and chastise its shortcomings. She was remarkably like the Georgia mother who was losing a fist-fight with her son when two strangers came up and began to handle the boy rather roughly. The rescued mother dashed into the house and reappeared with the family shotgun, ordering the intruders off the place. Critics of Georgia ran the risk of a fight with Rebecca Felton.

14

. . . . .
. . .
.

Journalist and Writer

ONE OF THE earliest and strongest of Mrs. Felton's ambitions was to become a writer. As a schoolgirl she worked hard at her compositions and speeches, read newspapers, and marvelled at the wisdom of their editors. When Dr. Felton entered politics, she immediately took over his letters to the press and seized every opportunity to send in one over her own name. Early in 1885 she probably encouraged him to start the *Courant,* for its first issue made it clear that she was going to take an active part in its publication. The editors were announced as "Dr. and Mrs. Wm. Felton." [1]

Many of the editorials were unmistakably hers. They dealt with topics she had labored on for years, and were written in her brisk, colloquial style.[2] Ex-Independent Emory Speer was ridiculed for "dancing a little jig" to the Bourbons' tune, and Joe Brown was given ironic praise for ordering his lobbyists to stop "honey-fuggling" the legislature with liquor.[3] One editorial made sport of "the ignorance and innocence of Neighbor Bill Arp," the folksy columnist of the *Constitution,* and another grew angry about the game of "thimble rig" that Gordon and other convict lease-holders were playing with unscrupulous penitentiary keepers.[4] When the *Wesleyan Christian Advocate* solicited funds for foreign missions the *Courant* suggested that the money could be better spent to "evangelize the heathen in California, Wyoming and the United States Congress." [5]

There is no reason to doubt her statement that after the legislature opened in the summer of 1885, the Doctor contributed nothing but advice and suggestions: at least his initialed editorials ceased to appear. From her correspondence it is evident that the business management of the paper was entirely in her hands

even when her husband was in Cartersville. She solicited adver-
tisements and subscriptions, persuaded Senator Colquitt to get the
Courant second-class mailing privileges, and dogged the Postmaster General for Government printing. And she could not begin her work on the paper until she had finished her household
chores and driven three miles into town.[6] The task was too
much even for her strength and enthusiasm, and in the fall of
1885 she broke down and took to her bed. After a few weeks
she was back at work, but the following March the Doctor as-
serted himself. The duties of the editress, he announced, were
too strenuous to risk her health any longer; the *Courant* would
be sold. Democratic editors spoke kindly of the fine paper she had
run, but it is doubtful they felt the loss of her stinging editorials,
especially at election time.[7]

In 1899 she took on her second newspaper job, one that was
to make her name and opinions heard in Georgia farmhouses from
the mountains to the Okefenokee. The Atlanta *Journal* was trying to increase the circulation of its *Semi-Weekly Edition* in the
rural areas, and Publisher Hoke Smith was considering a column
advising wives how to "brighten" the home. Would Mrs. Felton
write it for him? She would. A paying job was something you
didn't turn down, especially one on a newspaper.[8]

She had lots of advice to give about the home—and about
many other things. First of all, the wives must see that their
husbands put in such conveniences as electricity and waterworks.
A man should be ashamed to make his wife haul water from a
well in the yard. The women were cautioned, however, to be
careful about electricity; live wires were dangerous, especially
during a storm. Next, comfortable furniture must be bought. It
didn't need to cost too much, and a smart woman could weave
her own rugs. She ought to learn to sew also, and to teach her
daughters; but Mrs. Felton certainly hoped they would shun such
modern styles as those skin-tight dresses that made a woman look
like a pouter pigeon above the waist, and revealed the shape of
the lower limbs.[9]

She insisted that housewives were far too busy to take over entirely the job of brightening the home. They were urged not to
pay the slightest attention to Dorothy Dix, a better-known lady
columnist, who was always saying that even after a hard day
women should appear fresh and smiling for their husbands. If
the husband wanted everything neat and cheerful, let him pitch
in and do some work and smiling of his own. Daughters ought

to help, too, and without complaining. Recently she had been in a home where she had a hard time to keep from smacking the jaw of one impudent young thing.[10]

As long as she was telling the wife how to run her home, Mrs. Felton thought she might as well tell the husband how to run the farm. The chances were that he wasn't doing a very good job. If he was buying commercial fertilizer on credit, he'd better stop before the storekeepers got a grip on him where the wool was long enough to hold. He ought to diversify his crops so that he would have something to sell when the cotton season was bad. But above all, he must work more and do a little less complaining. Just the other day, she had driven by a house where the farmer and his sons were sitting on the porch looking at a cotton patch almost hidden by the weeds.[11]

She wanted the young people to listen to her too. There was so much badness going on in the world—so much more than there used to be. Girls must not go out alone at night, now that "lust and liquor had the right-of-way on country roads as well as city streets." They must stay out of those soft-drink parlors too, where dope could be slipped into an innocent looking soda. Never give a kodak picture of yourself to a man, because you might find it turning up after you have married someone else. If a girl thought dancing wasn't indecent, let her ask herself if she'd go down the church aisle with a man holding her the way he did in the "bunny hug" and "grizzly bear." Of course men were going to say that dancing was just a harmless exercise. Well, if that was so, why didn't they dance with each other?[12]

In the same caustic tone she warned the boys about smoking, gambling, and drinking. Even Coca-Cola was habit forming and led to a craving for stronger drink. Boys must not swear, especially in front of ladies, and they were too young to drive those dangerous automobiles. She knew they were going to complain that she didn't want them to have any fun, but there were lots of ways to have fun besides those that put broken-hearted parents into early graves.[13]

Of all Mrs. Felton's readers the group that won her sincerest concern was the Confederate Veterans. By the turn of the century many of them had become obvious burdens to their children and grandchildren, and were being eased into the lonely life of Old Soldiers' Homes. She took them under her ample wing, publishing their letters about wartime experiences, helping them to get pensions, and worrying about those long trips to reunions, and their parades in the summer sun. Of course she scolded them too. She was shocked to see "so much evidence of booze" at one reunion, and she spoke sharply to their Commander, General George Harrison, for coming out against National Prohibition. In a burst of anger she suggested that one old fellow's pension ought to be stopped if he kept using it to go on monthly sprees. It is doubtful that she induced any of them to take the temperance pledge, for she would have mentioned it in her column.[14]

Besides advising her various readers about their problems and behaviour, Mrs. Felton told them what was wrong with the country. In her opinion there was a great deal wrong. She was disturbed by those strange revolutionary ideas that were undermining established beliefs, especially in other sections. The spreading doctrine of socialism she considered nothing more than " a cloak" to rob the industrious and thrifty. It was absurd to talk about putting an end to poverty. Didn't the Bible say "The poor ye have with you always"? The trouble was that politicians, even in the South, were supporting radical legislation in order to get the working man's vote. She warned the Georgia Legislature that if it passed the Child Labor Law, cotton mills would hire Negro men and women instead of white boys and girls.[15]

It worried her to see how people were drifting away from religion. Even some preachers were saying that parts of the Bible weren't true. When she saw all those joy-riding automobiles on Sundays, she was reminded of the Biblical prophecy that "The chariot shall rage in the streets." She got no comfort from the fact that Catholicism was increasing in the big cities. Undoubtedly the Pope would soon be running the American Government. Immigrants were pouring into the country, and the Yankees were petting and pampering the Negro. Look how that pugilist Jack Johnson, black as the ace of spades, was allowed to parade his white wife, and Teddy Roosevelt sitting down to dinner with Booker T. Washington in the White House. Well, some states were already seeing the results of these absurd notions. California had been forced to pass laws to keep out the Japs, and Illinois was having worse race riots than any of the Southern states.[16]

She got no argument from her readers. These were their views, expressed more clearly and loudly. They came to look upon her as their oracle, and kept her mail heavy with their questions, which she answered readily, "especially when a stamp is enclosed for the return letter." No, all foreigners were not Jews;

nor was Woodrow Wilson a Catholic, although he did have other shortcomings. Was it all right for a girl to get engaged to two men? Certainly, if she wanted to start a shooting scrape. What did Mrs. Felton think ought to be done to a man who had shot his daughter suspected of immorality? "Lynch him," advised Mrs. Felton. They brought their troubles and needs to her and she tried to help. She sought homes for orphans and urged fugitive husbands to return to their wives. Stern moralist though she was, she helped a "fallen" woman find employment. (The man was probably to blame anyway.) Although she refused to act as a regular matrimonial agent for young girls, she did offer to forward letters from old maids to lonely, respectable bachelors. (People of that age were so timid about such things.) Over a hundred ladies availed themselves of this service.[17]

From all over the state came expressions of admiration and gratitude. One man wrote that he kept a scrapbook of her columns, and another called her the smartest woman in Georgia. A woman looked forward to meeting her in heaven, and a fisherman named his boat for her. Moved by her interest in the Veterans, one wrote to thank her in the name of the "few old stragglers still on this side of the river." Probably her most original compliment came from a son-in-law who thought her picture in the *Journal* resembled his wife's dear mother.[18]

A young railroad conductor spoke for those stubborn, reticent people when, helping her off his train, he asked, "Aren't you the Mrs. Felton who writes for us?" [19]

Letters from her readers indicate that she continued to write for them up until 1928, although not long after the war she gave up pasting her columns in scrapbooks. It may be she got out of that habit some time between October 1920 and August 1921 while she was contributing a weekly letter to the Atlanta *Sunday American*. There is no evidence that she gave up writing for the *Journal* during that period, although she had quarreled with Editor James Grey for omitting several of her pieces. Tartly she informed him that even if she didn't pet poodles and paint china like certain other women columnists, she wrote articles that were read and enjoyed by a large number of his subscribers, and she could prove it, too. In spite of this burst of resentment she probably continued her non-political columns in the *Journal* while giving vent to her antagonism towards Wilson and the League of Nations in her letters to the *American*. She needed this second outlet. The War, with its new weapons and mass

slaughter, had troubled her deeply, and she was convinced
that this country should never again make the tragic mistake
of meddling with Europe's evil affairs.[20]

The *American* welcomed Mrs. Felton as a staff member, and she
must have found the paper's atmosphere congenial and exciting.
Its owner, William Randolph Hearst, could match her hatred of
Wilson, Great Britain, and the New Internationalism. Like her,
he had not said all that he would have liked to say during the
war, but now he was throwing his large chain of newspapers
against the pro-League Democrats in the coming elections. Mrs.
Felton would have no articles refused by this paper.

Her attacks became as personal and savage as those she had
made on the Bourbons in the days of Independentism. She charged
that Wilson had lived high in Europe during the Versailles
Conference while his secretary Joseph Tumulty had run this
country like a dictator. Carefully she itemized and reported the
cost of his expensive junket. Then she turned to "crafty Eng-
land." It had charged for transporting American soldiers to
fight for its own selfish interests, and now it was using American money—loaned to make the world safe for democracy—to
build an army for subjugating smaller nations, just as it had
tried to subjugate this country in 1812. Digging into David
Lloyd George's past history, she came up with some disparaging
remarks the British Prime Minister had made about the Southern
Confederacy. She became a stout champion of Irish independence,
posing with the Lord Mayor of Cork on his visit to Atlanta. It
was good, even at eighty-six, to be in the midst of a hot fight
again.[21]

It was good to win too. In November Warren Harding, the
Republican Presidential candidate, easily defeated James Cox.
During the campaign Harding had been evasive on the League,
but in his inaugural address he announced that this country
would take no part in directing the affairs of Europe. Five
months later Editor Edwin Camp of the *American* wrote her that
because of falling advertising revenue, the paper would have to
discontinue her Sunday letter. Perhaps Camp had decided also
that her assignment had been carried out.[22]

Journalism could never have satisfied Mrs. Felton's literary ambitions. She was determined to leave a more enduring record of
her writing and opinions. Just before the Doctor's death she decided to do a history of their long, vain fight against the Bourbons.
Future generations of Georgians ought to know the truth about

Gordon's corruption, Colquitt's pious hypocrisy, and Brown's shrewd, unscrupulous tactics. Soon she would be the only one left who could tell the story of their iniquities, and if she remained silent, future histories would be clouded by "those eulogies and well-paid biographies" already written by Democratic party hacks.[23]

My Memoirs of Georgia Politics appeared in 1911. A number of people had been anticipating it—some, perhaps, with apprehension. She tried to add to their fears. When an Atlanta reporter asked what the book was like, Mrs. Felton whispered, "It's terrible." What was in it? "Nothing but the truth," she answered. She believed that. Shortly after the book came out, she dared anyone to point out a single misstatement in its six hundred pages. No one stepped forward.[24]

In a lengthy preface the author explained why Georgia had been controlled from 1866 to 1896 by "small men with large ambitions." After the War, Bullock's Scalawag administration implanted in white men of all political faiths an enduring fear of Negro domination. By putting an end to this unnatural regime, the Democratic Party had won a loyalty and support that could not be shaken by the subsequent corruption of its leaders. A few brave Independents, headed by Dr. Felton, had battled the powerful ring only to be maligned and driven from politics. Side by side with her husband she had fought these plunderers and demogogues. She knew the depth of their infamy, and now she was going to expose it.[25]

As a background for Dr. Felton's political crusades, she gave her recollections of Georgia politics up to 1874 and an account of the insidious influence of the Pacific Railroad lobby on state administrations during the following three decades. The Doctor's campaigns are then given in chronological order.[26]

Throughout the book Mrs. Felton chastised her enemies impartially. In her discussion of the Kirkwood Ring she took care of Colquitt, finally dismissing him with the contemptuous comment that he was either negligent or unfit to be governor.[27] She branded Hill as an opportunist and lobbyist because of his war on the Coalition. But the memory of old friendships was not easily pushed aside, and she suggested that by 1882 his mind was probably weakened by his fatal disease.[28] Although she declared that she never enjoyed discussing Gordon, she managed to go rather thoroughly into his career: his sly interest in the Ferry letter, the "sale" of the Senate seat, his trading of the presidency in the Hayes-Tilden crisis, and the cordial references to him in the Huntington letters. Besides a long chapter on his race for governor in 1886, she brought herself to devoting another one to his earlier sins.[29]

Although she condemned Brown heartily for his part in the Bullock administration, she made a calm and interesting analysis of his character, entirely free of her usual moral indignation.

> Ex-Governor Brown could buy men when they were willing to sell their influence for money or the offer of political position, but it was not the ex-governor's habit to sell his own influence for money. He left such money trading to smaller men and weaker natures. He knew a great deal of what Georgia politicians had done and were doing, and he always kept men near him who could be useful in ferreting out the invisible, if not the unknown. . . . He was an able man in intellect, either at home or in Washington.[30]

She did not offer as evidence of Brown's political skill those letters that passed between him and the Feltons in 1881.

The chapter which Mrs. Felton obviously did not enjoy writing was the one on Stephens and the governor's race of 1882. She stuck to her original statement that he had betrayed his friends to make sure of his victory, and she published those letters which Dr. Felton had persuaded her not to publish during the campaign. But Stephens had been dear to her, dearer than Hill could ever have been, and time and his death had softened her bitterness. Now she was willing to shift some of the blame to those designing men who had used him to their purposes. As a matter of fact, her account of Howard's visit to the Governor's Mansion just before Stephens' death reveals that she never really lost her affection for the strange little invalid.[31]

Mrs. Felton might have written a more convincing, readable book if she had been able to control her partisan feelings. It is difficult to believe that everyone who opposed the Doctor did so from low motives. Anxious to convict her enemies, she loaded her pages with evidence, and pressed points already made. She not only published the numerous Huntington letters along with her unflattering interpretations, but added thirty pages of derogatory comments from newspapers; and in her account of the Felton-Simmons brawl she gave all of the Doctor's long speech, a large part of Simmons', and again, considerable editorial opinion. Her intense animosity upset the continuity of some chapters. In the midst of punishing one culprit she would recall another, and go after him.[32]

Convinced of the truth of her accusations, she did not always bother to give the source of her information. She quoted public statements without saying how or where they were made, and sometimes neglected to give the name and date of a newspaper. Once she held back the name of a friend who had supplied a choice piece of news, and, in another place, she promised to furnish authority for a serious charge when it was called for.[33]

But in spite of these defects in tone and organization, the *Memoirs* made a valuable contribution to Georgia political history. There is justification for some of her large blocks of evidence. The state's newspapers had studiously ignored the Huntington letters, so widely publicized in the Northern press, and the abundant material she collected on the Bullock Bonds made a convincing story of Reconstruction pillage. Certainly the hitherto-unpublished Stephens letters revealed the farce behind the 1882 election.[34] And as biased and discursive as the book is, it did supply a needed antidote to the writings of such Bourbon penmen as Henry Grady, I. W. Avery, and Joseph Fielder.[35] Contemporary historians have made judicious use of the *Memoirs*.[36]

Although she promised a sequel to it, if Providence permitted, Mrs. Felton turned, in her second book, to an earlier period and nonpolitical theme. *Country Life in Georgia in the Days of my Youth* came out in 1919. In its preface the author announced she would tell how the people of the state lived in ante-bellum times before the coming of railroads, telegraphs, and telephones.[37] For about a third of the book Mrs. Felton furnishes some lively scenes of early Georgia. There are descriptions of an old field school, her father's country store, and the domestic routine of her grandmother.[38] She recalled vividly her trip on the first run of the Western and Atlantic Railroad from Marthasville (Atlanta) to Marietta twenty miles away.[39] Unfortunately she passed quickly over a rural funeral, a religious revival, and a picnic to nearby Stone Mountain; and she burdened one chapter with an account of the Yazoo Fraud, which troubled Georgia shortly after the Revolutionary War.[40]

After five chapters she may have found it increasingly difficult to remember additional happenings from those far-off days. At any rate, she moved on, without excuses, to the middle years and told of her trips to various Expositions, life in Washington during the 1870s, and how the Doctor was defrauded of the 1894 election—this last topic already well covered in the *Memoirs.* Had she written *Country Life* before age had begun to cloud her mind, she would undoubtedly have done a fuller, richer picture of ante-bellum Georgia.

Mrs. Felton's third book was largely the work of a collaborator, Carter Jones of the Atlanta *Georgian.* She had given him a series of interviews about the achievements of Georgia women. These were republished in 1930 with the title *The Romantic Story of Georgia Women.* The first two of the twenty short chapters deal briefly with Mary Musgrove, the Creek princess, and with Nancy Hart, the legendary heroine of Revolutionary days; and the last four present the rather sparse achievements of Georgia women in such fields as education, journalism, and literature. The remaining fourteen tell the story of one Georgia woman: Rebecca Felton. As might be expected, the autobiographical chapters contain little not already told more vigorously in her speeches, newspaper articles, and the other two books. But even to give interviews at ninety-four is a feat of strength and memory.

Mrs. Felton may not have written her books for money, but she saw no reason for neglecting that possibility—certainly she saw no reason for losing on them. She consulted Tom Watson about the most economical way to publish the *Memoirs,* and when it appeared, she publicized it by sending complimentary copies to prominent people all over the country.[41] Fortunately she was able to make an arrangement with the *Journal* to offer autographed copies of *Country Life* with a three years' subscription to the paper for two dollars and twenty-five cents. If the *Journal's* advertising can be believed, many copies were sold.[42]

There is no question, however, that in 1902 Mrs. Felton took up another of her literary activities to make money. She had heard that Watson was doing mighty well with his public lectures. There wasn't any reason why she couldn't do it too. Again she went to him for advice. He was most helpful and encouraging. She must not sign with a speaker's bureau, but make her own appointments. Through her connection with the *Journal,* she could get the necessary publicity. In booking her lectures, however, she must take care not to conflict with religious revivals and large social entertainments. If she handled things right, she ought to make one hundred to four hundred dollars a week.[43] His figures were high enough to dispell all hesitation, and within a few days she had secured three engagements.[44]

It is doubtful that she often made the minimum Watson had predicted. Sometimes she had to take a modest percentage of the receipts, the rest going to local hospitals and churches. The University of Georgia offered her twenty-five dollars to speak to its Summer School, and worthy organizations wrote that they could only take care of her expenses—but they did hope Mrs. Felton could come.[45] Apparently she always did. She spoke at county fairs, school commencements, and reunions of Confederate Veterans, on topics ranging from her own war experiences to the problems of the modern world.[46] The revenue might be disappointing, but it warmed her to see a room full of people waiting to hear her. She always enjoyed talking.

A revealing criticism of her public speaking has been found among her papers. A Michigan man attended one of her lectures in Macon and wrote her afterwards what he thought of it. The first forty-five minutes was fine, he said; she had held her audience spell-bound. But when she went on for an hour and a half, people around him began to grow restless, and his own bones ached terribly. He believed that if she would look over the speech, she would find she had largely repeated herself in the second half.[47] Stung by his criticism, she wrote a Macon friend asking whether others had found the talk boring. The loyal lady replied that everyone else had enjoyed all Mrs. Felton had said, and that she must pay no attention to the Yankee's impudence.[48]

But the outspoken gentleman cannot be convicted so readily of sectional prejudice. The manuscripts of Mrs. Felton's speeches run to alarming lengths and, like her books, reveal a tendency to repeat and digress. In speaking as well as in writing, she apparently could not remember that the interest of others in her subject was likely to be less than her own.

Her sharpest writing is found in her shorter compositions: the *Courant* editorials, the *Journal* columns, and especially her letters to editors. Confronted with space limitations, she could write concisely and in an orderly fashion, with sentences that cut like a razor stroke. She was far too earnest and dogmatic to be content with ambiguous phrases and flabby diction, revising even her personal letters until they were models of clarity and strength. In editorial controversy she was a skilled and deadly foe. Clark Howell once called her the finest polemist since Junius, and a lady admirer bragged that Mrs. Felton had made "many a man wince and some mend their manners." [49] She may not have mended the manners of Gordon, Candler, and Hawthorne to suit her own tastes, but she undoubtedly made them, and other worthies, wince more than once when they reached the editorial pages of their newspapers.

15

. . . . .
. . .
.

The Reward of It All

IN THE FALL of 1920 Georgia politics were in an uproar. Iso-lationism was the main issue in state and national campaigns, and Tom Watson, who had boldly condemned the war while it was being fought, was now condemning the men who made the peace. From public square and courthouse lawn he denounced Woodrow Wilson, the League of Nations, and the "hundred per-cent idiots" who supported it. The applause of his audience grew louder and louder. Although many of them had sent sons into the battles and cheered the final victory, now, in the apathy which follows war, they could believe their country had been tricked into fighting for the British Empire and the invest-ments of Wall Street. If they elected "Tom" to the Senate, he would see that it didn't happen again.[1]

Watson's eloquence and popularity would probably carry a fellow-Isolationist into the governor's office: ex-Senator Thomas Hardwick. Although Hardwick's opposition to Wilson's war meas-ures had cost him his seat in 1918, it had regained for him Watson's friendship, which he had lost in 1908 for refusing to attack Governor Hoke Smith. Riding now on the Watson wave he would probably be elected.[2]

Both candidates could count on Mrs. Felton's support. Her affec-tion for Watson had steadily increased. Since the Doctor's death she had asked and taken his advice about her lectures, her books, and the epitaph for her husband's tombstone.[3] She shared com-pletely his views on Wilson and the war, although she was too patriotic to express them while Americans were falling in battle. Nor would she follow Watson's suggestion to write a letter to his *Jeffersonian Magazine* condemning Wilson for not keeping up the grave of his first wife in Rome, Georgia.[4] But when peace came her voice rose as loudly as his in denouncing the League, and her attacks on the President became just as violent, although never as personal. The campaigns of 1920 became for her a crusade against the cruelty and wickedness of war.

She had opened a correspondence with Hardwick when he began to oppose Wilson in the Senate. In her letters she said the things she was unwilling to say in her *Journal* columns. He replied promptly, agreeing with all she wrote. During a Senate debate on the Sedition Bill he read one of her letters into the records. Mrs. Felton, he assured his colleagues, was considered the most brilliant woman in the state.[5] She endorsed him heartily for governor, even though he had voted against the Eighteenth and Nineteenth Amendments. Always a realist, she saw no reason for bickering over causes already won.

It was good to be in politics again, to have an issue and candidates that could stir her fighting blood. She hoped that Georgia women would be eligible to vote and stand for office in the coming elections, even though the die-hard legislature had not yet passed a law making the Susan Anthony Amendment operative on the state level. What wouldn't she give to be twenty-five years younger! She still remembered the prediction that she would be the first Georgia woman elected to Congress.[6] Not at eighty-five. But she could help send the right men there—and women too when they were allowed to run. She attended the State Democratic Convention with Watson and told the delegates that if they didn't behave she would spank them. They cheered her lustily.[7]

In the primaries, which decided elections in one-party Georgia, Watson easily defeated Hoke Smith, the incumbent, and Governor Hugh Dorsey. Hardwick led in his field, but by so slim a margin that a run-off was necessary between him and Clifford Walker, the State Attorney General. Watson called his supporters back with the cry that the battle was only half won.[8]

Mrs. Felton rushed into the fray. So the Walker people were saying that Hardwick was pro-German and had done nothing to help win the war? She would hoist them with their own petard. In an anonymous letter to the *Georgian* she asked "Was Cliff Walker a soldier or a slacker?" and proceeded to answer her own question. He was a slacker: he had spent the war in a safe political job, even though he was young and "had no wife or children." [9]

This time, however, Mrs. Felton had opened fire without examining her ammunition. Back came a letter from Dr. S. Y. Jameson, a Baptist preacher: Walker *was* married and had two small sons.[10] Far from being abashed, Mrs. Felton got off a wire to the *Georgian* in time for that day's edition. She admitted, rather concisely, that she had been misinformed about Mr. Walker's family. Then she returned to the attack with the absurd charge that Dr. Jameson had accused her of sympathizing with the infamous Bolshevik regime which was forcing unmarried women to bear children for the state. It is true the clergyman had repeated a popular slander that Hardwick was a paid attorney of the Soviet Government, but nowhere in his letter had he mentioned Mrs. Felton's name. In fact, he had accused one A. B. Smith of writing the letter against Walker. Jameson evidently felt that a refutation was not necessary.[11]

Unable to further this controversy, Mrs. Felton published another letter, signed this time, urging the voters to deliver the women of Georgia from the League of Nations. A majority of male Georgians complied. By ten o'clock on election night Hardwick was wiring his thanks for what he called "her great work" in their decisive victory.[12]

Mrs. Felton was delighted also with the result of the Presidential election, especially when Warren Harding invited her to Florida to learn her views on the nation's international problems. On her return she refused to reveal the conclusions she and the President had reached, but she did say that she was willing to risk him in the White House—adding that she had always been considered a "right good judge of character."[13]

With Watson and Hardwick running things in Georgia, she expected to be consulted about state affairs too. She must see that the women voted and ran for office in the next elections, now that the legislature had finally acted on the Nineteenth Amendment. Perhaps she could get Corra Harris to stand for Congress in the Seventh. But unfortunately for Mrs. Felton's plans, Watson and Hardwick were soon quarrelling again.[14] Georgia politicians could never pull very long in the same harness. In the 1922 race Watson's followers went over to Walker, and Hardwick was badly beaten. A number of women did vote, but none ran for any major office. Mrs. Felton became discouraged. Was there nothing ahead but retirement in the quiet of Cartersville?

And then, on September 26, the newspapers carried a headline that shattered the political set-up in Georgia to bits: "Thomas Watson, Dead."[15]

The papers pointed out that a colorful epoch in Georgia had

come to a close. For years Watson had controlled and voted the
balance of power in the state and had allowed no rival near
his throne. What would become of his political machine? Who
would succeed him in the Senate? And who would be appointed
to fill the office until the election? The *Journal* offered a possible
answer to the last question: "It is understood upon good authority that the name of Mrs. Felton will be presented to Governor
Hardwick at the proper time for appointment as Senator Watson's successor."[16]

If Mrs. Felton dwelt upon this item in the midst of her grief,
she can be pardoned. After all the defeats and frustrations . . .
in her old age . . . the first woman Senator.

Her practical mind must have readily grasped the situation.
Hardwick, hurrying home from New York, was bound to run,
and he would naturally make an appointment that would improve his chances. Would it be some man from the Watson
machine which had undoubtedly defeated him in the gubernatorial race? Or some woman? They had also voted against him.
She could only wait—and hope.

During the next few days the press suggested several men
the Governor might appoint, such as Roland Ellis of Macon, and
W. J. Vereen of Moultrie. Her name was not mentioned again.
Greater interest centered upon men that might run for the
office: Hardwick, of course, Hoke Smith, Clark Howell of the
Constitution, and Walter George, an ex-justice of the State
Supreme Court. On the train returning from the Watson funeral
politicians huddled here and there in the cars.[17]

By October 2 the situation was coming to a head. The *Journal*
announced that Hardwick was being urged to appoint Watson's
widow and that he was going to make an important statement
the following day. He made two: he appointed Mrs. Felton Senator
and announced that he would be a candidate for the office in the
election on October 17.[18]

Hardwick explained that he had offered the appointment to
Mrs. Watson, and when she refused because of poor health,
he had chosen "another noble Georgia woman, now in the sun-
set of a splendid, useful life." Obviously he wanted it known
that Mrs. Felton had been a warm friend of the man she had
succeeded. He said that almost the last letter Watson wrote
had been one to her in which he expressed his great esteem and
affection. The Governor regretted that Mrs. Felton could not serve

in her high office, but a successor would be elected before Congress met again.[19]

Mrs. Felton lost no time in wiring her acceptance. She thanked Hardwick in the name of the thousands of Georgia women who would reward him when he stood for office again. Rather significantly she made no comment upon his explanation that her honor could only be a nominal one.[20]

Friends, reporters, and photographers streamed in and out of her small house. Telegrams and letters arrived in sheaves, and the telephone rang continuously. Could Mrs. Felton send a picture for the Sunday paper? Would she care to say what bills she would sponsor if she were going to serve? Everyone seemed interested: the New York *Times,* Henry Ford's *Dearborn Independent,* International News. Pathé Exchange wanted to make a newsreel.[21]

Cartersville turned out for the presentation of her commission. Through a chilly, rainy night Mrs. Felton's "home-folks" came to crowd the Courthouse, fill the benches in the Superior Court Room, and stand along the walls. Corra Harris spoke briefly. She assured her audience that her old friend could have been elected as easily as she had been appointed. Hardwick had more to say. He admitted that he had opposed the Nineteenth Amendment, but was now convinced that it was "right." Therefore he had appointed Mrs. Felton to show that Georgia had accepted woman's suffrage as a fact. Cheering and applause swept the hall as he handed her the commission.[22]

At the rostrum she had to wait several minutes for quiet. She spoke to them as an older neighbor who had suffered with their parents and grandparents in the '60s. In a lighter vein she speculated on what the "millionaire" senators would think if they could see their latest colleague at her daily chores. Turning to Hardwick she explained that the only importance of her appointment lay in its recognition of women in government. When she finished, men and women pushed forward to shake her hand and say how happy they were over her great honor.[23]

Undoubtedly she was happy too; yet a *Journal* reporter thought she did not show "the same exuberance as her neighbors." [24] Perhaps her mind was not entirely on the homey ceremony. She may have been thinking of a similar but more impressive one that is held in a loftier hall, where the Vice-

President of the United States administers the oath of office
to a new Senator, and rows of dignified men listen to his maiden
speech. Mrs. Felton had probably decided already that she was
going to be enrolled in Washington with her peers.

Was she driven to make the effort by personal ambition
or by the insistence of her fellow-suffragettes that the first
woman Senator should be officially seated? Unquestionably she
was motivated by ambition. To reach any other conclusion one
would have to ignore the eagerness with which she had sought
honors and recognition throughout her life. Her desire to be
seated was, however, strengthened by the encouraging letters
from women all over America, and she should not be criticized
too severely for claiming, more than once, that she was only
carrying out their wishes.[25] In effect, she was campaigning
for an office, and candidates are not supposed to advocate their
own interests, but those of their supporters.

The success of her attempt would depend largely upon the
support of these women. Hardwick had made it seem mathemati-
cally impossible: her successor would be elected before Congress
convened. But Helen Longstreet, the General's strong-minded
young widow, had hit upon the extravagant idea that the President could call a special session to seat the first woman Senator.[26]
It would take pressure to get his consent, but politicians, especially those in the national field, were paying more attention
to the wishes of women.

Mrs. Longstreet, either with or without Mrs. Felton's permission,
called upon the women of the land to make their wishes known,
and they flooded Harding with letters. He refused. It would be
too expensive to summon Congress just to seat a single Senator.
That way seemed blocked.[27]

Meanwhile another solution had been suggested. Whoever was
elected Senator from Georgia must not present his credentials
until Mrs. Felton was sworn in and had sat for a day. It
would be either Hardwick or George. Mrs. Felton was not very
active in their contest. She published one letter endorsing Hardwick without attacking George.[28] Perhaps she could find nothing in his record or campaign to attack. He won by a huge
majority. The women had not fulfilled Mrs. Felton's promise that
they would "reward" Hardwick. The suffragettes perhaps could
not forgive him for having opposed their pet legislations, and
the rest were probably caught up in the George landslide.[29]

The women immediately petitioned their new Senator to let

Mrs. Felton "have her day in Washington." George assured them that he would be happy to help her, but he believed a bill would have to be passed by both houses of Congress before she could "qualify." The ex-Justice knew his Seventeenth Amendment: it specified that the term of an appointed Senator ended the day his successor was elected.[30] Her last chance seemed gone. The press ceased to mention "Senator Felton."

The excitement and suspense proved too much for her strength. Unable to throw off a bad cold she consented to enter an Atlanta hospital.[31] Had she given up? Evidently not. From her sick bed she wrote Harding on November 8 asking if he would not change his mind about the special session.[32]

The next day the newspapers supplied the answer. Harding was calling Congress into session on November 20, not to seat her, but to speed up some Republican-sponsored legislation.[33] The old lady stirred uneasily. Only eleven days off. New Senators would be sworn in and it would all be over. If she was going to do anything, she would have to get out of there. Two days later she was back in Cartersville.

And then on Tuesday, November 14, only six days before Congress was to open, hope came from an unexpected quarter. Georgia's Secretary of State, S. G. McLendon, a friend of Mrs. Felton's and an in-law of her sister's, announced that Walter George could not be certified in time to reach Washington the following Monday. Under state law, he could not be declared elected until the Governor, the Secretary of State, and the Comptroller General had canvassed his election returns. This had not been done, and Hardwick would not return from a trip to New York until next week. McLendon went on to say that if Mrs. Felton was in the Senate when it opened, he knew no reason why she could not be sworn in. The *Journal* immediately telephoned her. Had she heard McLendon's statement? She had, and she was packing her bags.[34]

Harding had blocked her the first time; George the second. Now it was Hardwick. He did not believe that Mrs. Felton would be accepted even if George was not there, and he wanted the state represented by two Senators on the opening day. On Wednesday he wired McLendon to hold the canvass without him. When McLendon replied that this would be illegal, Hardwick wired that he would be back in Atlanta on Saturday in time for George to catch an afternoon train. The *Journal* decided that "it did not look as if Mrs. Felton would be seated." [35]

She went right on with her packing. By then she had a plan of her own. There was only one way to settle the whole question: get George to hold up his credentials, present her own, and see if the Senate would accept them. She believed that George would do this. He was a nice young fellow, and besides, the women were working on him again. Sure enough, he telephoned late Wednesday night to say that he would have to be present on the opening day, but if she was willing to take the risk, she could present her credentials first and let the Senate decide. She was willing. Friday she caught the morning train.[36]

During the stop-over in Atlanta one of the reporters noticed that she looked weak and pale. Was her son going with her? No, she wouldn't let him. He had not quite recovered from a serious operation.

"But won't he be worried about you?" the reporter asked.

"Of course he will," she replied. "But you see I've always just gone ahead and done the thing I thought ought to be done." [37]

She took the train alone, an old lady of eighty-seven, still showing the effects of her recent illness, her mind made up to walk into the United States Senate and ask for a seat which she had been told was not hers. In her hand-bag she carried a cartoon from a Texas newspaper. It showed an elderly woman peering into a room where a number of men sat glaring at her. The caption asked, "Will the gentlemen offer the lady a seat?" She was going to Washington to find out.[38]

As her train moved north, the New York *Times* reported that the Senate was "all at sea." Republican leaders put their heads together. Mrs. Felton had no right to the seat. The Constitution proved that. Besides, the Senate Disbursing Officer had said he could not carry three Senators from one state on his payroll. To disregard the law, even to seat the first woman member, would be inviting other such cases at every session.[39]

But ought the Party to take action? A single Senator could ask the Rules Committee for a decision. That would take time, and George couldn't wait indefinitely. Who would make the motion? One member immediately announced that he was no candidate for the job. Someone asked Vice-President Coolidge how he would address Mrs. Felton when he met her on the floor. "Like an old friend," he answered promptly. Still, there were others who felt strongly about Senate law and precedent. Someone would raise the question.[40]

When the lady under discussion reached the Capital, she was

surprised to find no one waiting to meet her. Where were the newspapermen who had been writing so much about her? And the women who were going to give that big banquet? Well, she ought to go to the hotel and rest anyway; trains tired her now. At the Lafayette she asked not to be disturbed, but before long her telephone was ringing. The lobby was full of reporters who had expected her on a later train. What should the clerk do? Send them up, of course.[41]

She captivated veteran Washington correspondents, calling them "children," answering all their questions, posing for pictures with the warning that she "couldn't look pretty" at her age. One thought she was as picturesque as a grandmother in a rare old print. Other visitors came: apologetic ladies promising a limousine for the banquet tomorrow night. It is to be hoped that she got some rest the following day.[42]

Perhaps it was in the quiet of Sunday that she wrote the *second* speech.[43] She would have an acceptance speech ready, but for all her cheerful air, she wasn't at all sure she would have occasion to make it. The Washington papers had carried stories about the Republican meeting, the adverse opinion of Senate officials, and the warning that one Senator could block her. Even some of the women had doubted that she ought to risk being publicly embarrassed.

The very idea! As if she would come all that way and not even try for her seat. And she didn't propose just to sit there either and let them turn her down. She may have told George she'd let the Senate "decide," but if they didn't decide in her favor they were going to hear from her. She'd look like a fool unless she said something. Carefully she wrote down her angry objections and then went over them.[44]

With both speeches in her bag, she was the first "Senator" to reach the chamber on Monday morning. Theodore Tiller, the *Journal* correspondent, was waiting with news. He had heard that she might not get a chance to present her credentials that day, and that the Republicans were going to hold another "conference" on her case that afternoon. Mrs. Felton nodded. She would be there again tomorrow to present them. And if anyone objected, she would have something to say. As an ex-Senator she could claim the privilege of the floor, and that was exactly what she would do.[45]

Handing her wraps to a page, she walked down the aisle on the arm of Hoke Smith. Loud applause broke from the galleries.

They were filled with women wearing the colors of their various organizations. Smiling, she blew them a kiss before taking the seat of an absent Senator.[46]

Gradually the other seats filled. Senators she knew came over to speak to her. She made much of them, recalling days when they were all younger. The Senate was called to order at noon. The chaplain prayed that "nothing but good would come of these deliberations," and she, no doubt, added a silent amen. Little if anything came of the first session. Resolutions were passed on the deaths of Watson and another member, and the Senate adjourned to honor their memory. Tiller had been right.[47]

The following morning she was present again, in Watson's seat now, and looking completely at home there. The suffragettes were crowding into the galleries. Howard was up there. Disregarding her objections, he had arrived the day before. At twelve o'clock Cummins of Iowa took the chair. Where was Coolidge? Had he foreseen trouble?[48]

Cummins' gavel banged, and the Senate came to order. Lodge of Massachusetts announced that the two houses would meet in joint session at twelve-thirty to hear the President's message. Would there be time now to induct the new members? Cummins evidently thought that at least their commissions could be presented. Three were read: two from Pennsylvania and one from Delaware. Now there was only the one from Georgia left. William Harris, the State's Senior Senator, rose. The next name read would be a woman's.[49]

Harris gave the details of Mrs. Felton's appointment and asked that she be sworn in. He hoped no Senator would object. She would serve only for a day; George would present his commission tomorrow. Obviously nervous, Harris again hoped that there would be no objections. Then he waited. Cummins raised his head.[50]

"The Senator from Georgia will present the credentials of appointment," he ordered.

"They are in the hands of the Secretary of the Senate," Harris answered. Had she been accepted? No Republican was getting up.

"Mr. President," came a voice from the Democratic side of the floor. Thomas Walsh! Why was he interrupting? Cummins recognized the Senator from Montana, and Harris sat down.[51]

Walsh's words came seriously, slowly. He was sure that every member of the Senate was willing that Mrs. Felton have her seat for a day, but "it would do little credit to this body or to

her, if the Constitution we have all sworn to support forbids
it." Since grave doubts had been expressed about her eligibility,
he wished to offer some "reflections" on the question.[52]

Up in the galleries puzzled women were whispering. Was Walsh
going to object? If not, then why was he speaking? They would
have sworn her in if he had kept quiet. But Walsh was a Democrat, a liberal.

Before anyone could be sure, a message came from the House.
The President was ready to speak. Mrs. Felton marched out with
the others.[53]

She could hardly have paid close attention to Harding's long
speech on ship subsidy. Walsh had surely upset things. In another
minute she would have been called to the rostrum. Now, no matter what he said—even if he approved seating her—he had
opened the discussion and made it easy for some Republican to
ask for that ruling. Well, if anyone did she was going to answer him. There was her speech, written on two small cards.
At least she could start a good fight, for some Democrats were
bound to support her. She might not get the seat, but the Senate
wouldn't forget that she'd been there. Thank goodness Harding
was closing. She was getting mighty tired.

Back in the Senate chamber she settled down, to listen now.
Lodge proposed, rather ominously, that those Senators be in-
ducted whose "commissions will provoke no discussion." When
this was done, Walsh again took the floor.[54]

Steadily he built up the argument against seating her, quoting
the Seventeenth Amendment on the termination of a Senator's
appointment, citing decisions based upon that clause. But then
he took the other side of the question. He named several appointed
Senators who had served beyond election day, and he emphasized
that the law "abhors a vacancy." In closing, he revealed the purpose of his lengthy "reflections." If Mrs. Felton was seated, as he
believed she would be, he wanted it apparent that the Senate
had not been moved by a spirit of gallantry, but that being fully
advised of the issue, it had decided she was entitled to take her
seat.[55]

The great hall became still. Walsh hadn't objected. But if anyone rose now—Cummins' voice broke the silence.

"The Secretary will read the certificate of the Junior Senator
from Georgia."[56] A smile passed across Mrs. Felton's face.[57]

She walked to the rostrum with Harris. When Cummins raised
his hand to swear her in, she stuck out her own in greeting.

Smiling again, she corrected her mistake, and the brief ceremony ended.[58]

She did not make her acceptance speech that day; perhaps she was too weary. George must have agreed to wait a little longer, for she was again in his seat the following morning, and he was still somewhere in the background. When Cummins had called the session to order, he recognized "the Junior Senator from Georgia."[59]

Her opening remarks were witty and slyly ironical. She pointed out that contrary to precedent, she had been obliged to conduct her campaign for the Senate after she had been appointed. When she told about the cartoon in the Texas paper there was laughter from the floor as well as from the galleries. Hurriedly she assured the audience that the gentlemen had offered her not only a seat but "a beautiful, hospitable welcome." Next she thanked Hardwick for appointing "the old lady"; George, for letting her "have her day in the Senate"; and Harris for his courteous assistance.[60]

Then the old voice grew serious. She told the Senate it would not regret seating her. Ten million women voters had been heartened by "the romantic . . . historic event." She assured the gentlemen that she would bring no shame upon her office. The British House of Commons had accepted Virginia-born Nancy Astor as its first woman member, and the United States Senate need have no fear about "this relic of the old South." Finally, she promised them they could welcome with confidence the women Senators who would come after her.

> Let me say, Mr. President, that when the women of this country come and sit with you, though there may be very few in the next few years, I pledge that you will get ability, you will get integrity of purpose, and you will get unstinted usefulness.[61]

When the applause had died down, the patient George was sworn in, and the Senate got down, at last, to more mundane affairs.[62]

She and Howard left that afternoon for Georgia. Riding back through the darkness she must have re-lived, again and again, those past few days: the wearying delays, the suspense endured while Walsh spoke, but at last the summons to the rostrum. They had enjoyed her speech; more than they would have enjoyed the one she *didn't* make. And she was glad she hadn't had to make it, although it was a good speech too.[63]

The argument in it was brief and clear-cut: she had been officially appointed to Watson's seat, and no one else had appeared to claim it. Any legal obstacles in her way must be removed.

> If the Senate has no provisions in its regulations for attending to the mandate of a sovereign state in the Federal Union, it is obvious that such a solution is demanded.[64]

Her closing words would have brought war cries from the galleries and confirmed the wisdom of that Senator who had declined the job of speaking against her.

> With ninety-five Senators on the roll of the Senate, the temporary presence of one woman Senator, who asks nothing but a hearty welcome, and is pledged to hand you nothing more hostile than a hearty goodbye, should be granted; not as a favor or a compliment—not as a bequest to a charity patient; but as a tribute to the integrity, the patriotism, and the womanhood of the blessed wives and mothers of our common country.[65]

Yes, she was glad she hadn't had to make it. Everybody had been mighty sweet to her—mighty sweet.

16

· · · · ·
· · ·
·

If By Reason of Strength

IF MRS. FELTON was asked on her return from Washington, "What are you going to do now?" she may have given the same answer the aged Georges Clemenceau, France's war premier, gave: "I intend to live till I die." A very elderly person can hardly say more. But Mrs. Felton would not have meant that she was going to sit by and watch the younger generation run things. Even at eighty-seven, with her Senate commission in hand and her causes won, she had no idea of becoming a sort of national grandmother who wrote Mother's Day greetings for the Associated Press and made sentimental statements on her birthdays.[1] She certainly wasn't going to turn all her business affairs over to someone or resign from such positions as the trusteeship of the Girls Training School; she could sit at home and write her *Journal* columns and, through the newspapers, keep an eye on Cliff Walker, Will Harris, and those other politicians who worshipped Woodrow Wilson.

Of course there couldn't be many years left. For a long time she had been saying how old she was, and she had always believed death stayed close to everybody. But when you got tired so easily and had to be careful about stumbling, and couldn't read so well even with stronger glasses, well, she wasn't going to pull a chair up to the fire and wait for death to come.[2]

She could still read well enough to find in the newspapers people who needed her help. So the British were threatening to execute Eamon de Valera, the Irish patriot? She wired President Coolidge, begging him to intercede, and signed the telegram "Rebecca Latimer Felton, Former United States Senator."[3] The Federal Government seemed to be doing mighty little for those soldiers disabled in the last war. Her friend Senator Lodge would

150

help to get a larger appropriation for their vocational training.[4] Her concern for those younger veterans became as devoted as that she had shown for the old Confederates. They turned to her in serious troubles: a prisoner in Fort Leavenworth, an inmate of a mental ward who claimed he was sane, a Marine charged with raping a small Puerto Rican girl. She believed their stories and wrote letters in their behalf. Through her efforts the soldier at Leavenworth was released.[5]

Her mail usually brought something interesting. A Seventh Day Adventist tried to convert her, and an ex-member of the Ku Klux Klan informed her that a number of preachers could be found under the white robes.[6] A man insisted that Mrs. Felton had been too hard on a judge who wouldn't sentence a husband for whipping his wife. According to the writer, the woman had been spanked because she had beaten her old mother-in-law.[7] A girl in an insane asylum wrote a letter in verse.[8] Sometimes Mrs. Felton's correspondents preferred to remain anonymous, so that they could abuse her in safety for hating President Wilson, or for being so stingy.[9]

She wasn't stingy, but she certainly wasn't going to throw her money away after she'd worked so hard for it. Somebody was always trying to make her contribute to something she didn't believe in. There was the Stone Mountain Memorial that was going to include Gordon and leave off James Longstreet, and that Methodist Memorial Fund the bishops were raising for "political reasons." She wouldn't think of giving a cent to either of them.[10] The trouble was a lot of people didn't know the value of money because they didn't know what hard work was. All they wanted was one of those soft jobs the politicians were handing out. That was where all her taxes were going. Every year she went down to the courthouse and argued about her assessment, and she always put on her income tax returns such additional information as "I am an aged widow trying to manage my farm lands." But it didn't do a bit of good.[11]

People tried to take advantage of you when you became old and helpless. Look how the local Methodists had changed the name of Felton Chapel, built on land donated by her husband and herself. She'd written Bishop Beauchamp threatening to sue for her property if he didn't do something about this ingratitude.[12] Then there was that state legislator who said she ought not to have visited President Harding, because he was a Re-

publican. But she had quieted him with an article in the Macon
Telegraph.[13]

Nothing, however, made her so mad as the memorial ceremony
for Tom Watson held in Atlanta. Will Harris and his gang had
had the nerve to take charge of things, knowing that Watson had
hated them like poison. Naturally they had put her speech almost at the end of the program, forcing her to sit there and
listen to them make a political rally out of the occasion. In a letter to the Lincoln *Journal* she told the public how she had
been treated, and warned that a national campaign was already
under way to revive the League of Nations by nominating William McAdoo, Wilson's son-in-law, at the next Democratic National Convention. Harris was trying to corner the Georgia delegation for him.[14]

In February, 1924, Woodrow Wilson died. Death could
never sanctify an enemy for Mrs. Felton, especially when he left
followers to carry on his ideas in his name. She read in the papers
that Wilson had willed everything to his second wife except a
small annuity to his oldest daughter as long as she remained unmarried. The neglected grave of the first wife haunted Mrs.
Felton. It was time the people of Georgia were told, but she
must handle it carefully. She wrote a letter to the *Constitution*
suggesting that since Wilson had left no money for keeping up
the grave, the state might want to take it over as a historical
landmark. But Editor Howell, a good Wilsonian, was also interested in the next presidential convention. He praised her idea
but thought it should be proposed at "a more proper time." [15]
The best she could do was get the letter published, long after
the convention, in the *National Republican,* a Washington newspaper with almost no Georgia circulation.[16]

By now Mrs. Felton's fighting blood was up. She was even willing to accept Governor Alfred E. Smith of New York, a "Wet"
and a Catholic, as the Democratic nominee. With her eighty-
ninth birthday just ahead, she opened a lively fight against
McAdoo.

She attempted the almost impossible task of persuading the
W. C. T. U. not to come out against Smith. Hearing that it was
planning to endorse McAdoo at its next meeting, she wrote
begging the ladies not to support the League of Nations and a
man who was legal counsel for E. L. Doheney, a prominent
figure in the Elk Hill oil scandal. The meeting voted not to

read her letter, and to oppose her candidate. She made no further effort to placate her former allies; they were enemies now. In a letter to the press she repeated her charge against McAdoo and denounced the W. C. T. U. for voting to send their children to be sacrificed in Great Britain's wars.[17]

It would have required a Tom Watson, however, to convince the average Georgian that something as vague and far-off as the League of Nations was more dangerous than Catholicism and whisky. At the Convention the state's delegation stood solid for McAdoo until the end. After a long deadlock he and Smith withdrew to permit the nomination of John W. Davis, a weak compromise candidate.[18] Mrs. Felton could rejoice that Wilson's son-in-law would not go to the White House, but she could claim no credit for his defeat.

There was no time to brood over failure. Tom Hardwick had entered the Senate race, and, perhaps stirred by her grudge against Harris, she was determined to give her friend more help than she had given him in 1920 and 1922.

The Ku Klux Klan was going to be the main issue of the campaign.[19] This powerful and sinister order posed a problem for a Georgia candidate: to antagonize it might mean his defeat, yet to court its approval might implicate him in its subversive tactics. Most politicians tried to solve the problem by ignoring, in public, the Klan's existence.

When the Klan began to work against Hardwick, Mrs. Felton could come to but one conclusion: Harris was a member. Of course he had denied this; members were allowed to. But she had noticed that he hadn't repudiated its help.[20] With almost no supporting evidence she shared her conclusion with the press.[21] Several papers, mostly small weeklies, published her accusation, and one of her articles was reprinted as a circular and widely distributed by Hardwick's headquarters. Almost all of the dailies were willing to accept Harris' word that he had never been affiliated in any way with the Klan. His home town paper explained that Mrs. Felton was not to be taken seriously; she was trying to repay Hardwick for the Senate appointment.[22]

In the midst of the campaign Mrs. Felton welcomed a controversy that she had tried for some time to provoke. Always loyal to those who were loyal to her she had urged President Harding to appoint Helen Longstreet to the Gainesville postmastership, which she had lost when Wilson took office. In 1923 Mrs. Felton had published a letter from the late Senator Charles Townsend explaining that Harding had tried to make the appointment but had been blocked by both Georgia Senators. Fearing, perhaps, that Townsend's charge might lose Harris votes, Congressman Bell of the Gainesville district issued a statement that the two Senators could not have opposed Mrs. Longstreet because the Republicans had never suggested her for the office. Immediately Mrs. Felton published a letter with the dubious caption "Congressman Bell calls Mrs. Felton a Liar." [23] She even struck back, less viciously, at Walter George, when he confirmed what Bell had said. Admitting it was painful to take issue with him, she insisted nevertheless on her right to challenge anyone who questioned her veracity.[24]

A vast majority of the voters were either not convinced or not disturbed by Mrs. Felton's accusations. Hardwick carried only six small counties. Bartow, her home county, expressed a decided preference for Harris.[25]

Her political defeats did not upset her as much as her financial troubles. For several years the boll weevil had been taking an increasing toll of the South's cotton crop, and during the summer of 1924 almost no rain fell on Georgia's red fields. Mrs. Felton kept a close eye on her tenants. She was, as she once said, "a sharp old sister" in business matters. In early 1924 she decided to sue T. A. Jenkins, a white share-cropper, who had not settled her last year's accounts. To her surprise and indignation he had anticipated her and gone into bankruptcy. She immediately had him arrested for "stealing" corn left in the barn by his predecessor, only to hear the court acquit him. Then Jenkins had another surprise in store for her: he brought suit for malicious prosecution. After a long trial she won the case, but that did not bring her the rent or the consumed feed. And there were the lawyer's fees too.[26]

During these suits she was fighting feverishly to forestall a far greater loss. In 1912 she had bought, on the advice of J. S. Shingler of Ashburn, fifteen shares of stock in the Bank of Donaldson. For several years it had paid handsome dividends, as high as ten per cent in 1916, but in the early 1920's these cheques ceased to come. She tried to sell the stock, but even the bank's officials were uninterested. In 1924 the bank closed.[27]

Mrs. Felton must have known that Georgia bank stock carried a double liability, but she was horrified at the prospect of

paying it. She appealed to everyone: the State Department of
Banking, the Chief Justice of the Supreme Court, the public—
even to Governor Cliff Walker. None of them could offer her
any help or hope. She even wrote Shingler, reminding him that
he had recommended the stock. He replied that he had lost
everything in the bank's failure and in other reverses. Her violent letters to the press were returned unpublished. She got the
state legislator from Bartow to introduce a bill relieving her of
the penalty. It never got out of committee. She carried her
case all the way to the State Supreme Court, which ruled that
she must comply with the law. Her lawyer finally persuaded
her not to appeal to the United States Supreme Court.

In 1927, with the interest on her assessment mounting steadily
she gave up and paid. Bitterly she totalled her loss: $2500 for the
stock, $1500 for the penalty, $261.50 for interest, $33.75 for
court costs. And the lawyer's bill still to come. On her cheque
for the penalty she wrote "I do protest against this cruel order;"
and on the one for interest "To settle the interest claimed by
the State Banking Department for the rotten bank of Donaldson."
This outburst gave her only temporary relief.[28]

In December of 1926, just before she got the State Supreme
Court's decision, Howard, her last child, died. Four months.
later his wife was buried beside him. A second generation had
passed. She had only the two grandchildren William and Annie
Rebecca left.[29]

Her mind dwelt more and more upon death, not in fear but
almost in curiosity as to when it would finally come.[30] Two
years earlier she had written to another Lady Manager of the
old World's Fair, asking how many of them were still alive.
Only three.[31] And she had been the oldest of them all. She had
better make sure her affairs were in good shape. Her will had
been drawn up, but she wanted to add a couple of codicils. And
she might as well let that Marietta marble company go ahead
and build her mausoleum. There was no telling what they'd put
up if she wasn't here to watch them—also what they would
charge.[32]

But it was hard to think of going. Would people forget her
as soon as she was gone? She asked her *Journal* readers. From
all over the Southeast came letters, cards, and wires assuring
her that she would be fondly remembered.[33] It was some comfort.

But she was never one to stay despondent for long. In June,

1927, she made a witty speech at her ninety-second birthday
party given by the local chamber of commerce. Afterwards
she told a reporter she wasn't a bit worried about the younger
generation, not even about girls smoking.[34] His applause of her
"young ideas" was not echoed by some of her devoted readers.
A man wrote deploring her views on smoking, and a woman
urged her to prepare her soul for eternity.[35] Well, you couldn't
please everybody.

In December of 1927 she insisted on making a trip to Washington. A ceremony was to be held there which she was not going
to miss: the unveiling of a bust of Alec Stephens. By now the
old bitterness had faded, leaving only the memory of a kindly
little man in the days of the old National Hotel. She had been
proud to write an article about him which the *National Republic* Magazine was bringing out. Of course she was going to
be there when he was honored.[36] She had known him better than
anyone now living.

The unveiling, however, did not go to suit her. She was not
asked to speak, and the audience made much less of her than of
an ancient Negro woman who had belonged to the Stephens
family. Weary and unhappy, Mrs. Felton left immediately for
Georgia. It was her last visit to the Capital.[37]

She did not get out much that winter. During the long evenings she went over her papers. She was going to give them to the
University of Georgia. Duke University had wanted them—and
would have paid, too—but Georgia had given her an honorary
degree, and her husband had graduated there. She warned the
University that it must keep her things in a safe place. If it didn't,
"spite politicians" would destroy them, just as (she was convinced) they were destroying every copy of her *Memoirs* they
could get their hands on. Naturally they didn't want people to
know that they and others like them had been robbing the state
since the Civil War. It was all right here, in those papers. Somebody would use them some day to write the first true history
of Georgia. And she and Dr. Felton would get their proper
recognition in such a book.[38]

Night after night she opened faded envelopes and smoothed
out crumpled clippings. As she read, dead issues came alive
and old animosities burned again. Carefully she made notations
in the margins of scrapbooks and on the backs of old letters:
"consummate liar," "oh shame where is thy blush," "the letter
was missing after all," "how politicians cheated Mrs. Felton out

of her paid-up railroad stock." [39] An article or a letter con--
cerning Gordon invariably earned a comment: "Gordon's scheme
to defeat Lawton," "Gordon's fake appointment of his son,"
"how much money was paid Gordon I don't know." [40] He had
been dead for almost a quarter of a century. But she still remembered all her uncomplimentary stories about him.[41]

After her papers were packed, she clung to them. "I couldn't
let them go," she told Frank Daniel of the *Journal*. "When
they go, I go too." They did not go until after her death.[42]

Among the few items she added during the remaining two
years was a copy of her last political speech. In 1928 Al Smith
won the Democratic nomination, and civil war broke out in Georgia politics. Tom Hardwick was coming to Cartersville to speak
for him. Did Mrs. Felton feel up to saying a few words for
him at the rally? She certainly did, even if she offended the
newspaper, the preachers, and the W. C. T. U.[43]

She did not limit herself to a few words in reviewing her own
political career and in attacking Smith's enemies. On some of the
issues she completely reversed positions she had taken in the past.
In the 1870s she had encouraged Democrats to leave the party
and during the battle for woman's suffrage she had applauded
the W. C. T. U. for entering politics. Now, with the same ear-
nestness, she urged against both steps. But she was fighting different enemies in 1928; and she always fought with whatever
ammunition was available. Her final political effort, however,
was largely in vain. Smith lost both Cartersville and Bartow
County—although he did carry the state.[44]

A printed circular, dated August 1, 1929, tells of her last
controversy. For some time the Cartersville paper had been reporting that paving of the city's streets was going ahead and
that everyone was rejoicing over the wonderful improvement.[45]
Mrs. Felton, however, was far from elated. In an appeal addressed
to the Judge of the Superior Court she complained that the
city had taken her property for sidewalks without her consent,
and had assessed her outrageously for pavement she did not want.
It is doubtful that her protest retarded the march of progress
in Cartersville.[46]

She left almost no letters from her last year to round out
the story. But anecdotes and legends tell of a tiny, wrinkled old
lady, dressed in clothes of an earlier day, appearing unexpectedly in private homes and public places to talk of times
and people long gone or to complain of corrupt officials and shift-

less tenants bent on cheating widows and orphans. There are
tales of how she hoarded her money. Her next door neighbor
must save his newspaper for her; she couldn't afford to buy one.
And she couldn't see a bit of sense in riding the train to Atlanta
when the bus was cheaper. A family seated at dinner would look
up to find her standing in the door. Yes, she would have a bite.
Those biscuits were mighty good. They must wrap up a few for
"Grandma's" supper. But these stories are told kindly, just as
she was treated kindly. People in small towns cherish their aged
and their eccentric.

So she lived on, a small, black-clad figure from another day,
her indomitable spirit wearing out body and mind. Mercifully it
was the body that gave way first.

In March of 1929 it almost seemed that death grew impatient.
The quiet of a Cartersville Sunday morning was shattered by
the crash of two automobiles. Grandma Felton was in one of
them. Her grandson, only slightly injured, and others lifted her
carefully from the wreck and carried her to a nearby doctor's
office. She was bleeding profusely from four deep cuts on her
face. Poor old thing—was she still alive?[47]

The two doctors worked feverishly. An artery had been sev-
ered. Could she stand a general anesthetic? The old lady opened
her eyes. "Don't you put me to sleep," she said. "If I'm going
to die I want to know about it." She lay quiet and conscious
while a local anesthetic was injected and twenty-six stitches
were taken in her face.[48]

She was removed to the hospital and people waited for the
final news. They could hardly believe the doctor when he announced the next day that she would pull through—if he could
keep her from talking. Then on to her grandson's home, where
she must live now. She recovered so rapidly that in a few days
she was able to write to the marble company, protesting the high
charge for her mausoleum.[49]

The days dragged, but the months sped by. It was June already
and another birthday. Her ninety-fourth. The Atlanta Daughters of the Confederacy, whose chapter had been named for her,
were giving the party this year. As always, her speech brought
a lot of laughter and applause. She joked about her accident
and read a letter from an ex-Felton slave praying that God
would "strengthen her backbone and keep her climbing." There
had certainly never been any apparent weakness in her backbone,

and she obviously intended to keep on climbing. Perhaps she would celebrate her hundredth birthday, as people were prophesying.[50]

The Great Depression which struck in the late summer worried her, of course. She had been telling everybody they were living too high. On a trip to Atlanta she consulted banker Eugene Black about conditions. He asked what she thought. "I tell you what, Gene," she said with a rare burst of profanity, "things are in a hell of a shape." Thank goodness she didn't have any stocks to worry about. Her spare money was in cash and government bonds.[51]

In December she became front page news. A blimp landed in Cartersville, and its pilot invited her for a ride. Of course she would go. She'd ridden in every other kind of conveyance—oxcart, buggy, train, and auto—she might as well try this thing. When she returned, she assured everyone that she had enjoyed herself immensely—although she later admitted to a reporter that she enjoyed landing more than she did taking off.[52]

Actually she seemed to have regained some of her famous energy since the accident. She celebrated Christmas with her family and attended a gay New Year's party where she announced that she had seen ninety-four summers but not a single "winter of discontent." On Tuesday, January 14, she argued against "the paving mania" before the Grand Jury, and got ready for a trip to Atlanta the following day.[53]

The next morning, however, she felt a cold coming on. Hadn't she better give up the trip if she didn't feel well? The papers said the cold weather was on the way. No, she was all right. The trustees of the Girls Training School were meeting the next day, and she had other business to attend to. Why didn't she take the train this time? Because she was going by bus.[54]

She appeared in the *Journal* office that afternoon looking pale and listless. Friends gathered around her. She ought not to be out in such weather. Was she sick? Oh, she had a little cold. But when she reached Mrs. Sally Morrison's, where she was to spend the night, she felt much worse. "I believe this cold will kill me," she said as Mrs. Morrison hurried her to bed. Bronchial pneumonia set in during the night, and she was moved to the Davis-Fischer sanitarium.[55]

She made a brave fight. On Friday she was reported slightly improved. She wanted to live. When her pastor called she told him she had had a "close call," and he must pray for her. But she was not afraid. She had never been afraid. "If my time has come," she said, "I'm ready." The congestion in her chest became heavier, and by the following Tuesday she was conscious only at times.[56]

What scenes and faces crossed the tired mind in those last broken moments of light? Her hour of greatness in the Senate? The faces of the three men who had won her devotion—Watson, Stephens, her husband? One hopes her father's face came too, bringing with it the peace and love she had known so long ago. Then darkness settled to stay, although the sturdy heart beat on. She died on Friday, just before midnight.[57]

The newspapers ran front-page stories and appropriate editorials. The Cartersville paper announced "Felton Estate Valued More Than Quarter Million." Prominent people commented upon her life and character. Walter George said more in fewer words than the rest. "She had well defined and firmly fixed opinions upon social, moral, and political questions and was always ready to defend them." [58]

The body was carried to Cartersville on Saturday and services held on Sunday in the Sam Jones Memorial Church. The Atlanta trains had been bringing in huge floral pieces for two days. Wires came—from all over Georgia, from the nation, from Washington, where the Senate had adjourned the day before in her honor. The local telegraph operator had not handled so many wires since Sam Jones' funeral. Many dignitaries were there: the Chief Justice of the Supreme Court, the Chancellor of the University, the Mayor of Atlanta. Others sent their representatives.[59]

But the funeral of the first woman Senator was a small-town Southern funeral. It was the men and women of Bartow who came, in their Sunday neatness, to crowd the pews and sing "Rock of Ages" and "Abide With Me" as only small-town Southern congregations can sing those plaintive hymns. Her own preacher delivered a highly personal eulogy, and neighbors bore the coffin to the bank of flowers and the mound of red Georgia earth.[60]

There she would rest, at last, in the impressive mausoleum, near the grave of the Doctor. To the front of the lot stood the four small stones that had thrown their shadow across her long life.

Notes

CHAPTER I

1. Stiles Martin to author, April 5, 1956.
2. Newspaper clipping, Scrapbook XXIV, p. 26, Felton Collection,University of Georgia Library. All scrapbooks cited are in this collection. They are numbered from I to XXXVIII. Some have no page numbers. Unless otherwise indicated, all references to scrapbooks are to newspaper clippings.
3. E. Merton Coulter, *A Short History of Georgia*, pp. 212-17; John E. Talmadge, "The Burritt Mystery," *Georgia Review*, Vol. VII (Fall, 1952), pp. 332-41; James H. Johnston, *Western and Atlantic Railroad of the State of Georgia*, p. 6.
4. Eleanor Boatwright, "The Political and Civil Status of Women in Georgia, 1789-1860," *Georgia Historical Quarterly*, Vol. XXV (November, 1941), pp. 305, 313; Dorothy Orr, *A History of Education in Georgia*, pp. 19-20, 150-51, 153-54.
5. Rebecca Latimer Felton, *Country Life in Georgia in the Days of My Youth*, p. 17. Hereafter cited as *Country Life*. Lucy Talbot Swift to Eleanor Latimer, January 25, 1851, Felton Collection. Unless otherwise indicated, all letters, manuscripts and pamphlets cited are in this collection.
6. Franklin M. Garrett, *Atlanta and Environs*, Vol. I, p. 112.
7. Felton ms., "Some Influences That Mould Character"; Rebecca Latimer Felton, *My Memoirs of Georgia Politics*, pp. 18-19. Hereafter cited as *Memoirs*.
8. *Ibid.*, pp. 20-23; Atlanta *Georgian*, November 7, 1920.
9. Garrett, *Atlanta*, Vol. 1, p. 479.
10. Charles Latimer to Charles Latimer, Jr., September 9, 1861, in possession of Professor W. M. Henderson of the University of Georgia Law School, a great-grandson of Charles Latimer.
11. Charles Latimer to C. R. Hanleiter, May 26, June 11, 1858.
12. Felton mss., "Some Influences That Mould Character," "Women on the Farm"; Scrapbook XXIV, p. 38.
13. *Country Life*, p. 28; Scrapbook XXIV, p. 24; Eleanor Swift Latimer to R. L. Felton, March 6, 1857.
14. Felton mss., "Women on the Farm," "Southern Women in the Civil War."
15. Scrapbook XXIV, p. 26; Scrapbook XI, p. 39.
16. *Memoirs*, p. 17; *Country Life*, pp. 50-51.
17. *Ibid.*; Garrett, *Atlanta*, Vol. I, p. 184.
18. Scrapbook XXIV, p. 56; Felton ms., "Some Influences That Mould Character."
19. *Ibid.*; Cartersville *News-Tribune*, January 30, 1930.
20. *Country Life*, p. 60.
21. *Ibid.*

161

22. *Ibid.*, pp. 61-62.
23. *Ibid.*
24. Scrapbook XXIV, p. 38; bound volume of sheet music.
25. Scrapbook XXIV, pp. 30, 187; Scrapbook XXX, p. 19.
26. Felton ms., "Mrs. Felton Describes Christmas Seventy Years Ago."
27. Augusta *Chronicle and Sentinel,* (Weekly) July 11, 1852; *Catalogue*

of *Madison Female College* (Madison, 1953), loaned the author by Mrs. Louise McHenry Hickey, Madison, Ga.
28. *Ibid.*
29. Bound volume of sheet music; sketchbook; Felton ms., "The Spirit of Improvement."
30. Felton ms., "Some Influences that Mould Character."

CHAPTER II

1. William Tappan Thompson, *The Courtship of Major Jones* (New York, 1872), p. 33.
2. Boatwright, "The Economic and Political Status of Women in Georgia," loc. cit., pp. 313-14.
3. Augusta *Chronicle and Sentinel* (Weekly), August 11, 1852.
4. *Ibid.*
5. William P. Roberts, "The Public Career of Dr. William Harrell Felton," a Ph.D. dissertation, University of North Carolina, 1952, pp. 1-8.
6. William H. Felton, *An Address Delivered at the Annual Commencement of the Madison Female College,* pp. 1-6, 10.
7. *Ibid.* p. 11.
8. Cassville *Standard,* September 30, 1852; Francis S. Bartow to W. H. Felton, August 29, 1852; *Marriage Book,* 1846-1856, Ordinary's Office, Decatur, Ga.

9. *Country Life,* pp. 42-44; Roberts, "Dr. Felton," pp. 1-7.
10. *Ibid.*, pp. 1-4; Lucy Josephine Cunyus, *The History of Bartow County, formerly Cass,* p. 283.
11. *Ibid.; Journal of the Georgia Legislature, 1851-1852,* pp. 67, 867.
12. Herman Clarence Nixon, *Lower Piedmont Country,* pp. 9-15.
13. Scrapbook XIII, p. 88; Charles Latimer to R. L. Felton, September 7, 1855; Eleanor Swift Latimer to R. L. Felton, December 15, 1854.
14. Cassville *Standard,* January 29, 1857; Cunyus, *Bartow County,* pp. 19-22.
15. *Ibid.;* Scrapbook XVI, p. 89.
16. Atlanta *Georgian,* November 8, 1922.
17. Scrapbook IX, pp. 62, 157; Scrapbook XXXII, unnumbered page; bound volume of sheet music.
18. Roberts, "Dr. Felton," pp. 7-8.
19. T. Conn Bryan, *Confederate Georgia,* p. ix.
20. Cassville *Standard,* August 8, 1860.

CHAPTER III

1. *Memoirs,* p. 25.
2. In a eulogy of Robert E. Lee after the war, Dr. Felton maintained that although Lee opposed secession, "he was the son of Virginia, and therefore the servant of Virginians." These may also have been Dr. Felton's sentiments. See his pamphlet *A Sermon on the Life and Character of Robert E. Lee.*
3. Cunyus, *Bartow County,* pp. 209-17; *Country Life,* pp. 87-88; Felton ms., "Address to the U.D.C. Assembly."
4. *Ibid.*

5. Roberts, "Dr. Felton," p. 7; Cartersville *Express,* July 18, 1878; J. J. Goodrum to R. L. Felton, June 6, 1919; *Country Life,* pp. 101-03.
6. Charles Latimer to Charles Latimer, Jr., September 9, 1861; Eleanor Swift Latimer to R. L. Felton, April 14, 1861.
7. William Pittenger, *Daring and Suffering, A History of the Andrews Raid into Georgia,* pp. 97-111; Scrapbook XXX (unnumbered pages).
8. Bryan, *Confederate Georgia,* pp. 76-77.

9. "Mrs. Felton's War Memoirs," Atlanta *Journal*, November 11, 1928; Scrapbook XXIV, p. 33.
10. *Ibid.;* Scrapbook XXXII, p. 7.
11. *Ibid.*
12. *Ibid.*
13. "Mrs. Felton's War Memoirs," Atlanta *Journal*, October 14, 1928; ms. of signed contract.
14. Scrapbook XXX, p. 9.
15. *Ibid.*
16. *The War of the Rebellion: A Compilation of the Official Records of the Union and Confederate Armies,* Series I, Vol. XXXVIII, Part I, p. 76.
17. Atlanta *Journal*, February 12, 1902.
18. *Ibid.*
19. Mrs. Felton did not learn until later that her parents had been caught in Sherman's bombardment of Atlanta and had refugeed to Crawfordville, Ga. See Scrapbook X, p. 47. William T. Swift to R. L. Felton, September 13, 1864.
20. Scrapbook XXI, p. 23.
21. William T. Swift to R. L. Felton, September 13, 1864; Milledgeville *Confederate Union*, September 26, 1864; Scrapbook XXIV, p. 103.
22. *Ibid.;* Atlanta *Journal*, October 4, 1902; Moultrie *Observer*, May 23, 1922.
23. *Ibid.; Country Life*, p. 86.
24. Moultrie *Observer*, May 23, 1922.
25. Scrapbook XXXI, p. 63; *Country Life*, pp. 90-91.

26. Scrapbook XXXII, p. 27.
27. Felton ms.
28. Cartersville *Express*, April 17, 1866; Cunyus, *Bartow County*, p. 24; Rebecca Latimer Felton, *The Romantic Story of Georgia Women*, p. 23. Hereafter cited as *Romantic Story*.
29. Dr. John Westmoreland to R. L. Felton, June 25, 1865; R. L. Felton to Julius Brown, March 2, 1903.
30. Isaac W. Avery, *The History of Georgia from 1850-1881*, pp. 338-39; Wirt Armistead Cate, *Lucius Q. C. Lamar, Secession and Reunion*, p. 119; Scrapbook XXIV, p. 143; Andrew Sparks, "Is There $50,000 in Gold Buried under Highway 41?" Atlanta *Journal*, September 16, 1951; note on back of letter, Julius Brown to R. L. Felton, March 2, 1903.
31. *Romantic Story*, p. 23; Circular announcing opening of Feltons' school.
32. Cunyus, *Bartow County*, pp. 256, 261; Cartersville *Express*, January 16, April 17, June 19, 1866.
33. *Ibid.* March 6, 1866, April 14, 1870, July 1, August 8, 1871; W. H. Felton, *A Sermon on the Life and Character of Lee*," loc. cit.; Felton ms., "Brandy, A Report for the Cartersville Temperance Club."
34. "Mrs. Felton's War Memoirs," Atlanta *Journal*, December 9, 1928; Cartersville *Standard and Express*, September 18, 1873.
35. *Ibid.;* Felton ms.

CHAPTER IV

1. Julia Collier Harris, *The Life and Letters of Joel Chandler Harris* (Boston, 1918), pp. 50-51.
2. Rudolph von Able, *Alexander H. Stephens*, p. 247; Allen P. Tankersley, *John B. Gordon, A Study in Gallantry*, p. 222; Louise Biles Hill, *Joseph E. Brown and the Southern Confederacy*, p. 247.
3. Augusta *Chronicle and Sentinel* (Weekly), May 10, 1865; Judson C. Ward, Jr., "Georgia Under the Bourbons," a Ph.D. dissertation, University of North Carolina, 1947, p. 10.
4. Coulter, *History of Georgia*, pp. 340-59; Tankersley, *Gordon*, pp. 239-45.

5. Hill, *Brown*, pp. 293-98; Haywood J. Pearce, *Benjamin H. Hill, Secession and Reconstruction*, pp. 204-08.
6. Coulter, *History of Georgia*, pp. 353-56; Avery, *History of Georgia*, pp. 439, 456, 472.
7. Alexander Mathews Arnett, *The Populist Movement in Georgia*, pp. 20-21; Atlanta *Constitution*, October 4, 1872.
8. Raymond B. Nixon, *Henry W. Grady, Spokesman of the New South*, p. 306; Pearce, *Hill*, p. 231.
9. Coulter, *History of Georgia*, pp. 356-57; Tankersley, *Gordon*, pp. 263-64.
10. Hill, *Brown*, pp. 298-305.

11. Avery, *History of Georgia,* pp. 472-76; Tankersley, *Gordon,* p. 266.

12. Ward, "Georgia Under the Bourbons," pp. 72-73; Arnett, *Populist Movement,* pp. 33-34.

13. *Ibid.;* Atlanta *Constitution,* December 4, 1873, February 8, 1874; *ibid.,* (Weekly) March 3, June 2, 1874; for comments of Atlanta *Herald* see Cartersville *Standard and Express,* July 15, 1874.

14. *Ibid.,* January 15, June 24, July 15, 1874; Rome *Commercial* quoted in Cartersville *Standard and Express,* July 8, 1874.

15. Ward, "Georgia Under the Bourbons," pp. 78-79; Cartersville *Standard and Express,* September 16, 1874; clippings Rome *Courier,* Rome *Commercial* and Marietta *Journal,* Scrapbook I (pages unnumbered).

16. Cartersville *Standard and Express,* April 1, June 3, August 5, 1874; the Doctor's announcement in the Cartersville *Sentinel* is discussed in *Standard and Express,* April 1, 1874.

17. Nellie Latimer McLendon to R. L. Felton, June 10, 1874.

18. Cartersville *Standard and Express,* August 5, 1874.

CHAPTER V

1. Clippings, Rome *Commercial,* Marietta *Journal,* and other papers, Scrapbook I, (pages unnumbered).

2. Clippings, Atlanta *Herald* and other papers, Scrapbook I; Dalton *North Georgia Citizen,* reprinted in Cartersville *Standard and Express,* September 30, 1874.

3. *Ibid.;* Atlanta *Constitution,* September 18, 1874; Scrapbook I.

4. *Ibid.; Memoirs,* pp. 212-13; (copy) W. H. Felton to Colonel R. H. Jones, September 10, 1876; L. N. Trammell to Colonel R. H. Jones, September 8, 1876.

5. Cartersville *Standard and Express,* September 16, 1874; Scrapbook I.

6. Clippings, Cartersville *Sentinel,* Cedartown *Record,* and Atlanta *News,* Scrapbook I. Brown had forced Abrams to give up the editorship of the Atlanta *News* by foreclosing a note. See Nixon, *Grady,* p. 104. Clipping, Rome *Courier,* Scrapbook I.

7. Ms. of the Executive Committee's proposal to Dr. Felton; Cartersville *Standard and Express,* October 7, 1874; clipping, Atlanta *Herald,* Scrapbook I.

8. Clippings, Rome *Courier* and Atlanta *Herald,* Scrapbook I; Cartersville *Standard and Express,* October 21, 1874; Atlanta *Constitution,* October 27, 28, 1874.

9. Clippings, Atlanta *News,* and other papers, Scrapbook I; *Memoirs,* pp. 152-53.

10. A. R. Wright to R. L. Felton, November 11, 1874; *Memoirs,* pp. 153-63.

11. *Ibid.*

12. *Ibid.,* pp. 158-59; clippings, Atlanta *News,* Scrapbook I; Atlanta *Constitution,* November 7, 1874.

13. Clipping, Augusta *Chronicle and Sentinel,* Scrapbook I.

14. *Memoirs,* pp. 144-47.

15. B. H. Hill to R. L. Felton, October 23, 1874; H. V. M. Miller to R. L. Felton, October 24, 1874.

16. John B. Gordon to R. L. Felton, October 24, 1874; *Memoirs,* p. 478.

17. Atlanta *Constitution,* November 1, 1874.

18. Clippings, Atlanta *Constitution,* Atlanta *News,* and others, Scrapbook I; *Memoirs,* p. 146.

19. *Ibid.,* pp. 148-49.

20. Clipping, Atlanta *Herald,* Scrapbook I.

21. Lizzie J. Smith to R. L. Felton, June 22, 1876; B. H. Hill to R. L. Felton, May 22, 1875; John Stephens to R. L. Felton, November 20, 1875. Her news letter appeared in these papers over the pen name "Occasional."

22. Clipping, "Occasional," to Atlanta *Constitution,* Scrapbook I.

23. Allan Nevins, *Hamilton Fish, The Inner History of the Grant Administration* (New York, 1936), pp. 146-48; Cate, *Lamar,* pp. 230-31.

24. Clippings, "Occasional," Atlanta *Herald,* and Atlanta *Constitution,* Scrapbook I.
25. *Ibid.*
26. *Country Life,* p. 133; *Memoirs,* pp. 164-65.
27. Dolly Blount Lamar, *When All Is Said And Done,* p. 59. Allen P. Tankersley says that "a careful examination of the Felton papers . . . shows that prior to 1878 the Feltons and the Gordons lived on friendly, if not intimate terms." See *Gordon,* p. 318. The Papers contain a rather limited and formal correspondence between the two families up to 1878: the ambiguous letter from Gordon about speaking against the Doctor, which incensed Mrs. Felton; a letter from Gordon to Dr. Felton on an item of Congressional business; and a note from Mrs. Gordon to Mrs. Felton thanking her for an expression of sympathy in the death of a Gordon baby.
28. *Country Life,* pp. 124-29; Lamar, *When All Is Said And Done,* p. 55.
30. Clipping, Atlanta *Constitution,* Scrapbook I.
30. Clipping, "Occasional," Atlanta *Constitution,* Scrapbook I.
31. Scrapbook I.
32. *Congressional Records, Containing the Proceedings and Debates of the 44th Congress,* Vol. IV, Part I, pp. 160, 320, 331, 357, 450, 570; Part II, pp. 1727-29; Part IV, pp. 3789-91; clipping, Darien *Gazette,* Scrapbook I.
33. Clippings, Rome *Courier,* Augusta *Chronicle and Sentinel,* Atlanta *Herald,* Scrapbook I.
34. Cartersville *Standard and Express,* August 24, 1876.

CHAPTER VI

1. B. H. Hill to W. H. Felton, August 7, 1876.
2. Scrapbook I.
3. Clipping, Atlanta *Commonwealth,* Scrapbook I.
4. Milton Candler to W. H. Felton, September 6, 1876.
5. (Copy), unsigned, to Milton Candler, September 7, 1876.
6. Robert Toombs to R. L. Felton, September 21, 1876.
7. B. H. Hill to R. L. Felton, October 15, 1876.
8. Scrapbook I.
9. (Copy), R. L. Felton to B. F. Sawyer, September 9, 1876.
10. Clipping, Rome *Courier,* October 13, 1876, Scrapbook I.
11. Clipping, Rome *Bulletin,* Scrapbook I.
12. Scrapbook I.
13. T. E. Hanbury to R. L. Felton, October 16, 1876.
14. Clippings, Cartersville *Express,* Atlanta *Constitution,* and Atlanta *Herald,* Scrapbook I.
15. Clipping, "Occasional," Rome *Bulletin,* Scrapbook I.
16. Scrapbook I; Harry Bernard, *Rutherford B. Hayes and His America,* p. 399.
17. Cartersville *Courant,* February 26, 1885; Felton ms., "Address."
18. *Ibid.*
19. Atlanta *Constitution,* April 7, 8, 15, 20, May 2, 1877.
20. R. L. Felton, "Alexander Stephens as I Knew Him," *National Republic,* February, 1922, pp. 19, 54; *Memoirs,* pp. 345-46.
21. Cartersville *Express,* August 9, 1877; A. H. Stephens to R. L. Felton, August 19, 1877; R. M. Johnston to R. L. Felton, August 16, 1877.
22. "R.A.F." in Cartersville *Express,* March 3, 1878; Scrapbook XIII, p. 100; A. H. Stephens to W. H. Felton, undated.
23. J. A. Erwin to R. L. Felton, March 8, June 6, 1878; C. H. C. Willingham to R. L. Felton, March 17, 1878; Cartersville *Express,* March 17, 1878.
24. Emory Speer to W. H. Felton, January 31, 1877; A. H. Stephens to Henry Casey, June 14, 1878, published in Atlanta *Constitution,* June 16, 1878; H. V. M. Miller to R. L. Felton, June 5, 1878.

25. Clipping, Rome *Bulletin,* May 28, 1878, Scrapbook III (unnumbered pages).
26. Atlanta *Constitution,* July 2, 1878.
27. Clipping, "Special Dispatch to the *Constitution,* July 11," Scrapbook XVIII, pp. 2-3.
28. *Ibid.*
29. *Ibid.*
30. *Ibid.*
31. Scrapbook XVIII, pp. 5, 7, 25.
32. *Ibid.*
33. *Ibid.,* pp. 5, 31, 48, 54.

34. *Ibid.,* pp. 48, 51, 54, 56, 68.
35. (Copy) R. L. Felton to Evan Howell, September 17, 1878; Atlanta *Constitution,* September 11, 19, 1878.
36. Scrapbook XVIII, pp. 23, 27, 48, 65, 67.
37. *Memoirs,* pp. 481-82.
38. *Ibid.,* p. 199; Cartersville *Express,* November 14, 1878. Told to the author by the late Justine Erwin Talmadge of Athens, Georgia.
39. Atlanta *Constitution,* November 7, 1878.

CHAPTER VII

1. *Memoirs,* p. 478.
2. Felton ms., "A Party Without Principles."
3. Clipping, Augusta *Chronicle and Constitutionalist,* Scrapbook XXV, p. 55; Atlanta *Constitution,* February 28, 1879.
4. J. D. Head to R. L. Felton, December 9, 1878; (copy) John Young Brown to J. D. Head, December, 1878; (copy) J. D. Head to John Young Brown, December 9, 1878.
5. Amos T. Akerman to R. L. Felton, December 21, 1878.
6. Cartersville *Free-Press,* January 9, 23, 27, February 13, 20, 1879.
7. Macon *Ledger,* qouted in Cartersville *Free-Press,* January 23, 1879.
8. Clipping, "Editorial Correspondent, January 22, 1879, A.W.R.," Scrapbook XVI, p. 1.
9. *Memoirs,* pp. 482-83. According to the Columbus *Enquirer-Sun,* Gordon never denied asking Ferry for the letter. See Scrapbook XVI, p. 85.
10. Macon *Telegraph and Messenger,* February 13, 1879.
11. Clipping, "Washington, D. C., February 19, 1879, Editor of *Chronicle and Constitutionalist,*" Scrapbook XVI, p. 302.
12. Atlanta *Constitution,* February 25, 1879.
13. *Ibid.,* February 28, 1879.
14. Scrapbook XVI, p. 412.
15. Macon *Telegraph and Messenger,* February 21, 1879.
16. *Ibid.,* March 2, 1879.

17. Clipping, "March 4, 1879, to the Editor of the *Chronicle and Constitutionalist,*" Scrapbook XVI, p. 40.
18. Clipping, "March 8, 1879, to the *Chronicle and Constitutionalist,*" Scrapbook XVI, p. 41.
19. Cedartown *Advertiser,* quoted in Atlanta *Constitution,* March 9, 1879; Covington *Standard* and LaGrange *Reporter,* quoted in Atlanta *Constitution,* March 13, 1879; Atlanta *Constitution,* February 28, 1879; Louisville *News and Farmer,* quoted in Atlanta *Constitution,* March 12, 1879.
20. DeKalb County *News and Messenger,* Conyers *Weekly* quoted in Atlanta *Constitution,* March 9, 1879.
21. Scrapbook XVI, p. 45.
22. Kenneth Coleman, "The Administration of Alfred Colquitt as Governor of Georgia," a Master's thesis, University of Georgia, 1940, pp. 32-62; Scrapbook XXV, pp. 4, 6, 19, 20; Cartersville *Free-Press,* March 20, 1879.
23. Scrapbook XXV, pp. 17-18, 36-37; Cartersville *Free-Press,* February 12, 26, 1880.
24. Atlanta *Constitution,* May 20, 21, 22, 23, 1880.
25. *Ibid.,* April 8, 1880.
26. Americus *Times-Recorder,* May 26, 1880; Scrapbook XVIII, pp. 89-92.
27. Scrapbook XXV, pp. 99, 100.
28. Atlanta *Constitution,* May 22, 23, 24, 25, June 3, 8, 1880.

29. Scrapbook XVIII, pp. 51; Atlanta *Constitution*, May 23, 1880.

30. Athens *Southern Watchman*, reprinted in Cartersville *Free-Press*, June 17, 1880. It is true that Gordon was not taking over the presidency of the Western and Atlantic Railroad, as the *Watchman* had reported, but he never explained how Grady, who had just left him, knew that Newcomb was going to offer him a job, and that Brown was going to succeed him.

CHAPTER VIII

1. Ward, "Georgia Under the Bourbons," p. 106; Coleman, "The Administration of Alfred Colquitt," pp. 32-44; Scrapbook XXV, pp. 9, 84-86.
2. Atlanta *Constitution*, May 23, June 30, 1880; Leola Spears, "The Senatorial Career of Joseph E. Brown," a Master's thesis, University of Georgia, 1954, pp. 28-32.
3. Cartersville *Free-Press*, July 3, 10, 17, 24, 1880.
4. *Ibid.*, May 27, 1880.
5. *Ibid.*, June 10, 1880.
6. *Ibid.*, July 15, 1880.
7. A. H. Stephens to R. L. Felton, June 30, 1880.
8. B. H. Hill to R. L. Felton, undated.
9. *Memoirs*, p. 403.
10. C. Vann Woodward, *Tom Watson, Agrarian Rebel*, pp. 73-74.
11. *Memoirs*, pp. 309-10.
12. (Copy) Joseph E. Brown to W. H. Felton, August 17, 1880.
13. *Ibid.*
14. Joseph E. Brown to R. L. Felton, August 17, 1880.
15. *Ibid.*, October 11, 1880.
16. *Memoirs*, p. 312; Cartersville *Free-Press*, September 2, 9, 1880.
17. A. H. Stephens to R. L. Felton, September 14, 1880.
18. *Memoirs*, pp. 311-12; Roberts, "Dr. Felton," pp. 236-37; Cartersville *Free Press*, October 28, 1880; Cartersville *Express*, November 4, 1880.
19. B. H. Hill to W. H. Felton, November 11, 1880.
20. Roberts, "Dr. Felton," pp. 232-33.
21. Cartersville *Free-Press*, November 11, 1880.
22. *Ibid.*
23. R. L. Felton to A. H. Stephens, January 1, 1882, Stephens Papers, Library of Congress.
24. *Memoirs*, pp. 326-27.
25. Atlanta *Constitution*, October 21, November 11, 18, 1880; Hill, *Brown*, p. 321.
26. B. W. Frobel to A. H. Stephens, December 4, 1880, Stephens Papers, Library of Congress.
27. Joseph E. Brown to A. H. Stephens, October 15, 1880, Stephens Papers, Library of Congress.
28. "From the Washington World," reprinted in Cartersville *Free-Press*, December 23, 1880.
29. *Ibid.*, March 17, 1881.
30. Cartersville *Free-Press*, April 4, 28, July 14, September 8, 15, 22, October 6, 1881.
31. A. H. Stephens to R. L. Felton, March 10, 15, 17, September 11, October 8, 20, 25, December 20, 1881.
32. Cartersville *Free-Press*, December 22, 1881.

CHAPTER IX

For a condensed treatment of the Governor's race of 1882 see John E. Talmadge, "The Death Blow to Independentism in Georgia," *Georgia Historical Quarterly*, XXXIX (December, 1955), pp. 37-47.

1. D. B. Sanger and T. H. Hay, *James Longstreet*, pp. 382-87; Atlanta *Constitution*, December 14, 20, 29, 1881.
2. *Ibid.*, January 3, 5, 1882.
3. B. H. Hill to W. H. Felton, January 3, 1882.
4. *Memoirs*, p. 418.
5. R. L. Felton to A. H. Stephens, January 14, 1882, Stephens Papers, Library of Congress; Atlanta *Constitution*, January 7, 10, 19, 22, 1882.
6. *Ibid.*, January 7, 25, February 10, 15, 18, 1882.

7. James Hook to W. H. Felton, August 6, 1881.
8. James Atkins to W. H. Felton, January 25, 1882.
9. A. H. Stephens to R. L. Felton, October 28, 1881.
10. James Longstreet to O. P. Fitzsimmons, December 17, 1881.
11. A. H. Stephens to R. L. Felton, December 8, 1881.
12. *Ibid.,* January 10, 1882.
13. R. L. Felton to A. H. Stephens, January 14, 1882, Stephens Papers, Library of Congress.
14. A. H. Stephens to R. L. Felton, February 21, 1882.
15. Atlanta *Constitution,* March 4, 10, 15, 1882.
16. R. L. Felton to A. H. Stephens, January 14, 1882, Stephens Papers, Library of Congress.
17. A. H. Stephens to R. L. Felton, March 13, 1882.
18. *Ibid.,* March 19, 28, April 3, 24, 1882.
19. Augusta *Chronicle,* March 19, 1882; Atlanta *Constitution,* April 4, 23, 25, 28, May 4, 1882.
20. A. H. Stephens to R. L. Felton, May 7, 1882.
21. Atlanta *Constitution,* May 7, 1882.
22. J. S. Hook to W. H. Felton, January 24, 1882.
23. *Memoirs.,* pp. 365-67.
24. *Ibid.*
25. *Ibid.*
26. *Ibid.*
27. Cartersville *Free-Press,* May 18, 1882.
28. A. H. Stephens to R. L. Felton, May 18, 1882.
29. A. H. Stephens to W. H. Felton, May 18, 1882.
30. Evan Howell to A. H. Stephens, May 19, 1882, Stephens Papers, Library of Congress.
31. A. H. Stephens to C. E. Smith, May 22, 1882, published in Atlanta *Constitution,* May 23, 1882; A. H. Stephens to W. H. Hiddell, June 11, 1882, Stephens Papers, Pennsylvania Historical Society.
32. Atlanta *Constitution,* May 23, 24, 25, 26, 28, 31, 1882.
33. Augusta *Chronicle and Constitutionalist,* quoted in Cartersville *Free-Press,* June 29, 1882; Macon *Telegraph,* quoted in Cartersville *Free-Press,* September 4, 1882; Atlanta *Constitution,* August 25, 1882; W. T. Wofford to A. H. Stephens, September 10, 1882, Stephens Papers, Library of Congress.
34. H. V. M. Miller to W. H. Felton, May 25, 1882; James Hook to R. L. Felton, June 19, 1882; Cartersville *Free-Press,* July 13, 17, 1882.
35. Von Able, *Stephens,* p. 309.
36. Macon *Telegraph,* reprinted in Cartersville *Free-Press,* September 28, 1882.
37. *Memoirs,* pp. 373-75.
38. *Ibid.*
39. Atlanta *Constitution,* September 1, 1882; telegram R. L. Felton to A. H. Stephens, September 1, 1882.
40. A. H. Stephens to W. H. Hiddell, June 11, October 9, 1882, Stephens Papers, Pennsylvania Historical Society.
41. *Ibid.,* October 27, 1882.
42. Roberts, "Dr. Felton," p. 31; Atlanta *Constitution,* October 5, November 8, 15, 16, 1882; Cartersville *Free-Press,* September 28, 1882; C. D. Forsyth to W. H. Felton, July 26, 1882; anonymous telegrams, Felton Collection.
43. A. H. Stephens to R. L. Felton, December 20, 1881.
44. *Memoirs,* pp. 382-83.
45. Atlanta *Constitution,* March 2, 4, 6, 9, 1883.
46. *Ibid.;* Von Able, *Stephens,* pp. 316-17.

CHAPTER X

1. Cartersville *Free-Press,* March 8, 1883.
2. Cartersville *Express,* April 22, 1884; R. M. Johnston to R. L. Felton, August 1, 1883.
3. James Longstreet to R. L. Felton, January 2, 1883; (copy) W. H. Felton to James Longstreet, September 6, 1883.
4. P. W. Alexander to R. L. Felton, April 23, May 23, 1884; Henry Watterson to R. L. Felton, July 5, 1884;

Charles Dana to R. L. Felton, July 5, 1884.

5. Conyers, *Solid South,* quoted in Cartersville *Free-Press,* December 6, 1883.

6. R. M. Johnston to R. L. Felton, May 18, 1883.

7. *Memoirs,* pp. 547-49.

8. *Ibid;* Roberts, "Dr. Felton," pp. 360-62, 392-400; W. H. Hiddell to R. L. Felton, September 29, 1884.

9. *Memoirs,* pp. 556-57; Roberts, "Dr. Felton," pp. 360-62, 392-400.

10. R. L. Felton to W. H. Felton, September 15, 1889; W. H. Felton to R. L. Felton, July 21, August 5, 1885.

11. Cartersville *American,* January 13, 1885; Cartersville *Courant,* February 7, 26, September 17, October 15, 1885.

12. Felton ms., "Her Most Valuable Property."

13. *Memoirs,* pp. 556-623; Atlanta *Constitution,* August 5, 11, 12, 1887; Atlanta *Journal,* August 10, 11, 1887.

14. *Ibid.*

15. *Ibid.*

16. *Ibid.*

17. *Ibid.*

18. *Ibid;* Atlanta *Constitution,* August 12, 1887.

19. Woodward, *Watson,* p. 120.

20. Nixon, *Grady,* p. 226.

21. A. O. Bacon to W. H. Felton, May 15, 1886.

22. *Memoirs,* pp. 94-119; Tankersley, *Gordon,* pp. 293-98.

23. Ward, "Georgia Under the Bourbons," pp. 180-81; Nixon, *Grady,* pp. 226-30.

24. *Ibid.;* Atlanta *Constitution,* May 19, 24, 25, 26, 27, June 1, 13, 1886.

25. Scrapbook XXVIII, p. 5; Ward, "Georgia Under the Bourbons," pp. 184-85; J. F. Hanson to R. L. Felton, May 20, 1886; Patrick Walsh to R. L. Felton, May 20, 1886; W. H. Hiddell to R. L. Felton, May 26, 1886.

26. Mrs. Felton's letters signed "Plain Talk" were reprinted in a pamphlet, *General J. B. Gordon as a Financier and Statesman.*

27. Atlanta *Constitution,* June 14, 1886.

28. Cartersville *American,* June 22, 1886.

29. *Ibid.;* C. Vann Woodward, *Reunion and Reaction, The Compromise of 1877 and the End of Reaction,* pp. 82, 123-24; Tankersley, *Gordon,* p. 298.

30. Atlanta *Constitution,* June 18, November 13, 1886.

31. Scrapbook XII, p. 29.

32. Scrapbook X, p. 75.

33. Atlanta *Constitution,* May 23, 1886.

34. Woodward, *Watson,* pp. 129-45.

35. *Ibid.,* pp. 162-64.

36. *Ibid.;* J. E. Brown to L. N. Trammell, June 23, 1888, Trammell Papers, Emory University.

37 Woodward, *Watson,* p. 167.

38. *Ibid.,* pp. 164-68, 240-41, 268-75.

39. Atlanta *Journal,* July 15, 1889; Roberts, "Dr. Felton," pp. 408-15; Cartersville *Courant-American,* November 6, 1890; *Memoirs,* pp. 641-63.

40. *Ibid.,* pp. 654-56; Felton ms., "Why I Voted With the Populist Party"; Cartersville *Courant-American,* August 30, September 6, November 8, 1894; T. E. Watson to W. H. Felton, September 6, 1894.

41. H. A. Scomp to W. H. Felton, November 9, 1894; J. A. Cunningham to W. H. Felton, November 8, 1894; W. H. Hiddell to W. H. Felton, November 7, 1894.

42. W. P. Frye to R. L. Felton, December 4, 1894.

43. W. H. Dudley to R. L. Felton, November 19, December 1, 1894; J. K. Davis to R. L. Felton, December 20, 1894; H. C. Lodge to R. L. Felton, December 26, 1894.

44. Felton ms.; *Memoirs,* pp. 668-69.

45. *Ibid.,* pp. 667-68.

46. *Ibid.;* R. L. Felton to W. H. Felton, March, 1895.

47. W. H. Dudley to R. L. Felton, December 26, 1885, February 29, 1886.

48. *Memoirs,* pp. 670-72; Atlanta *Constitution,* April 11, 1886.

49. W. H. Dudley to R. L. Felton, May 18, 1886.

50. *Ibid.;* J. K. Davis to W. H. Felton, June 26, 1886.

51. Atlanta *Journal,* July 7, 1886; *Memoirs,* pp. 672-78.

52. M. L. Palmer to W. H. Felton, May 18, 1896.

CHAPTER XI

1. L. M. McLaws to R. L. Felton, August 8, 1890.
2. Joseph E. Brown to R. L. Felton, August 12, 1890.
3. *Country Life,* pp. 108-11.
4. Telegram, Phoebe Cousins to R. L. Felton, April 16, 1891.
5. Bertha Palmer to R. L. Felton, May 4, 1891.
6. Francis Willard to R. L. Felton, April 24, 1891; Charles Dana to R. L. Felton, April 24, 1891; (copy) J. E. Brown to T. W. Palmer, April 24, 1891.
7. Mrs. John A. Logan to R. L. Felton, April 27, 1891; Mrs. Virginia Meredith to R. L. Felton, May 5, 1891.
8. Bertha Palmer to R. L. Felton, May 4, 1891, December 29, 1893.
9. Isabella Hooker to R. L. Felton, January 29, 1891.
10. R. L. Felton to E. A. Latimer, May 21, 1894; R. L. Felton to W. H. Felton, May 3, 1894.
11. R. L. Felton to W. H. Felton, March 15, 1893.
12. R. L. Felton to H. E. Felton, March 26, 1893.
13. R. L. Felton to W. H. Felton, December 15, 1892.
14. *Ibid.,* March 15, 1893.
15. Telegrams, W. H. Felton to R. L. Felton, April 5, 6, August 15, 1893.
16. Emma Thompson to R. L. Felton, July 7, 1895.
17. *Country Life,* pp. 113-15.
18. Sam Jones to R. L. Felton, March 13, 1889; J. E. Brown to R. L. Felton, January 7, 1888.
19. J. H. Peyton to R. L. Felton, September 19, 1905; H. H. Cabiniss to R. L. Felton, October 8, 1892; envelope, Etna Life Insurance Company, notation on back, January 6, 1892; W. E. Candler to R. L. Felton, November 8, 1904.
20. Undated clipping, Atlanta *Sunday American.*
21. Atlanta *Constitution,* August 19, 1906.
22. Eula T. Willingham to R. L. Felton, October 4, 1909.
23. W. D. Totten, Jr., to R. L. Felton, October 4, 1909.
24. Cartersville *News,* September 30, 1909.
25. Scrapbook XVII, p. 73.
26. Cartersville *News,* June 9, 23, 1910.
27. Corra Harris, *The Co-Citizens,* pp. 21, 22, 26; Corra Harris to R. L. Felton, January 1, 1915; H. E. Maule to R. L. Felton, December 29, 1915; Atlanta *Journal,* June 22, 1921.
28. Lucian Lamar Knight, *A Standard History of Georgia and Georgians,* Vol. II, p. 876.
29 Roberts, "Dr. Felton," p. 452.
30. *Memoirs,* pp. 10-11.
31. M. R. Turner to R. L. Felton, April 24, 1902.

CHAPTER XII

1. (Copy) R. L. Felton to Isabella Hooker, December 8, 1890.
2. *Memoirs,* p. 444.
3. Scrapbook XXIV, p. 186; ms. "The Convict System of Georgia."
4. *Ibid.;* Mrs. W. H. Felton, "The Convict System of Georgia," *The Forum,* January 1887, Vol. II, pp. 484-86.
5. *Memoirs,* p. 470.
6. C. E. Felton to R. L. Felton, December 8, 1886; G. W. Cable to R. L. Felton, July 24, 1886.
7. Josephine Bone Floyd, "Rebecca Latimer Felton, Political Independent," *Georgia Historical Quar-* *terly,* Vol. XXX (March, 1946), p. 30.
8. Scrapbook IX, p. 187.
9. Scrapbook XVII, pp. 205-06.
10. *Romantic Story,* p. 27.
11. Mrs. J. J. Ansley, *History of the Georgia Woman's Christian Temperance Union, from its Organization, 1883-1907,* pp. 121-23.
12. *Country Life,* pp. 207-13.
13. Coulter, *History of Georgia,* pp. 396-98.
14. This description of a prohibition address by Mrs. Felton is based upon the following manuscripts of

speeches: "The Address at Madison," "From A Woman's Standpoint," "Woman's Relation to the Temperance Movement," "A Mother's Appeal," "The Effects of Drunkenness on the Future of a Child."

15. Scrapbook XVII, p. 31; R. L. Felton to Mrs. J. J. Ansley, October 3, 1910.
16. G. M. Napier to R. L. Felton, July 23, 1894; Scrapbook XVII, pp. 28-30.
17. Felton ms.
18. M. C. Mewborn to R. L. Felton, November 11, 1899; Frances Willard to R. L. Felton, November 30, 1888.
19. *Romantic Story,* p. 27.
20. Ansley, *History of Georgia W.C. T.U.,* p. 143.
21. Atlanta *Journal,* November 1, 1898.
22. Scrapbook XXXI, p. 47.
23. Cartersville *Courant,* February 11, 1886; *Country Life,* p. 297.
24. Mrs. Felton's arguments for woman's suffrage are taken from the following manuscripts: "The Subjection and Enfranchisement of Women," "A Few Plain Facts," "The Question," "To the General Assembly of Georgia."
25. Scrapbook XXIV, p. 56.
26. Scrapbook XXVII, pp. 35, 54.
27. Macon *News,* May 16, 18, 1915; M. R. Brown to R. L. Felton, May 13, 25, 1915.
28. *Ibid.*
29. Atlanta *Constitution,* July 7, 1914.
30. *Ibid.,* July 30, 1915.
31. A few notes made on Miss Rutherford's speech and the sketches of the hat are on a sheet of Georgia Legislature stationery.
32. Atlanta *Constitution,* July 30, 1915; Scrapbook XXIV, pp. 111-12; Felton ms., "How They Do It in Georgia."
33. *Ibid.*
34. *Ibid.*
35. Scrapbook V, p. 64.
36. Felton ms., "Some Reasons Why the General Assembly Failed to Ratify."
37. Felton ms., "Concerning Rev. W. A. Candler's Plan."
38. Bartow *Tribune,* May 15, 1920.
39. Atlanta *Constitution,* September 13, 1889.
40. Harry A. Alexander to R. L. Felton, January 19, 1893; Harry Hodgson to R. L. Felton, May 29, 1893; University of Georgia *Pandora,* 1893.
41. Felton ms., "Editor of the *Constitution,* June, 1898"; Felton ms., "Intercollegiate Athletic Contests."
42. Felton ms., "Why They Forbid the Girls"; W. B. Hill to R. L. Felton, July 3, 1893.
43. Felton ms., "Women in the University."
44. *Country Life,* pp. 170-92.
45. Scrapbook XVII, pp. 24-25.
46. Clipping, New York *Mail and Express,* July 3, 1901.
47. J. J. Slocum to R. L. Felton, June 12, 1913; Wilmer Moore to R. L. Felton, August 23, 1918; *Romantic Story,* pp. 46-47.
48. Clipping, "The Grand Old Lady of Georgia," *Business Woman,* Scrapbook XXXVIII, p. 25.

CHAPTER XIII

1. *Country Life,* pp. 98-100; Scrapbook XXIV, p. 13.
2. Cartersville *News and Courant,* October 10, November 8, 1891; Scrapbook IX, p. 51. Although less violent than Mrs. Felton, her friend Corra Harris largely shared this view. See her article "Black and White" in *Saturday Evening Post,* November 15, 1931.
3. J. Pope Brown to R. L. Felton, June 30, 1897.
4. Atlanta *Journal,* August 12, 1897.
5. H. C. Hanson to R. L. Felton, August 17, 1897 (pasted in Scrapbook VIII, p. 58). Newspaper clipping, "To the Editor of the Macon *Telegraph,*" August 18, 1897.
6. Atlanta *Constitution,* November 11, 1898.
7. Hugh T. Lefler and Albert R. Newsome, *The History of a State* (Chapel Hill, 1954), p. 522; Atlanta *Journal,* November 11, 14, 1898.

8. *Ibid.,* November 15, 21, 1898.
9. New York *Tribune,* November 11, 1898.
10. Atlanta *Constitution,* December 19, 1898.
11. *Ibid.,* December 22, 1898.
12. *Ibid.,* December 26, 29, 1898.
13. Atlanta *Journal,* April 13, 14, 15, 16, 17, 18, 1899.
14. Atlanta *Constitution,* April 23, 1899.
15. *Ibid.,* April 24, 1899.
16. Editorials quoted in Atlanta *Journal,* April 25, 26, 1899.
17. Atlanta *Journal,* May 2, 1899.
18. *Atlantic Monthly,* July, 1902, Vol. 90, pp. 65-73.
19. Madison Bell to R. L. Felton, July 29, 1902.
20. Atlanta *Constitution,* August 3, 1902.
21. J. W. Renfroe to R. L. Felton, August 5, 1902; Lily Johnson to R. L. Felton, August 6, 1902; Felton ms., undated; John S. Cohen to R. L. Felton, August 8, 1902.
22. Atlanta *Constitution,* August 5, 1902; Henry M. Bullock, *A History of Emory University,* pp. 240, 356.
23. C. Vann Woodward, *The Strange Case of Jim Crow,* pp. 51-52; Atlanta *Journal,* May 5, 1913: Scrapbook XI, p. 33.
24. Scrapbook XXIV, pp. 69, 78; Felton ms., "Women on the Farm."
25. Scrapbook XXXVI, (pages unnumbered); Scrapbook XXXII, p. 12; Scrapbook XXVII, p. 34.
26. Clark Howell to R. L. Felton, January 3, 1903; Atlanta *Constitution,* January 8, 1893.
27. *Ibid.,* January 9, 10, 13, 14, 1893.
28. Felton ms., "The Future of Methodism."
29. B. F. Hayes to Walker Lewis, July 20, 1897; Walker Lewis to B. F. Hayes, July 22, 1897; B. F. Hayes to R. L. Felton, July 22, 1897; Scrapbook XXII, pp. 21, 107.
30. Clement C. Carey to R. L. Felton, December 11, 1897.
31. *Ibid.,* December 4, 8, 11, 1897; Atlanta *Journal,* November 24, 26, 27, 29, December 7, 1897.
32. *Ibid.*
33. Alfred M. Pierce, *Giant in the Sky,* pp. 77-81; *Country Life,* pp. 157-70; Atlanta *Journal,* May 26, 1898.
34. *Ibid.*
35. Sam Adams to R. L. Felton, May 30, 1902.
36. Scrapbook XXI, p. 41; Scrapbook XXIV, p.4.
37. C. Vann Woodward, *Origins of the New South,* Vol. IX, in *A History of the South,* pp. 131-33.
38. Claire DeGraffenreid, "The Georgia Cracker in the Cotton Mill," *Century* Magazine, Vol. XLI (February, 1891) , pp. 483-98.
39. J. F. Hanson to R. L. Felton, April 4, 1891, March 3, 1891.
40. D. N. Speer to R. L. Felton, May 5, 1891.
41. Scrapbook XXVII, p. 27.
42. *Ibid.*
43. Atlanta *Journal,* June 13, 1903.
44. Charles D. Tuller to R. L. Felton, June 15, 1903.
45. See penciled note on back of ms. reply to Miss DeGraffenreid.

CHAPTER XIV

1. Cartersville *Courant,* February 7, 1885.
2. *Ibid.,* August 20, 27, September 3, October 15, 1885.
3. *Ibid.,* February 26, October 10, 1885.
4. *Ibid.,* September 3, 1885.
5. *Ibid.,* January 7, 1886.
6. *Ibid.,* August 20, 27, 1885; newspaper clipping; J. E. Wood to R. L. Felton, March 3, 1885; J. H. McLean to R. L. Felton, June 19, 1885; A. H. Colquitt to R. L. Felton, March 10, 1885; A. E. Stevenson to R. L. Felton, July 18, 1885.
7. Cartersville *Courant,* September 24, 1885, March 4, 1886; Savannah *Morning News,* March 7, 1886.
8. Hoke Smith to R. L. Felton, August 2, 1899. For a more detailed treatment of Mrs. Felton's work on the Atlanta *Journal* see John E. Talmadge, "Rebecca Latimer Felton," *Georgians in Profile, Historical Es-*

says in Honor of Ellis Merton Coulter, pp. 277-302. Since no files of the *Journal's* semi-weekly or tri-weekly editions have been found, all references to her column are made to undated clippings in her scrapbooks.

9. Scrapbook IX, pp. 9, 19, 53; Scrapbook XXIV, pp. 107, 116, 144.

10. *Ibid.,* pp. 60, 174, 194.

11. Scrapbook XXI, p. 91; Scrapbook IX, p. 17.

12. *Ibid.,* pp. 74, 84; Scrapbook XXIV, pp. 152, 165; Scrapbook V, p. 8.

13. *Ibid.,* pp. 45, 88; Scrapbook XXIV, pp, 17, 110; Scrapbook XXXII, p. 34.

14. *Ibid.,* pp. 1, 200, 204-05; Scrapbook IX, p. 15; Scrapbook XXI, p. 13; Scrapbook XXIV, pp. 4, 22.

15. *Ibid.,* p. 4; Scrapbook V, p. 46; Scrapbook XXXI, p. 47.

16. *Ibid,* p. 1; Scrapbook XXIV, pp. 15, 71, 78, 98; Scrapbook IX, p. 8; Scrapbook XXI, p. 36; Scrapbook XXX, p. 7; Scrapbook XXVII, pp. 66-67; Scrapbook XXXII, p. 12.

17. *Ibid.,* p. 180; Scrapbook XXXI, pp. 57, 91; Scrapbook XXIV, pp. 68, 73, 112.

18. *Ibid.,* pp. 110, 184; Scrapbook IX, pp. 71, 145; Scrapbook XXXII, p. 8; Ulysses Roach to R. L. Felton, October 7, 1922; Nola Wooten to R. L. Felton, no date; Mary Felton to R. L. Felton, March 28, 1920; C. O. McMichael to R. L. Felton, November 29, 1918; A. J. Alford to R. L. Felton, April 11, 1903.

19. Newspaper clipping.

20. Scrapbook X, pp. 113, 114; Scrapbook XXIV, pp. 11, 49; (copy) R. L. Felton to James Grey, February, 1919; Atlanta *Sunday American,* October 17, 1920.

21. Scrapbook X, pp. 34-35, 38-39, 46-47, 51; Scrapbook XX, pp. 14, 18-19.

22. Richard Morris, *Encyclopedia of American History* (New York, 1953), p. 318; Edwin Camp to R. L. Felton, August 4, 1921. Although Mrs. Felton quarrelled with the *American* also about omitting one of her articles, there is no evidence that this argument cut short her stay on

that paper. See note on back of her letter to Edwin Camp, October 19, 1920.

23. *Memoirs,* pp. 5-11; Scrapbook V, p. 57; Scrapbook XXVII, pp. 46-47.

24. *Ibid.*

25. *Memoirs.,* pp. 5-11.

26. *Ibid.,* pp. 17-143.

27. *Ibid.,* pp. 257-97.

28. Ibid., pp. 399-427.

29. *Ibid.,* pp. 82-89, 151, 302-10, 478-546, 624-40.

30. *Ibid.,* p. 527.

31. *Ibid.,* pp. 370-71, 345-98.

32. *Ibid.,* pp. 94-143, 585-623.

33. *Ibid.,* pp. 286, 453, 531, 536.

34. *Ibid.,* pp. 47-78, 352-59, 362, 369-70, 392-93.

35. In a single paragraph, Avery uses twelve highly flattering adjectives to describe Gordon's character, *History of Georgia,* p. 564.

36. Arnett, *Populist Movement,* p. 229; Woodward, *Watson,* p. 491.

37. Scrapbook X, p. 57; *Country Life,* p. 5.

38. *Ibid.,* pp. 39-41, 46, 58-59.

39. *Ibid.,* pp. 50-52.

40. *Ibid.,* pp. 11-15, 49, 65, 66.

41. T. E. Watson to R. L. Felton, February 11, 1911; Felton ms., "Editor of the Atlanta *Constitution."*

42. Scrapbook XXXI, p. 38.

43. T. E. Watson to R. L. Felton, July 9, 1902.

44. Georgia Watson to R. L. Felton, August 23, 1902; W. E. Hollingsworth to R. L. Felton, August 1, 1902; J. E. Clark to R. L. Felton, August 30, 1902.

45. T. J. Woofter to R. L. Felton, March 7, 1906; Harris Jordan to R. L. Felton, July 15, 1903.

46. M. E. Parker to R. L. Felton, May 15, 1903; J. D. Gunn to R. L. Felton, November 14, 1903; Mrs. A. H. Smith to R. L. Felton, August 29, 1902; W. E. Hollingsworth to R. L. Felton, April 3, 1903.

47. C. H. Dickenson to R. L. Felton, February 14, 1892.

48. Sallie Hill to R. L. Felton, February 19, 1892.

49. Clark Howell to R. L. Felton, April 20, 1888; Belle Bayless to R. L. Fel-

ton, August 9, 1920. Corra Harris describes the style of Susan Walters, Mrs. Felton's prototype, as "not lit-erary, but . . . versatile in wit and sarcasm and outrageous veracity." See *The Co-Citizens*, p. 23.

CHAPTER XV

For a briefer treatment of Mrs. Felton's fight for the Senate see John E. Talmadge, "The Seating of the First Woman in the United States Senate," *Georgia Review*, Vol. X (Summer, 1956), pp. 168-74.

1. Woodward, *Watson*, pp. 471-72.
2. *Ibid.*, pp. 410, 473.
3. T. E. Watson to R. L. Felton, January 10, 1910, February 10, 1911.
4. A good example of the conflict between Mrs. Felton's pacifism and patriotism is found in her statement that although she could not "cheer" at the prospect of Americans dying in France, she was convinced that if the Germans invaded America, they would find "Jericho a hard road to travel," Scrapbook XXVI, p. 11; T. E. Watson to R. L. Felton, October 2, 1916; *Jeffersonian*, October 26, 29, 1916.
5. T. W. Hardwick to R. L. Felton, April 8, 1915, January 1, 14, April 4, 17, 24, 1918; *Cong. Rec.*, 65th Cong., 2nd Session, pp. 5939-40.
6. Helen Longstreet to R. L. Felton, October 2, 1915.
7. Atlanta *Georgian*, October 10, 1920.
8. *Ibid.*, September 7, 10, 19, 1920.
9. *Ibid.*, September 27, 1920.
10. Atlanta *Constitution*, September 29, 1920.
11. Atlanta *Georgian*, September 29, 1920.
12. *Ibid.*, October 5, 1920; telegram, T. W. Hardwick to R. L. Felton, October 6, 1920.
13. Warren G. Harding to R. L. Felton, October 29, 1920; Scrapbook XXXVIII, p. 21.
14. Emma C. Connaley to R. L. Felton, August 8, 1922; Atlanta *Georgian*, September 2, 6, 7, 12, 14, 1922; Tom Loylass to R. L. Felton, September 21, 1922; Columbus *Enquirer-Sun*, September 22, 1922.

15. Atlanta *Georgian*, September 26, 1922.
16. Atlanta *Journal*, September 26, 1922.
17. Atlanta *Georgian*, September 27, 28, 29, 30, October 1, 1922.
18. Atlanta *Journal*, October 2, 3, 1922.
19. *Ibid.*
20. *Ibid.*
21. Four folders of congratulatory letters and telegrams; Atlanta *Journal*, October 15, 1920; clipping, *Dearborn Independent*, Scrapbook XXXVIII, p. 29; New York *Times*, October 4, 1922; James Buchanan to R. L. Felton, October 12, 1922.
22. Atlanta *Journal*, October 7, 1922.
23. *Ibid.*
24. *Ibid.*
25. Atlanta *Journal*, October 15, 1922; Atlanta *Georgian*, November 20, 1922.
26. Two telegrams, Helen Longstreet to R. L. Felton, October 4, 1922.
27. New York *Times*, October 8, 1922; Warren G. Harding to R. L. Felton, November 16, 1922; Atlanta *Journal*, October 19, 1922.
28. Atlanta *Journal*, October 14, 1922; T. W. Hardwick to R. L. Felton, October 16, 1922.
29. Atlanta *Journal*, October 19, 1922.
30. *Ibid.*, October 20, 1922.
31. *Ibid.*, October 29, 1922.
32. Warren G. Harding to R. L. Felton, November 16, 1922.
33. Atlanta *Journal*, November 9, 12, 1922. Harding refused, politely but firmly, to call the session; see Warren G. Harding to R. L. Felton, November 16, 1922.
34. Atlanta *Journal*, November 14, 1922.
35. *Ibid.*, November 15, 16, 17, 1922.
36. *Ibid.*, November 16, 1922; the Hon. Walter George to author, December 10, 1952.
37. Atlanta *Georgian*, November 17, 1922.
38. Newspaper clipping.

39. Atlanta *Georgian,* November 18, 1922; New York *Times,* November 18, 1922.

40. *Ibid.,* November 19, 1922; Washington *Post,* November 18, 19, 20, 1922.

41. Atlanta *Georgian,* November 20, 1922; Abby Baker to R. L. Felton, November 7, 1922; Atlanta *Journal,* November 19, 1922.

42. Washington *Star,* November 18, 1922.

43. The exact time that Mrs. Felton wrote the two speeches cannot be determined. It is, however, not unreasonable to assume that on Sunday she wrote the speech castigating the Senate. One of the two copies is on Lafayette Hotel correspondence cards. She could not have read the articles in the Washington papers or learned the doubts of the women until after she arrived. On the other hand she seemed to indicate in her interview with the *Journal* on Monday morning that she had already written it. Copies of the speech are in the Felton Collection.

44. *Ibid.*

45. Atlanta *Journal,* November 20, 1922.

46. Washington *Star,* November 20, 1922; Washington *Post,* November 21, 1922; Atlanta *Georgian,* November 20, 1922.

47. *Ibid.; Cong. Rec.,* 67th Congress, 3rd Session, p. 3; Washington *Star,* November 21, 1922; Washington *Post,* November 22, 1922; Atlanta *Geor-*

gian, November 21, 1922.

48. *Cong. Rec.,* 67th Congress, 3rd Session, p. 8.

49. *Ibid.*

50. *Ibid.*

51. *Ibid.*

52. *Ibid.,* pp. 8, 11.

53 Atlanta *Georgian,* November 22, 1922, reported that when Walsh began his speech, many senators believed "he was planning to keep Mrs. Felton from being seated." It is impossible to say at what point in his speech Walsh was interrupted, but since the call from the House came at 12:25 p.m., and some time had been consumed in reading the commissions from four senators, it is unlikely that he had reached that point where he began to present the arguments for seating her.

54. *Cong. Rec.,* 67th Congress, 3rd Session, p. 11.

55. *Ibid.,* pp. 11, 14.

56. *Ibid.,* p. 14.

57. Washington *Post,* November 22, 1922.

58. Atlanta *Georgian,* November 22, 1922.

59. *Cong. Rec.,* 67th Congress, 3rd Session, p. 23.

60. *Ibid.*

61. *Ibid.*

62. *Ibid.*

63. Felton ms.

64. *Ibid.*

65. *Ibid.*

CHAPTER XVI

1. (Copy) Mother's Day telegram for the Associated Press, Scrapbook XXI, p. 40.

2. In 1923 she admitted she had "begun to stumble" and that she was "less able to get about." See William Witham to R. L. Felton, August 8, 1923, and Lillian Todd to R. L. Felton, December 30, 1923.

3. (Copy) Telegram, R. L. Felton to Calvin Coolidge, October 6, 1923.

4. H. C. Lodge to R. L. Felton, November 22, 1923.

5. Mrs. P. S. Connor to R. L. Felton, December 26, 1923; Roy Ritchie to R. L. Felton, February 11, 1923; Wil-

liam Long to R. L. Felton, June 10, July, 1924.

6. C. P. Down to R. L. Felton, December 14, 1925; J. O. Jett to R. L. Felton, undated.

7. L. O. Hollis to R. L. Felton, May 14, 1925.

8. Anonymous letter, July 19, 1922.

9. Anonymous letters, October 1, 1920, January 14, 1921.

10. Hollis Randolph to R. L. Felton, June 6, 1923; John Paschall to R. L. Felton, April 6, 1925; Felton ms., "A Word with the Methodists of the Cartersville Methodist Church."

11. Felton ms., "To Editor of Bartow Tribune"; (copy) income tax return of 1917.
12. (Copy) R. L. Felton to H. B. Mays, November 11, 1926; W. B. Beauchamp to H. B. Mays, November 16, 1926.
13. Macon *Telegraph,* December 19, 1923.
14. Scrapbook XXIII, pp. 35-36.
15. Felton ms., "The First Georgia Woman to Reach the White House"; Clark Howell to R. L. Felton, April 1, 1924.
16. Mrs. R. M. Pritchett to R. L. Felton, February 8, 1925.
17. (Copy) R. L. Felton to James Boykin, undated; Felton ms., "The McAdoo Candidacy and the Women's Vote."
18. Atlanta *Georgian,* July 8, 9, 1924.
19. T. W. Hardwick to R. L. Felton, July 24, 1924.
20. Mrs. Felton argued that even if Harris denied membership in the Klan, as members were permitted to do, he evidenced "gratitude for such support . . . and endorsement of the Klan's motives and plans of operation in Georgia." See ms. "The Ku Klux Klan in Georgia."
21. In the Felton Collection there is a photostatic copy of a transfer of membership for "William Harris" from the Cedartown (Harris' home town) branch to the Atlanta branch. It is impossible to say whether Mrs. Felton obtained the document before she first made her charge; Columbus *Enquirer-Sun,* September 8, 1924.
22. W. J. Vereen to R. L. Felton, August 23, 24, 1924, gives a list of papers to which Mrs. Felton should send her "disclosure"; Israel Mannheim to R. L. Felton, August 25, 1924; J. M. Elder to R. L. Felton, July 28, 1924; clipping, Cedartown *Standard,* September 4, 1924.
23. Felton ms., "Congressman Bell Calls Mrs. Felton a Liar." No information has been found as to what paper this letter was published in, but Hardwick wrote that he had read her attack on "Harris and Bell." See T. H. Hardwick to R. L. Felton, August 24, 1924.
24. Paid advertisement, Bartow *Tribune-News,* September 4, 1924.
25. Atlanta *Georgian,* September 11, 1924; Bartow *Tribune-News,* September 11, 1924.
26. Legal brief, "T. A. Jenkins v. Mrs. Wm. H. Felton"; Cartersville *News-Tribune,* October 24, 1926; John A. Sibley to R. L. Felton, September 17, October 28, 1926; (copy) R. L. Felton to Samuel H. Sibley, April 2, 1924.
27. Folder of information on her Bank of Donaldson controversy. The following documents cover the main points: Hooper Alexander to R. L. Felton, February 28, April 2, May 2, 1927; Samuel H. Sibley to R. L. Felton, September 29, 1927; C. N. Davis to R. L. Felton, April 24, 1925, June 6, 1927; Clifford Walker to R. L. Felton, February 2, 1925; Richard Russell to R. L. Felton, March 7, 1925; L. E. Heath to Representative Tritt, July 14, 1925; circular "What Are the Superintendents of Georgia's Banks Employed to Do?"
28. Cancelled cheques, dated May 20, 1927, and June 20, 1927, both payable to Hooper Alexander.
29. Scrapbook XXVII, p. 57; Hooper Alexander to R. L. Felton, April 27, 1927.
30. In June, 1927, Mrs. Felton wrote that both her "strength and hearing" were failing. See Lucy Fears to R. L. Felton, July 2, 1927.
31. Susan Gale Parlin to R. L. Felton, February 8, 1925.
32. John A. Sibley to R. L. Felton, March 18, 1927. The work on the mausoleum was completed by the end of 1927. See C. W. DeFoor to R. L. Felton, January 1, 1928.
33. Folder of telegrams, letters, cards.
34. Atlanta *Journal,* June 10, 1927.
35. E. L. Vining to R. L. Felton, June 18, 1927; Mrs. B. Maulti to R. L. Felton, June 22, 1927.
36. Rebecca Felton, "As I Remember Stephens," *National Republic,* February 28, 1927; Felton ms., "Hon. A. H. Stephens' Birthday."

37. *Ibid.*
38. Scrapbook XXVIII, p. 57; Willis M. Boyd to R. L. Felton, February 2, 1925; R. L. Felton to T. W. Reed, January 1, 1927, August 20, 1928.
39. John B. Gordon to R. L. Felton, October 24, 1874; Scrapbook XIII, p. 24; A. H. Colquitt to W. H. Felton, August 9, 1878; circular addressed to "Dear Sir" and signed J. T. Haley and H. B. Wallis, August 2, 1887.
40. Scrapbook X, p. 71; F. H. Fitzhugh to W. H. Felton, February 9, 1879; W. H. Huff to W. H. Felton, October 26, 1877.
41. R. L. Felton to T. W. Reed, January 29, 1927.
42. Atlanta *Journal,* January 26, 1930.
43. Cartersville *News-Tribune,* September 20, 1927; Felton ms.
44. *Ibid.*
45. Cartersville *News-Tribune,* January 26, 1928.
46. Circular, "Mrs. Felton Appeals to Hon. Claude C. Pittman, Judge of Superior Court, August 1, 1929."
47. Cartersville *News-Tribune,* March 7, 1929; Atlanta *Journal,* June 10, 1929.
48. *Ibid.*
49. *Ibid.;* M. L. McNeel to R. L. Felton, May 31, 1929.
50. Atlanta *Journal,* June 10, 1929; Cartersville *News-Tribune,* June 13, 1928.
51. Told to the author by the late Henry Grady Black. Mrs. Felton's will, on file at the Bartow County Court House, gives United States Government and municipal bonds as the only securities in the list of assets.
52. Atlanta *Journal,* January 26, 1930.
53. *Ibid.,* January 25, 26, 1930.
54. *Ibid.*
55 *Ibid.*
56. *Ibid.*
57. *Ibid.*
58. Cartersville *News-Tribune,* January 31, 1930; Atlanta *Constitution,* January 25, 1930; Atlanta *Georgian,* January 25, 1930; Atlanta *Journal,* January 25, 1930.
59. *Ibid.,* January 26, 1930.
60. *Ibid.*

Bibliography

I. PRIMARY SOURCES

1. Manuscripts and Private Papers

Rebecca Latimer Felton Collection, University of Georgia Library, Athens. The larger part of this collection was given to the University by Mrs. Felton shortly before her death in 1930. The smaller part was placed on deposit with the Library by her grandson's widow Mrs. Lillian Felton in 1952. The total collection is made up of letters from 1851 to 1930; forty-one scrapbooks of newspaper clippings and a few letters; and such miscellaneous items as loose newspaper clippings, tax assessments and returns, receipted bills, cancelled cheques, sheet music, greeting cards, etc.

Alexander H. Stephens Papers, Library of Congress, Washington. Contains a few letters from Mrs. Felton to Stephens from 1880 to 1882.

Alexander H. Stephens Papers, Historical Society of Pennsylvania, Philadelphia. The correspondence between Stephens and W. H. Hiddell throws light upon the Stephens-Felton controversy.

Warren A. Candler Papers, Emory University Library, Atlanta. Contains a letter from Mrs. Felton to Candler on Ku Klux Klan activities in Georgia during the 1920's.

Thomas H. Watson Papers, University of North Carolina Library, Chapel Hill. Contains no letters from Mrs. Felton but furnishes background information on the Populist Movement in Georgia.

2. Published Writings of Rebecca Latimer Felton

My Memoirs of Georgia Politics. Atlanta: Index Publishing Co., 1911.

Country Life in Georgia in the Days of My Youth. Atlanta: Index Publishing Co., 1919.

The Romantic Story of Georgia Women. Atlanta: Atlanta *Georgian and Sunday American*, 1930.

Sermon and Address by Hon. W. H. Felton and his Wife Mrs. W. H.
  Felton on the Life and Character of General Robert E. Lee. Carters-
  ville, 1915. A pamphlet.
A Petition from the Woman's Christian Temperance Union of Geor-
  gia. Atlanta, 1886. A pamphlet.
On the Subjectation and Enfranchisement of Women. A pamphlet.
"The Convict System of Georgia," in *Forum,* Vol. II (1887).
"As I Remember Stephens," in *National Republic,* February, 1928.

3. NEWSPAPERS

Atlanta *Constitution,* 1873-1930.
Atlanta *Georgian* and Atlanta *Sunday American,* 1920-1930.
Atlanta *Journal,* 1886-1930.
Augusta *Chronicle and Sentinel,* 1852, 1865.
Bartow *Tribune,* 1914-1915.
Bartow *Tribune-*Cartersville *News,* 1915-1923.
Cartersville *Express,* 1866-1871, 1875-1881.
Cartersville *Standard and Express,* 1871-1875.
Cartersville *Free-Press,* 1878-1883.
Cartersville *American,* 1884-1886.
Cartersville *Courant,* 1885-1886.
Cartersville *Courant-American,* 1887-1898.
Cartersville *Courant American-News,* 1898-1901.
Cartersville *News and Courant,* 1901-1907.
Cartersville *News,* 1907-1915.
Cartersville *Tribune-News,* 1923-1930.
Cassville *Standard,* 1852, 1857-1860.
Macon *News,* 1915.
Macon *Telegraph and Messenger,* 1879.
New York *Times,* 1922.
Washington *Post,* 1922.
Washington *Star,* 1922.

4. PUBLIC RECORDS

DeKalb County Marriage Book, 1846-1856. Ordinary's Office, Decatur.
The War of the Rebellion: A Compilation of the Official Records
  of the Union and Confederate Armies. Washington, 1890-1901.
  Series I, Vol. XXXVIII, Part I.
United States Congress, *Congressional Records,* 44 Cong. (1876); 67
  Cong. (1922).

II. SECONDARY SOURCES

1. CRITICAL STUDIES

Ethridge, Willie Snow, "The Lady from Georgia," in *Good House-*
  keeping (January, 1923).

Floyd, Josephine Bone, "Rebecca Latimer Felton, Political Independent," in *Georgia Historical Quarterly*, Vol. XXX (March, 1946).

—————, "Rebecca Latimer Felton, Champion of Woman's Rights," in *Georgia Historical Quarterly*, Vol. XXX (June, 1946).

Hunter, Mrs. Joan (Conerly), "Rebecca Latimer Felton." A Master's Thesis, University of Georgia, 1944.

Roberts, William P., "The Public Career of Dr. William Harrell Felton." A Ph. D. Dissertation, University of North Carolina, 1952.

Talmadge, John E., "The Death Blow to Independentism in Georgia." In *Georgia Historical Quarterly*, Vol. XXXVI (December, 1952).

—————, "Rebecca Latimer Felton, Georgian." In *Georgia Review*, Vol. IV (Spring, 1955).

—————, "The Seating of the First Woman in the United States Senate." In *Georgia Review*, Vol. X (Summer, 1956).

—————, "Rebecca Latimer Felton." In *Georgians in Profile: Historical Essays in Honor of Ellis Merton Coulter,* edited by Horace Montgomery. Athens: University of Georgia Press, 1958.

2. Books and Articles

Ansley, Mrs. J. J., *History of the Georgia Woman's Christian Temperance Union, from its Organization, 1883-1907.* Columbus: Gilbert Printing Co., 1914.

Anthony, Katharine, *Susan B. Anthony, Her Personal History.* Garden City: Doubleday, 1954.

Arnett, Alexander Mathews, *The Populist Movement in Georgia* (Studies in History, Economics and Public Law, Columbia University, Vol. CIV). New York: Columbia University Press, 1922.

Avery, Isaac W., *The History of Georgia from 1850 to 1881.* New York: Brown and Derby, 1881.

Barnard, Harry, *Rutherford B. Hayes and His America.* Indianapolis: Bobbs-Merrill, 1954.

Boatwright, Eleanor, "The Political and Civil Status of Women in Georgia, 1783-1860." In *Georgia Historical Quarterly*, Vol. XXV (December, 1941).

Brooks, Robert Preston, *The Agrarian Revolution in Georgia (Bulletin of the University of Wisconsin,* No. 639). Madison, 1914.

Bryan, T. Conn, *Confederate Georgia.* Athens: University of Georgia Press, 1953.

Bullock, Henry M., *A History of Emory University.* Nashville: Parthenon Press, 1936.

Coulter, E. Merton, *A Short History of Georgia.* Chapel Hill: University of North Carolina Press, 1937.

Cunyus, Lucy Josephine, *The History of Bartow County, formerly Cass.* Cartersville: Tribune Publishing Co., 1933.

Dabney, Virginius, *Liberalism in the South.* Chapel Hill: University of North Carolina Press, 1932.

DeGraffenreid, Claire, "The Georgia Cracker in the Cotton Mill," in *Century* Magazine, Vol. XLI (February, 1891).

Fielder, Herbert, *A Sketch of the Life and Times and Speeches of Joseph E. Brown.* Springfield: Springfield Printing Co., 1883.

Garrett, Franklin M., *Atlanta and Environs,* Vol. I. New York: Lewis Historical Publishing Co., 1954.

Harris, Corra, *The Co-Citizens.* Garden City: Doubleday, Page, 1915.

Hill, Louise Biles, *Joseph E. Brown and the Southern Confederacy.* Chapel Hill: University of North Carolina Press, 1939.

Johnson, Amanda, *Georgia as Colony and State.* Atlanta: Walter W. Brown Publishing Co., 1938.

Knight, Lucian Lamar, *A Standard History of Georgia and Georgians,* Vol. II, IV. Chicago: Lewis Publishing Co., 1917.

Lamar, Dolly Blount, *When All Is Said and Done.* Athens: University of Georgia Press, 1952.

Madison Female College Catalogue, 1852. Madison, Ga., 1853.

Nixon, Herman Clarence, *Lower Piedmont Country.* New York: Duell, Sloan and Pearce, 1946.

Nixon, Raymond B., *Henry W. Grady, Spokesman of the New South.* New York: A. A. Knopf, 1943.

Orr, Dorothy, *A History of Education in Georgia.* Chapel Hill: University of North Carolina Press, 1950.

Pearce, Haywood J., Jr., *Benjamin H. Hill, Secession and Reconstruction.* Chicago: University of Chicago Press, 1928.

Pierce, A. M., *Giant in the Sky; The Life of Bishop Warren Aiken Candler.* Nashville: Abingdon Press, 1948.

Pittenger, William, *Daring and Suffering, a History of the Andrews Raid into Georgia.* New York: War Publishing Co., 1887.

Sanger, Donald B., and Hays, Thomas R., *James Longstreet.* Baton Rouge: Louisiana State University Press, 1952.

Schlesinger, Arthur M., *The Rise of the City (A History of American Life,* Vol. X). New York: Macmillan Co., 1933.

Sledd, Andrew, "The Negro: Another View," *Atlantic Monthly,* Vol. XC (July, 1902).

Tankersley, Allen P., *John B. Gordon: A Study in Gallantry.* Atlanta: Whitehall Press, 1955.

Taylor, A. Elizabeth, "The Origin and Development of the Convict Lease System in Georgia." In *Georgia Historical Quarterly,* Vol. XXVI (March, 1942).

⸺⸺⸺, "The Abolition of the Convict Lease System in Georgia." In *Georgia Historical Quarterly,* Vol. XXVI (September, 1942).

⸺⸺⸺, "Development of the Woman's Suffrage Movement in Georgia." In *Georgia Historical Quarterly,* Vol. XLII (December, 1958).

————, "The Last Phase of the Woman's Suffrage Movement in Georgia." In *Georgia Historical Quarterly,* Vol. XLIII (March, 1959).

Thompson, C. Mildred, *Reconstruction in Georgia, Economic, Social, Political, 1865-1872* (Studies in History, Economics and Public Law, Vol. LXIV, Columbia University). New York: Columbia University Press, 1915.

Von Able, Rudolph, *Alexander H. Stephens.* New York: A. A. Knopf, 1946.

Wade, John Donald, *Augustus Baldwin Longstreet: a Study of the Development of Culture in the South.* New York: Macmillan Co., 1924.

Woodward, C. Vann, *Origins of the New South, 1877-1913 (A History of the South,* Vol. IX). Baton Rouge: Louisiana State University Press, 1951.

————, *Reunion and Reaction, The Compromise of 1877 and the End of Reconstruction.* Boston: Little Brown, 1951.

————, *The Strange Case of Jim Crow.* New York: Oxford University Press, 1955.

————, *Tom Watson, Agrarian Rebel.* New York: Macmillan Co., 1936.

3. UNPUBLISHED MANUSCRIPTS

Coleman, Kenneth, "The Administration of Alfred H. Colquitt as Governor of Georgia." A Master's Thesis, University of Georgia, 1940.

Spears, Leola, "The Senatorial Career of Joseph Emerson Brown." A Master's Thesis, University of Georgia, 1954.

Ward, Judson C., Jr., "Georgia under the Bourbons, 1872-1890." A Ph. D. Dissertation, University of North Carolina, 1947.

Womack, Margaret Anne, "Mildred Lewis Rutherford." A Master's Thesis, University of Georgia, 1946.

Index